Foreword

For the first time in history whole cultures, and not just privileged segments, are characterized by the prospects and problems of wealth. One arena where the obstacles and opportunities of wealth come to the surface most saliently is that of estate planning. The substantial and exponentially growing affluence enjoyed by an increasing number of families raises to an unprecedented prominence the question of how properly to allocate wealth in the light of death and taxes. Especially in the United States, with our unique confluence of meritocracy and mutual assistance, the leading spiritual question about material life revolves around how to freely yet benevolently allocate financial resources during the final one-third of our life span.

What are some of the indicators of the changing material horizon of wealth and philanthropy that comprise the new environment for estate planning? First, there are now over 5 million households with net worth at or above $1 million, the number having grown at approximately 14% annually over the past decade. Second, the IRS reports there were 142,566 tax returns with adjusted gross income of $1 million or more in 1997, as compared to 110,912 in 1996 and 86,998 for 1995—a 64% increase in just two years. Third, in 1994 households in the top 1% of the income distribution donated 33% of our nation's charitable contributions, up from 25% in 1991. Fourth, from 1992 to 1995 the value of final estates increased 17%, the amount going to taxes rose 18%, the amount passed to heirs increased 14%, and the amount bequeathed to charity grew 28%. Fifth, estates valued at $20 million or more actually allocate more of their total value to charity (41%) than to heirs (24%). Sixth, according to the wealth transfer simulator developed by my colleague, John Havens, and me, the 55-year period from 1998 through 2052 will witness between $41 trillion and $136 trillion (1998 dollars) transferred by final decedents, with between $6 trillion and $25 trillion bequeathed to charity—even without assuming that individuals become more philanthropically inclined than they were in 1995.

Equal in importance to this material horizon is the social-psychological or spiritual horizon that now, and into the future will incline wealth holders to allocate a substantial proportion of their financial resources to charity. I suggest six elements of this spiritual horizon. First is the well-recognized desire to minimize estate taxes. When confronted with the decision whether to devote a sizable portion of their wealth to government or to self-chosen charitable purposes, wealth holders are prone to choose the latter. Second, wealth holders are disposed to be institution builders. In the realm of philanthropy this means they tend to aspire to "making a difference" not just by supporting existing charitable causes but by producing novel charitable ventures or new directions within existing enterprises. Third, wealth holders encounter what I call the spiritual secret of money, that natural tendency for those who are financially secure to entertain the deeper questions about the use of money. Being able to have what one wants in the material realm does not automatically lead to deepening what one wants for oneself and others—but it does make that question more intrusive. Fourth, there is the simple question of death. As wealth holders enter the later years of their life and begin to reorient their time and consciousness away from accumulating wealth, their mortality looms larger. This evokes a review of the moral legacy they wish to leave behind and of the moral countenance with which they hope to face eternity. Fifth, there is the experience of life's blessings. Wealth holders, along with the rest of us, are galvanized to provide gifts to others to the extent we recognize how much our own life has been marked by grace, blessing, and fortune. Finally there is the elementary yet often unspeakable satisfaction that derives from even the most rudimentary experience of focused giving. Once tasted, this satisfaction inspires additional giving in amounts and ways that magnify the sweet happiness of life.

Although the foregoing material and spiritual environments naturally predispose some wealth holders to be conscientious about their legacy, most are simply not well enough acquainted with their own material and moral potential for allocating their wealth in a way that serves their deeper essence. Scott Fithian's *Values-Based Estate Planning* provides the most psychologically sophisticated and technically adroit methodology I have yet encountered for coaching wealth holders to begin and then continue to make wise decisions about allocating their wealth.

Over the past two years I have observed Scott as he developed and relentlessly improved the principles and procedures enunciated in the following pages. What I have learned from a decade-and-a-half of research on wealth and philanthropy is thoroughly congruent with the principles and procedures Scott sets out for helping the growing number of increasingly wealthy individuals channel wealth into a thoughtful legacy. His central premise is that wealth holders achieve far happier personal outcomes and make far more productive public contributions when financial professionals offer wealth holders an informed process of inductive decision making. As such, Scott places wealth holders front and center as informed and intelligent agents. Under the guidance, but never the dominance, of properly trained financial professionals, wealth holders are capable of discerning their values and aspirations, reviewing their finan-

cial status, and charting a legacy for themselves, their heirs, and those beyond their kin for whom they care.

In the end Scott's unique contribution is straightforward. First, he
abandons those relentless vestiges of either telling wealth holders far too
much or far too little about how to translate their material wealth into a
self-fashioned legacy. Second, he rejects the notion that wealth holders are
either not smart enough or good enough to decide for themselves how
best to chart their estates. Third, and most importantly, he offers a way for
wealth holders to discern who they have been, who they are, and who
they want to become; how many financial resources they truly command
now and into the future; and what strategies—both experimental and established—they can pursue to allocate their wealth consistent with their
best lights. By offering wealth holders the opportunity to deliberate freely
and intelligently about their anxieties and aspirations, Scott's approach
makes it far more likely they will embark on a wiser, more satisfying, and
more gracious legacy.

Paul G. Schervish
Boston College
November 1999

Preface

This book is written for advisors who serve, or would like to serve, the needs of affluent clients. It is intended for all professional backgrounds. The common denominator is twofold—a *desire* and the *ability* to put the fulfillment of client goals and objectives above all else.

Through years of working with high net worth families, I have encountered numerous obstacles to effective planning. In fact, most of my professional colleagues would agree that people, in general, are averse to estate planning.

I believe the main reason is that for most people, the process is complex and confusing. Because clients don't understand it, they consequently believe they can have little, if any, control over the process. This lack of understanding and control leads to a situation where they either start the process only to stop or totally avoid planning at all.

Although most people find estate planning difficult to understand, the majority of those we encounter have a reasonably good handle on who they are and what is important to them.

With that in mind, this book is based on a revolutionary new planning methodology: values-based estate planning. Values-based estate planning is a step-by-step process that helps your clients define and express their values and objectives regarding money.

When you think about it, doesn't if seem strange to have to call attention to the role of values in estate planning? Shouldn't everything we do in life be based on our values, especially when it comes to the truly important decisions we make?

To understand the concept, consider the meaning of each underlying term:

Value:	A principle, standard, or quality considered worthwhile or desirable
Base:	A fundamental part
Estate:	Everything one owns
Plan:	A program or method thought out ahead of time for the accomplishment of a goal.

Now consider the resulting definition when these underlying terms are combined:

Values-based estate planning—A clearly thought out program, based upon principles, standards, and qualities considered worthwhile and designed for the accumulation, management, and transfer of everything one owns.

The concept is profound, yet simple. The focus is on what your client values, rather than the value of what your client owns. Through this process, clients gain confidence as their financial affairs and personal values become aligned.

This topic is particularly timely, given the immense intergenerational transfer of wealth that has begun from parents of baby boomers to the boomer generation. People in general are becoming more knowledgeable and savvy regarding their financial decisions. Increasing numbers are accumulating significant wealth from inheritance, through innovation and hard work, and as a result of good investment decisions. These wealth holders are beginning to pay closer attention to what their ultimate legacies could and should be, and they are seeking the advice of competent professionals to help them achieve their highest financial and philanthropic aspirations.

Many boomers who will receive this wealth are wondering how it will affect their and their children's lives, and if there are ways they can use some of what they have accumulated to influence society in a positive way. This book holds the key to helping advisors as they work with individuals and families who are seeking answers to these questions.

This is not a "numbers" book. It doesn't cover technical aspects of estate planning and related planning strategies. Rather, the book explores values-based planning concepts and explains how advisors can help individuals and families apply them to simplify and control the planning process.

In reading this book, advisors will learn to do the following:

1. Help clients discover and solidify their deepest values, convictions, and objectives as they relate to their money
2. Help clients express those values and objectives in a clearly written *Family Financial Philosophy* mission statement
3. Show clients—and other advisors with whom they may have relationships—how to use the mission statement to direct the planning process
4. Dramatically increase the percentage of recommendations clients actually implement
5. Build deep-rooted client relationships that will stand the test of time

These are not untried or new ideas. They are, rather, the culmination of more than 15 years in the field as a financial consultant, seeking the most efficient and effective ways to help clients achieve their highest dreams and goals.

I hope you'll try them on for size. Let me know how they work.

Acknowledgments

I could fill many pages with acknowledgment of those who have influenced this book—a daunting and impractical task. However, I feel compelled to name and thank four amazing people whose efforts have turned this dream of mine into a reality.

Literally dozens have contributed conceptually to this book. But above all others, JoAnne Vose is responsible for its actual completion. Somehow, she managed to transform my raw ideas and thoughts into clearly articulated prose. She lifted my spirits when they were down and managed the reality of each new deadline as it approached. Her perseverance, focus, and commitment to the project brought us together through many iterations to these pages. Thanks, Jo . . . here's to our next book.

My friend Paul Brooks is the driving force and innovator behind the emerging social capital industry. Paul has been planting the seeds of social capital for nearly two decades now. It is my great fortune to have encountered Paul and his vision when I did. Thank you for entrusting a few of your precious seeds to me.

I have participated in The Strategic Coach for the past six years. Its founder, Dan Sullivan, has encouraged and nurtured my entrepreneurial instincts and spirit through his uniquely effective approach to managing one's professional and personal life. Thanks, Dan, for your continually evolving innovation and inspiration.

My friend and mentor Dr. Paul Schervish, and his research on what motivates the affluent, especially as it relates to their philanthropy, has been instrumental in shoring up my confidence and refining my ideas. As a member of the training faculty for The Legacy Institute and The Legacy Leadership Forum, Paul has been a constant source of information and inspiration. I am proud to count him as my friend and humbled to view him as a colleague. Thank you for your confidence.

Finally, I acknowledge the multitude of professional advisors who have supported my efforts over the past several years. In particular, I want to recognize and thank the members of The Legacy Leadership Forum for believing in me.

I also pay tribute to all other professionals who have paved the way for values-based estate planning. I'd love to name names, but there are just too many, and I don't want to risk offending by virtue of omission. You'll find them in the best law firms, financial service offices, accounting firms, nonprofit organizations, trust departments, investment and insurance firms, and forward-thinking companies that consult on behalf of all the aforementioned—all over the country, and indeed, the world.

They are consummate advisors, helping their clients achieve their highest financial goals and fulfill their wildest philanthropic dreams. They are, at this very moment, changing the face of philanthropy and making values-based estate planning an accepted industry standard.

My thanks to you all, for lending your integrity, energy, enthusiasm, years of experience, and fine reputations to this mission.

—SCF

Contents

PART I

The Seven Principles of Values-Based Estate Planning

CHAPTER ONE

Eternal Planning: Why Clients Are Trapped

How long does it take to develop an effective estate plan? Although many possible answers come to mind, one stands out—a lifetime. Client procrastination, changing tax laws, and inertia all contribute to a process that has no apparent beginning or end.

1.1 BASIC ESTATE PLANNING STEPS

In its most basic form, estate planning consists of three steps:

1. Establishing objectives
2. Designing a plan to fulfill the objectives
3. Implementing the plan

In order for effective estate planning to occur, each level must be negotiated successfully in the proper order. Each step builds upon the last; the earlier steps create an essential foundation for those that follow. All three steps are highly interdependent.

Logic suggests that it makes no sense to design a plan before clear objectives are established. Likewise, it is not possible to implement a plan until the client has a plan to implement. Nevertheless, these seemingly senseless initiatives are attempted regularly. Plans are designed without clear objectives, and strategies are implemented before an overall plan is in place.

Technical as it may be, the plan design step actually creates a safety zone in which clients can hide. In this realm clients continually evaluate how various strategies may work, but they are not forced to consider why they work. They consider one strategy after another, but they are not forced to make decisions. The plan design step fosters procrastination and results in what may be viewed as *eternal planning*.

1.2 WHY CLIENTS ARE TRAPPED IN ETERNAL PLANNING

Although every client has his or her distinct reasons for procrastination, a number of common factors may contribute to the client being trapped in eternal planning.

(a) Estate Planning: A Difficult Topic at Best

When it comes right down to it, most people are not excited about the entire subject of estate planning. It forces them to face difficult issues related to death and taxes, family dynamics, and financial situations. In fact, some people go so far as to define estate planning as *planning to die efficiently*—not a particularly appealing image.

In truth, estate planning is not a topic most clients enjoy. The issues they are forced to address create anxiety. As a result, they enter the process with significant reservation, commonly motivated by a major life change such as marriage, the birth of a child, the death of a parent, or a substantial change in financial status.

In the minds of many, death is a remote, future event, not something they want to confront proactively. Many prefer to ignore its eventual reality altogether. In practice, many clients are motivated to begin planning their estate only when their peers begin to die. Unfortunately, this generally means they have waited too long, missing numerous opportunities along the way.

Whatever the reasons, more inertia is associated with estate planning than with any other area of planning. Procrastination is not only a problem—it is the standard.

And the eternal planning process begins.

(b) Loss of Control and Lack of Understanding

It has been said that people prefer to deal with things they can understand or control, preferably both. In reality, few clients have a clear understanding of what estate planning involves. Even fewer feel as if they are in control of the process.

Rest assured that if clients do not understand it and cannot control it, they will try to avoid it. As a result, the primary goal of most people once they enter the estate planning process is to get out of it as soon as possible.

Some clients will attempt to maintain control over various aspects of the process. The greater the degree of control the client attempts to maintain, the greater the potential for indecision. Ultimately, indecision evolves into paralysis, and the planning process stops short or slowly fizzles away.

There are three general areas over which clients often try to maintain control:

1. Their financial resources
2. The people and the process
3. The flexibility to make changes

(i) Loss of control over financial resources. One of the greatest fears clients face is losing control of their financial resources. Because estate planning often requires a shift in ownership of assets, clients are constantly aware of their diminished access to and control over financial resources. Even a simple transfer of ownership from one spouse to another suggests a shift in control within the family. The sense of loss of control over financial resources can be a major obstacle to the planning process.

(ii) Loss of control over people and process. Clients do not post their net worth statements on their front doors for the world to see. This is because financial affairs represent one of the most private aspects of their lives.

Unfortunately, effective estate planning requires clients to reveal many private elements of their financial lives to professional advisors and others. It also requires them to expose their values and beliefs regarding the accumulation, use, management, and distribution of financial resources. As clients divulge this information, they begin to feel an increased sense of losing control. As long as the client controls the information, the client is in control of the people and the process.

As clients release more and more information to advisors, a shift in power occurs. The advisors are in an increasingly powerful position to make specific recommendations and control the timing and movement of the process.

A similar shift in power occurs with children and other heirs. As clients release information, they expose themselves to second-guessing and their decisions to increased scrutiny.

(iii) The flexibility to adapt and change. One of the most common fears expressed by clients has to do with losing the flexibility to adjust as changing circumstances dictate. Often they are very concerned with retaining sufficient control to change their plans well into the future.

And the eternal planning process continues.

(c) Planning Dilemmas

Advisors often speak with clients as if every decision were black and white—good plan, bad plan, right answer, wrong answer. In reality, the estate planning process is filled with inherent dilemmas that may require a choice between two desirable outcomes or objectives that are in direct opposition to one another.

(i) Dilemma: client versus heir.   Many clients face a difficult choice between providing for their own needs and providing for the needs of their heirs. They want to ensure their own financial security and also provide a financial head start for heirs. However, they may have to recognize that providing such a head start could come at the expense of enjoying their desired lifestyle.

Thanks to medical innovations and wellness programs, more clients than ever face the possibility of outliving their financial resources. The sooner they begin transferring financial resources to heirs, the greater the likelihood this may occur. At the same time, if clients wait until death to transfer financial resources to heirs, they may wind up leaving a pile of money to "children" who are in their sixties and seventies.

(ii) Dilemma: children versus grandchildren.   The natural expansion of the family presents numerous planning dilemmas. As children grow older and grandchildren enter the picture, a variety of conflicts arise. A client's desire to provide a financial legacy for grandchildren may conflict with the client's desire not to interfere in his or her children's financial affairs.

(iii) Dilemma: financial security versus tax efficiency.   Many clients are forced to realize an obvious conflict between tax-effective estate planning and maintaining financial security. Tax-effective strategies often require the irrevocable separation of clients from their money. As a result, some of the most powerful estate planning tools present clients with an annual dilemma. Consider the $10,000 annual gift tax exclusion. Should clients make the gift and potentially save $5,000 in estate and gift tax, or should they retain the resources to protect their future lifestyle?

(iv) Dilemma: heirs versus charity.   Most clients see charitable giving as an alternative to inheritance. While they may want to contribute to their favorite charities, they cannot reconcile the perceived corresponding decrease in inheritance for heirs.

(v) Dilemma: client versus charity.   Many clients prefer to make charitable contributions during their lifetime, when they can measure the impact of their generosity. At the same time, lifetime contributions require clients to contemplate personal needs for financial security. They may want to make gifts today, but they also want to protect their lifestyle.

(vi) Dilemma: heir versus heir. More often than not, clients find themselves with children who have entirely different financial needs and circumstances from one another. This is one of the most common planning dilemmas. The client wants to treat heirs fairly, but that may not necessarily translate into equal distributions from the estate.

(vii) Dilemma: charity versus charity. At an increasing rate, charitable organizations compete for the same charitable dollars. As a result, client allegiances are frayed and torn as they attempt to choose among many charitable organizations about which they care.

(viii) Dilemma: spouse versus spouse. Perhaps the most common planning dilemmas result from differences of opinion between spouses. Opinions about whether to provide heirs with an equal or fair inheritance. Opinions about an appropriate role for philanthropy in the estate plan. Opinions about what is required to maintain a suitable lifestyle. Opinions about appropriate investment risk tolerance. These differences of opinion, however minor, tend to undermine planning before it begins.

These and other dilemmas create roadblocks to effective planning.

And the eternal planning process continues.

(d) Complexity

Estate planning is a highly technical process that involves tax codes, planning strategies, legal documents, and financial products. It has become an industry of specialists in generation skipping, business continuation, charitable planning, insurance planning, asset management, and more.

Some clients spend countless hours with advisors reviewing potential strategies and alternatives, attempting to become experts themselves so that they may rely on their own knowledge and instincts in making decisions. They believe that as soon as they fully understand every aspect of the situation, they will make the decision. Not surprisingly, that point of understanding rarely occurs. Likewise, the decision is not made.

Estate planning has become so complicated that the solution often seems worse than the problem. It should come as no surprise to advisors that many clients have trouble swallowing the medicine.

The truth is that the majority of clients never will understand the complex issues involved in estate planning, such as the inherent ever-changing tax laws, and the various planning strategies. Their lack of understanding will continue to create anxiety—anxiety that leads to fear; fear that leads to indecision; indecision that leads to planning paralysis.

And the eternal planning process continues.

(e) Too Much Jargon

Much like the medical profession, the estate planning industry has a tremendous compulsion to use jargon—names created by advisors for advisors but mistakenly used with clients every day. As a result, clients may feel as if they have entered a foreign country.

> . . . so, the NIMCRUT is connected to the ILIT, and the ILIT is connected to the IDIT, and the IDIT is connected to the FB, and the . . .

The client may never understand what all these acronyms and fancy names mean. Some advisors don't understand what they mean.

When it comes to their health, patients often take their medicine just because the doctor told them to take it. In the worst-case scenario, they may get a second opinion. Ultimately, most people act on the advice of the health care professional. After all, it may be a life or death matter.

Even though estate planning also is a matter that deals with life and death, clients routinely ignore the advice they receive from their advisors. Some seek a second opinion, or a third or even a fourth. Why? Often it is the result of ineffective communication. The client simply cannot decipher the code.

And the eternal planning process continues.

(f) Separation from Resources

As was stated earlier, and will be repeated often in this book, tax-effective wealth transfer planning strategies frequently require one very important thing—the irrevocable separation of clients from their money, as soon as possible, forever.

This poses a problem for many as it conflicts with a basic human instinct, that of self-preservation. Most clients lack confidence with regard to what is required to maintain their financial independence for life. Their default answer is that they need all of what they have. Since they cannot define how much they will need, rest assured, they will need it all. Any course that potentially reduces their financial independence is avoided.

Estate planning constantly reminds clients of the necessity to part with their financial resources. Each time they are faced with the possible diminishment of their financial independence, anxiety is created. This anxiety leads to indecision, which derails the planning process.

And the eternal planning process continues.

(g) Emotional Barriers

Many advisors believe their clients are not charitably inclined. This belief arises from years of experience in which clients summarily dismiss charitable giving as a component of their estate plan with no apparent explanation. In most of these cases, the advisor asks the client something like this:

> "Tell me, Scott, would you like to benefit any charities through your estate plan?" A typical reply might be, "Well, I'm really more concerned right now with making sure that my wife and I are financially secure and that we can provide a suitable inheritance for our children."

Based on the client's less-than-enthusiastic response to a general question, advisors typically assume the client has no charitable intent. As a result, charitable giving is taken off the list of potential planning issues.

The problem with this approach is that it assumes the client has already developed philanthropic awareness. It assumes the client has been able to overcome his or her natural emotional barriers to charitable giving—beliefs, for instance, that gifts are in opposition to other planning objectives, that philanthropy is only for the wealthy, or that charity is a subsidized form of government bureaucracy.

Even the most sophisticated clients often misunderstand the role that charitable giving can play in the estate planning process. As a result, charitable planning strategies such as charitable remainder trusts all too often are quickly dismissed by the client and advisor with no real examination.

And the eternal planning process continues.

(h) Advisor Bias

Every advisor has experienced the dreaded second opinion. Clients seek second opinions for several reasons: Either they lack confidence in the advisor's ability or they fear professional bias or they are simply confused.

As Stephen Covey put it, "People see the world not as it is, but as they are." Consider the wide range of professionals represented in the estate planning field:

- Insurance agents
- Investment brokers
- Estate planning attorneys
- Tax accountants
- Nonprofit planned giving officers
- Trust officers
- Family business consultants

What if a client poses a single problem to these seven professionals? Chances are, the client will get seven solutions: one from an insurance perspective, one from an investment perspective, one from a legal perspective, one from an accounting perspective, one from a fund-raiser's perspective, one from a trust officer's perspective, and one from the family office consultant's perspective. This should come as no surprise. Each advisor has been trained to use the tools of his or her profession to resolve client problems. Insurance agents typically are not trained in the intricacies of law, and lawyers typically are not trained to analyze and sell life insurance. Each advisor has his or her unique bias.

Clients are right to be concerned about the motivation behind each recommendation. Is the recommended strategy good for the client, good for the advisor, or both? Is the suggested solution merely a trick to sell a product? Is the charity just looking for a gift? Does the plan really need to be this complicated?

Clients seek second opinions in an effort to eliminate advisor bias. Unfortunately, they often fail to realize that every additional advisor they approach has his or her own biases. As a result, the quickest way to eliminate bias is to do nothing.

When confronted with advisor bias, more often than not the result is no result. Advisor bias leads to indecision, and indecision leads to planning paralysis.

And the eternal planning process continues.

(i) Ending the Game

As strange as it may seem, for some clients the prospect of completing their estate plan is a reason to fan the coals of the eternal planning process. They are afraid of reaching the end. They believe that once the plan is complete, death is inevitable. As a result, they undermine the process and avoid decisions. They will even change advisors just to repeat the process all over again. Some people may believe subconsciously that the eternal planning process will result in eternal life. In reality, it results in an incomplete plan with a devastating impact on financial resources and surviving family members.

And the eternal planning process continues.

CHAPTER TWO

Eternal Planning: Why Advisors Are Trapped

D o not assume that the client alone is responsible for estate planning obstacles. Advisors play a significant role in perpetuating the eternal planning process. A number of common factors contribute to why advisors also find themselves trapped within this process.

2.1 WHY ADVISORS ARE TRAPPED

It is fair to say that competent advisors know many of the right questions to ask a prospective client. They also know many of the possible answers to each question. Where they have trouble is matching the correct answers with the right clients.

(a) A Propensity to Make Assumptions

Rather than take valuable time to ask the questions, many advisors take a lot for granted. They believe that over the years they have seen it all. When they meet a prospective client for the first time, they place him or her into a category, along with other current and past clients who appear similar. Then they make numerous assumptions based upon this initial assessment. More often than not, some of these assumptions are incorrect. Eventually, if the assumptions are not corrected, they derail the planning process and facilitate eternal planning.

Clients are not just innocent bystanders in the crusade to gloss over objectives and jump to plan design. In many ways, they contribute to the situation. Clients tend to assume their advisors know what they want to do. They transfer the entire burden to the advisor, oversimplifying the planning process and discounting nonfinancial issues. They convince themselves that estate planning is a cookie-cutter process where one size fits all.

(b) Preoccupation with Strategies

For most advisors, creating a sustainable competitive market advantage is a primary concern. In estate planning, this often means staying abreast of the latest and greatest planning techniques and strategies.

Most advisors will agree that establishing clear and concise objectives is fundamental to effective planning, at least in theory. In practice, a majority of effort is devoted to plan design with a secondary emphasis on plan implementation. Far too little time is spent in developing objectives. This theoretically important area of planning seems to be viewed as a necessary evil by clients and advisors alike.

This is not to say that most plans are developed without objectives. The problem is with how those objectives are established. In many cases, the origin and appropriateness of the objectives are questionable. In reality, clients have little or no idea about what can be accomplished in estate planning. They have no concept of the possibilities. They are unaware of what other people in similar situations have done. As a result, they look to their primary advisor for advice because, after all, the advisor is the expert.

Herein lies the problem. Competent estate planning advisors are comfortable dealing with objective, technical planning issues within their respective areas of practice. Drafting legal documents, identifying strategies, evaluating insurance products, defining investment risk tolerance, or analyzing alternative financial outcomes are within familiar territory. Advisors generally are not comfortable managing subjective areas of planning, such as dealing with emotion, understanding family values, or managing conflict.

In their defense, most estate planning advisors receive minimal or no training with respect to these less technical issues. They are taught the technical areas of planning, strategies, and products. They are taught to be objective, or they are taught to sell. They are not taught to probe, listen, and empathize.

To see what advisors focus on at any point in time, review the agenda for any major industry conference. The majority of time is devoted to technical issues or sales issues. What new strategies can I learn? How can I sell more insurance? How can I raise more money for my organization? How can I gather more assets?

In the last few years, this trend has begun to shift modestly. However, the industry has a long way to go. Advisors are at risk when they are in front of their clients, particularly when other advisors are present. In these situations, natural survival instincts intervene and most advisors fall back on what comes most naturally to them.

Consider the issue of planning strategies. Advisors often attempt to help clients establish objectives by reviewing the appropriateness of various strategies. They fire one idea after another at the client and then watch for reactions—good or bad. Invariably, people end up with exploding headaches as a result of the complexity and confusion. Not only did they not understand the fifth strategy, they didn't even understand the first.

Sometimes this takes place in a single meeting and sometimes over the course of months or even years. The advisor continues to present a sequence of strategies. Each strategy is designed to resolve an assumed problem.

Increasing the complexity, clients often are barraged by several advisors with different strategies and differing objectives—all tools that have been designed to solve problems that have not yet been clearly defined.

It is important to note that clients do not necessarily object to this focus on strategies. In many ways, they actually enjoy it, even if they don't understand it. The reason should be obvious. While they are evaluating the benefits and features of various strategies, clients are not forced to make any decisions. Each strategy appears like a lifeboat floating on the water, providing temporary refuge from the decisions lingering beneath the surface.

Each new strategy gives clients one more reason to remain in the eternal planning process, contemplating what they might do.

(c) Mistaking Confusion with a Need for More Information

Advisors often mistake confusion with the need for additional information. Technology has blessed advisors with an infinite capacity to organize and generate information.

The personal computer has caused considerable damage to the life insurance industry over the past 10 years. By providing agents with the ability to generate their own insurance illustrations, the industry has shifted its focus from client objectives to features and benefits. On any given case, an agent can generate 5, 10, or even more illustrations, each with only minor variables, magically adjusting the proposal until the client buys the product.

The legal industry has suffered much the same fate, and perhaps has not seen the worst yet. Considerable time and money have been spent applying technology to estate planning. Many lawyers have automated document drafting to the extent that there is virtually no limit to the variations they can generate, or to their length. It is not uncommon for a client's estate planning documents to stand four or five inches high when stacked. Really complicated cases can stand over a foot.

The fund-raising industry has participated in this information overload through its rapid embrace of planned giving strategies. Rather than just asking for a gift, they provide the prospective donor with four or five planned gift illustrations.

No matter where you look, an advisor's ability to generate and distribute information has increased dramatically over the past 10 years. All too often, when confronted with an indecisive client, the solution is to provide just one more alternative. Each new layer of information gives the client another reason to put off a decision. Perhaps by waiting a while longer, yet another proposal will appear. Most of the time, this is a correct deduction.

(d) Advisor Bias

Advisors face biases that complicate the planning process. Sometimes another advisor, with different opinions, challenges a recommendation. This recommendation inevitably comes with the second advisor's own bias, further complicating and extending the process.

(e) Codependency

Keep in mind that advisors often are reluctant to move clients into implementation too quickly. They too are comfortable in the safety zone. Combine this with an advisor who is paid for plan design, and in many cases no one has adequate motivation to move the process forward.

These advisors will be paid regardless. In some cases, they will be paid even more if they don't ever complete the plan as, for instance, in the case of settling a messy estate and its resulting costs. In such a case, the advisors may be happy to revisit, reevaluate, and reconsider strategy after strategy.

(f) The Economics of Success

Consider the typical sales process, which begins with an assumed problem. This assumption may be on the part of the advisor or the client. The key is that the problem may not have been substantiated. Once the initial assumption is made, a strategy, or more than one, is selected to solve the problem.

Once the strategy is presented, the sale begins. Remember that salespeople do not get paid unless clients implement strategies that require their products.

The focus and emphasis is on the sale.

2.2 THE TRADITIONAL PLANNING PROCESS

Consider the steps in the traditional planning process, from the bottom up:

1. Data gathering
2. Review of the current plan

3. Establishing goals and objectives
4. Developing observations
5. Plan design and implementation
6. Administration

Historically, as much as 80 percent of the planning process has been devoted to the top two levels: (5) plan design and implementation and (6) administration.

Why do you suppose this is the case?

Because, for the most part, the advisor is compensated for the work completed during plan design and implementation. Unfortunately, the first four categories all too often are regarded as less important.

2.3 THE DISCOVERY PROCESS

The Legacy Planning System reverses the typical process. The first four steps become the focus, and 80 percent or more of the emphasis is devoted to data gathering, reviewing the current plan, establishing goals and objectives, and developing observations.

This part of the process holds the key elements to successful planning. Similar to the use of the term in law, *discovery* establishes facts and clarifies ambiguities. This is where the process needs to begin.

As stated previously, obstacles to effective estate planning are many and varied. In fact, professional advisors generally agree that most people are averse to estate planning. The underlying reason is that the process is complex and confusing. Because clients don't understand it, they consequently believe they can exercise little if any control over the process. This lack of understanding and control leads many to start the process only to stop out of frustration, or to avoid planning altogether.

Although most clients find estate planning concepts and strategies difficult to grasp, the majority have a reasonably clear understanding of who—and what—is most important to them.

The Legacy Planning System is a step-by-step approach—a *system*—that advisors can learn and use to accomplish the following:

- Help clients discover and solidify their deepest values, convictions, and objectives as they relate to their money
- Help clients express those values and objectives in a clearly written Family Financial Philosophy mission statement
- Serve as the team leader in advising clients—and clients' other advisors—on how to use the mission statement to direct the planning process

2.4 THE SEVEN PRINCIPLES
OF VALUES-BASED ESTATE PLANNING

Estate planning is a particularly timely subject given the immense inter-generational transfer of wealth that has begun from parents of baby boomers to the boomer generation. Estimated at $10.4 trillion in a 1990 Cornell University study, Boston College researchers Paul Schervish and John Havens now estimate amounts as low as $41 trillion and as high as $136 trillion will be transferred between now and 2052. See Foreword for more details on this new study.

People in general are becoming more knowledgeable and savvy regarding their financial decisions. Increasing numbers are accumulating significant wealth from inheritance, through innovation and hard work, and as a result of good investment decisions. These wealth holders are beginning to pay closer attention to what their ultimate legacies could and should be, and they are seeking the advice of competent professionals to help them achieve their highest financial and philanthropic aspirations.

The seven principles that follow explore values-based planning concepts and explain how advisors can help wealth holders use their values to simplify the planning process, ensure lifetime financial independence, and control their ultimate family and social capital legacies.

These principles, or planning "rules," will lead advisors and clients through a successful and gratifying process. They provide the framework for putting clients at the center of—and in control of—their planning.

1. *Understand the Hierarchy of Planning Objectives.* A "pyramid of planning objectives" provides a logical and effective progression for the planning process. The value that clients place on (1) financial independence, (2) family legacy, and (3) social capital legacy will lay the foundation for all their planning decisions.

2. *Master the Concept of Social Capital.* The concept of social capital redefines wealth and its potential impact on society. Most simply, social capital is that part of an individual's wealth that will be distributed either as taxes or charitable gifts.

3. *Define the Family Financial Philosophy.* Wills and trusts describe *how* estate assets will be distributed. A Family Financial Philosophy explains *why*. This written wealth mission statement expresses clients' values and goals as they relate to wealth and money.

4. *Quantify Financial Independence.* The first step in the planning process requires clients to define and quantify precisely how much wealth they will need to achieve and maintain financial independence for the rest of their lives.

5. *Identify an Appropriate Family Legacy.* Most people want to leave some part of their estate to family members or others who are important to them. Because passing "value without values" can be detrimental to heirs, it is important to examine issues related to inheritance and specify an appropriate amount for each.

6. *Maximize the Social Capital Legacy.* Will the social capital legacy be in the form of taxes or charitable gifts? Clients can choose! Decisions regarding the distribution of excess wealth become easier when they are values-driven.

7. *Build a Virtual Planning Team.* The ideal estate planning team is multidisciplinary, with each advisor bringing a unique ability to the mix. Using the values and objectives expressed in the Family Financial Philosophy mission statement as a guide, the planning team works collaboratively to recommend the best possible plan.

POINTS TO PONDER

- The amount of wealth held by individuals and families is increasing at an extraordinary rate.
- The amount of wealth held by younger people, especially those in the high-tech industry, is astounding.
- Many of the new wealth holders are not from affluent families. A US Trust survey indicates that 70 percent is first-generation wealth. Their inexperience leads to a variety of unfamiliar and uncomfortable issues and problems.
- There is much discussion regarding what constitutes an appropriate inheritance.
- Many are concerned about protecting financial independence, especially in relation to the prospective cost of long-term care as they age.
- Few families have any concept of what "appropriate inheritance" means.
- Regardless of how much wealth families have (the reality), they often feel they need more (the perception). This incongruity can lead to planning paralysis.
- Many advisors lack the necessary skills to motivate clients to develop clear, concise objectives. When it comes to "soft" issues, they admittedly don't know how to carry on the conversation.
- Most people have no idea what they could accomplish in the estate planning process.

- Given the opportunity to explore values, most people will identify an appropriate role for philanthropy.
- Excess wealth provides the working capital for philanthropy. Unfortunately, the vast majority of people believe they have little or no excess wealth.
- Values-based planning offers a way to help link values with wealth-planning decisions.

As more and more resources are distributed through a planning process based on values, the inevitable growth in philanthropy and its impact on society is sure to be monumental. The results will be good for individual clients . . . good for advisors . . . and good for society at large.

CHAPTER THREE

Principle #1

Understand the Hierarchy of Planning Objectives

The *pyramid of planning objectives* provides a logical and effective progression for the planning process. The value that clients place on (1) financial independence, (2) family legacy, and (3) social capital legacy will lay the foundation for all estate planning decisions to follow.

3.1 UNDERSTANDING THE CONCEPT

Three levels of a pyramid reflect the client's hierarchy of objectives as they relate to the accumulation, preservation, use, and distribution of wealth. The primary objective at the bottom level is the client's need to establish and maintain financial independence. The middle level addresses the client's desire to leave a family legacy. At the top of the pyramid is the client's wish to make a difference—to have a positive impact on society through a social capital legacy.

This order of priorities is fundamental, in that it first secures the basic needs of clients and those closest to them. Advisors are cautioned not to change this natural order. They should not let anyone convince them or their clients that tackling these issues in a different order makes better sense.

Regardless of what the client is considering, the levels are negotiated in this same order. First, what does the potential decision do to the client (and spouse, if applicable)? Second, how does it affect the ability to leave an appropriate and satisfactory legacy for heirs? Third, what other positive outcomes might be achieved for society after the first two levels have been addressed?

Each level of the pyramid demands two separate measurements of good planning: (1) How do clients accomplish their objectives at each specific level effectively? (2) How will accomplishing those objectives affect the sense of significance they feel, or would like to feel, at each level?

It is important to note that although the three levels appear to be separate and distinct, they actually overlap, and in some cases conflict. These conflicts or dilemmas are to be expected and arise often in the planning process. For example, in order to increase the amount of property passing to heirs from the estate, the client must begin making gifts today. However, what if investments perform poorly and the client runs out of money? Dilemmas like this are difficult, because they pit key objectives against one another.

With every decision an advisor helps his or her clients make, three simple rules apply:

1. When it comes to money, the clients' needs are always most important.
2. When it comes to money, the clients' heirs are the second most important.
3. When it comes to money, everyone else is third.

The same order applies to everyone. The amount of wealth clients choose to allocate at each of the three levels is a function of their values combined with their available financial resources.

3.2 THE PLANNING PYRAMID: A HIERARCHY OF PLANNING OBJECTIVES

Again, the planning process is driven by three intrinsic objectives: (1) the need to assure financial independence; (2) the desire to leave a family legacy; and (3) the desire to have a positive impact on society through a social capital legacy. These objectives tend to be at work unconsciously, even if not expressly understood and articulated. Clients will apply them intuitively to financial decisions. However, because most people have not clearly defined these important objectives, the planning process often is frustrated by indecision, which too often leads to planning paralysis.

Instinctively, a client may try to evaluate a proposed idea based on how it might affect these three objectives. Yet because the objectives are vague, or more often totally nonexistent, the client makes no decision at all.

(a) Financial Independence

The first and most basic planning objective should be to identify and maintain lifetime financial independence. Simply stated, financial independence is achieved when the client has accumulated and preserved all he or she could possibly ever need to maintain a desired lifestyle. Generally expressed as a combination of annual income and a specified minimum resource base, a financial independence goal answers the question, "What do I want from my wealth for the rest of my life?"

(b) Family Legacy

Once they define and achieve financial independence, clients gain the necessary self-confidence to shift attention to wealth distribution, generally called estate planning. This level of planning determines the *family legacy*—what heirs will receive. In an effective, comprehensive plan, the family legacy is predetermined as an appropriate transfer to heirs. During this phase of the process, advisors help clients deliberately and carefully specify an inheritance amount for each estate beneficiary.

(c) Social Capital Legacy

Once financial independence and the desired family legacy for heirs both are secured, clients will experience a greater sense of freedom to consider what their potential *social capital legacy* might be. The social capital legacy is derived from that part of the estate not needed to maintain financial independence and not designated for family legacy. There are two forms of social capital—voluntary and involuntary. Voluntary social capital comprises those dollars over which clients make a conscious decision to take distribution responsibility. Either taxes or charitable contributions, this part of the estate wealth represents the lasting impact clients may have on society by directing their social capital in a manner that reflects their personal value systems. These social capital dollars are self-directed.

Involuntary social capital may be described as those dollars and assets extracted under the default plan—tax. This represents the mandatory redistribution of social capital wealth when clients fail to take personal responsibility for their wealth distribution. These are government-directed social capital dollars.

In the most effective estate plan, each objective—financial independence, family legacy, and social capital legacy—is carefully examined and specified.

General Observation . . . on the priorities of wealth

When it comes to money, the clients' needs are always most important.

When it comes to money, the clients' heirs are the second most important.

When it comes to money, everyone else is third.

3.3 IDENTIFYING PLANNING MOTIVATION: WHY CLIMB THE PYRAMID?

One of the most important aspects of estate planning or wealth transfer is establishing a planning focus. What is the client's motivation for planning?

The dominant motivation for planning often will be one of the following five planning goals.

1. *Financial Independence Goal.* The motive is to maintain maximum access to financial resources, regardless of the impact on family wealth transfer. The client with this primary goal is most concerned about maintaining a sense of personal or family financial security. Maximizing inheritance for heirs, reducing transfer taxes, or making charitable gifts are secondary issues. If the client values financial independence above all other planning goals, strategies should focus on maximum control over financial resources.

2. *Tax-Effectiveness Goal.* The client desires to transfer financial resources from one generation to another while minimizing the amount of resources lost to tax. This client is most concerned with reducing the amount of tax paid, as wealth is transferred to the next generation. He or she prefers strategies that reduce tax above strategies that maximize inheritance and is likely to favor strategies that convert taxes into charitable contributions.

3. *Maximum Inheritance Goal.* The motive is to maximize the amount of wealth transferred from one generation to another, regardless of how much wealth is lost to tax. This client doesn't care how much tax is paid, as long as heirs receive the largest possible share of the wealth. The client wants to focus on strategies that reduce tax and/or transfer assets to charity, but only if those strategies do not reduce the inheritance for heirs.

4. *Social Capital Goal.* The client desires to convert taxes into charitable gifts, regardless of how much wealth is transferred to heirs. This client is most concerned about converting potential taxes into charitable contributions, even if those contributions reduce what is transferred to heirs. The client's primary value is social capital, and he or she is content to have heirs receive what is left after eliminating taxes to the greatest extent and making charitable gifts. This client prefers social capital planning strategies to more conventional planning strategies.

5. *Wealth Control Goal.* The motive is to convert taxes into charitable gifts, after securing the desired inheritance for heirs. This client wants to maintain control over the distribution of the estate. After establishing a minimum acceptable family legacy, planning efforts should focus on converting taxes into self-directed charitable contributions. Total control over financial resources is the goal.

Advisors must determine which of these five goals best represents any given client's perspective. The differences are subtle, but important. Whatever motivates the client to plan is what provides the focus for future planning decisions.

3.4 THE ESTATE PLANNING PROCESS: DEFENSIVE VERSUS OFFENSIVE PLANNING

Effective estate planning is the process of transferring what clients have . . . to whom they want . . . using the ways they want . . . when they want . . . at the lowest possible cost. Advisors can utilize defensive or offensive strategies in accomplishing the planning objectives. A combination of defensive and offensive strategies also may be appropriate.

Defensive estate planning strategies secure and maintain financial independence, coordinate the distribution of the estate, protect against administrative expense and delay in settling the estate, manage family business value and succession, protect assets from lawsuits, and maintain control over personal affairs. The primary focus of defensive planning is to preserve and distribute wealth.

Offensive estate planning strategies minimize taxes or convert taxes into charitable gifts, or both. The primary focus of offensive planning is tax-effectiveness.

In estate planning, cost refers to taxes, probate, administration, and the cost of planning. Most estates are subject to probate, administration, and the cost of planning at some level. However, only estates of a certain size are subject to tax.

The size of an estate often determines whether the plan requires defensive or offensive strategies, or both. Generally speaking, the larger the estate, the more likely offensive planning will be required.

This discussion does not include information on the Internal Revenue Code. However, one simple rule regarding the size of an estate is relevant: If a client is single in the year 2000, and the estate exceeds $675,000, offensive planning has a potential role. If a client is married, the figure is $1,350,000. In either instance, basic trust planning will solve most of the estate planning problems. Under present regulations, these exemption amounts are scheduled to increase over time, reaching $1 million and $2 million respectively by the year 2006.

If the client's estate is below this threshold, defensive planning likely will address planning needs adequately. If the estate size is above the threshold and therefore subject to tax, offensive planning strategies will offer tax-effective solutions. An offensive approach will help clients achieve their goals on each of the three planning pyramid levels.

3.5 CLIMBING THE PYRAMID: HOW COMPLEX IS THE JOURNEY?

Clients often complain about the complexity of the estate planning process. Yet, in reality, the complexity of an estate plan is largely a function of the client's goals and objectives. The process begins with asking the client this fundamental question: "What is the appropriate allocation of your financial resources among the three potential beneficiaries of your estate: (1) your heirs, (2) the IRS, and (3) charity?"

A *Planning Index* provides insight with respect to the level of effort needed to accomplish a client's planning goals and objectives. It also indicates whether offensive planning strategies are appropriate.

(a) The Planning Index

Generally speaking, the required level of effort for an estate plan can be determined by using two formulas:

$$\text{Factor} = [((\text{TE} \times 2) + \text{NTE}) \times \text{FLG}] + [\text{TE} \times (\text{FLG} \times \text{SCG})]$$
$$- ((\text{NTE} + \text{FE}) \times 2)$$

and

$$\text{Planning Index} = \text{Factor}/(\text{TE} + \text{NTE}),$$

whereby

$\quad\quad$ TE = taxable estate: total current financial resources included in the taxable estate

NTE = nontaxable estate: total current financial resources outside the taxable estate, and therefore, available for tax-free transfer to heirs

FLG = family legacy goal: desired percentage of TE and NTE passing to heirs

SCG = social capital goal: desired percentage of social capital allocated as charitable gifts

FE = federal exemption: total amount of financial resources that may be transferred to heirs, estate tax–free, under federal gift and estate tax laws

The higher the index, the more complex the required planning and the more likely offensive planning strategies will be necessary to accomplish the client's goals.

The Planning Index is detailed in Exhibit 3.1. A client's index is calculated by dividing the factor determined in the formula by the total available financial resources—in other words, TE + NTE. The higher the index, the more effort the plan requires. Generally speaking, an index of 6 or more requires lifetime planning.

The size of a client's estate and the client's family legacy goal are important factors in determining the required level of complexity to accomplish client objectives. The social capital goal increases the level of complexity only when the family legacy goal is high.

Consider three examples:

Example 1

Married, Taxable Estate ($10,000,000), Nontaxable Estate ($0)
(Goals: 75% heirs, 0% tax, and 25% charity)
$19,900,000 = [(($10,000,000 \times 2) +0) \times 75\%)]$
$+ [\$10,000,000 \times (75\% \times 100\%)] - (($0 + \$1,300,000) \times 2)$
(Planning Index 8) 198% = ($19,900,000/$10,000,000)

Factor/(TE + NTE)	Index
281% or more	10
230%–280%	9
181%–229%	8
154%–180%	7
134%–153%	6
122%–133%	5
113%–121%	4
106%–112%	3
101%–105%	2
100% or less	1

Exhibit 3.1 The Planning Index

Example 2
Single, Taxable Estate ($5,000,000), Non-taxable Estate ($500,000)
(Goals: 50% heirs, 50% tax, and 0% charity)
$4,200,000 = [(($5,000,000 × 2) + $500,000) × 50%)]
          + [$5,000,000 × (50% × 0%)] − (($500,000 + $625,000) × 2)
(Planning Index 1) 76.4% = ($4,200,000/$5,500,000)

Example 3
Married, Taxable Estate ($3,000,000), Nontaxable Estate ($0)
(Goals: 25% heirs, 0% tax, and 75% charity)
$350,000 = [(($3,000,000 × 2) + $0) × 25%)]
          + [$3,000,000 × (25% × 100%)] − (($0 + $1,250,000) × 2)
(Planning Index 1) 0% = ($350,000/$3,000,000) The actual result is negative 11.7%, however, negative numbers are assigned 0%)

(b) Lifetime Planning Strategies

Climbing the pyramid of planning requires a clear definition at each level. When and how clients climb the pyramid depends on each client's Planning Index. The higher the level of complexity, the greater the likelihood lifetime planning will be necessary.

With few exceptions, the primary advantage of planning over an entire lifetime is time. The more time a strategy has to work, the more effective it will be.

In order to take advantage of lifetime planning strategies, the client must apply planning resources. These resources represent dollars not required to support financial independence. Therefore, in order to maximize the advantages of lifetime planning, clients must first determine what they need to maintain financial independence, so that they can establish what they do not need.

(c) Testamentary Planning Strategies

The lower the Planning Index, the less likely additional lifetime planning strategies will be required to accomplish a client's goals. In low-complexity situations, planning goals may be accomplished entirely through testamentary planning. As previously suggested, it is simple to eliminate the estate tax by leaving 100 percent of the estate to charity at death. Only minimal lifetime planning is required, and maximum flexibility is retained.

(d) The Cost of Waiting

Those who procrastinate pay a heavy price. As the sloping line in Exhibit 3.2 indicates, over time, the benefits of planning suffer from diminishing

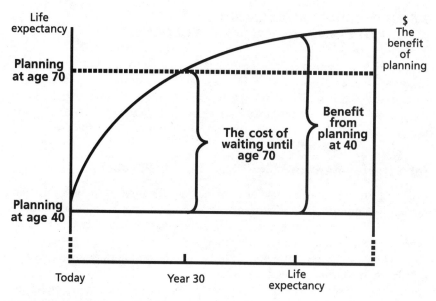

Exhibit 3.2   The Cost of Waiting

returns. Virtually every planning strategy available works better the sooner it begins. In fact, the best time to begin planning is yesterday. Today is second best. One thing is sure: The cost of waiting will exceed the cost of planning today. If a client's goals score high on the Planning Index, it is important to begin the process soon. The most successful results depend on it.

(e) Planning Index Summary

In planning an estate, both advisor and client should start with the end in mind. Define family and social capital legacies and build a plan to achieve those goals. The desired allocation of the estate among heirs, tax, and charity will determine the level of planning effort required. Stated simply, the client determines how complex the plan must be when he or she establishes these basic objectives.

The higher the Planning Index, the more likely lifetime planning strategies will be required to accomplish the objectives. Many lifetime planning strategies require an irrevocable application of planning resources. Planning resources are equal to total financial resources minus all assets required for financial independence. Therefore, lifetime planning is controlled intrinsically by the client's self-confidence regarding financial independence.

3.6 UNPACKING THE PYRAMID:
UNDERSTANDING THE INTERRELATIONSHIPS

In seeking to understand the pyramid, it is essential for advisors and clients to understand the relationships between and among the three levels. To a certain extent, the issues of each level are felt through the entire structure of the pyramid. Rather than strictly defined borders between each level, there is a gray area where many issues overlap and sometimes conflict.

(a) Effectiveness and Significance at Each Level

Financial success and a sense of personal significance often are characterized independently of one another. Some would argue that the first part of life is all about achieving success, and the second part is about turning that success into a sense of significance.

However, an equal capacity for both success and significance exists in all phases of one's financial life. The very process of working to become "successful" often results in feelings of "significance"—as in, for example, building a business, climbing the corporate ladder, or making wise investment decisions.

Early on, many strive to achieve financial independence—to succeed. Significance, although it may be felt, is a by-product of achieving success. The degree of significance individuals feel is, at least in part, a function of how effective they perceive themselves to be.

Once it is clear that the achievement of financial success is no longer a concern, the focus may shift fairly easily to how they can gain a greater overall sense of significance.

(b) Financial Independence: Effectiveness and Significance

How does effectiveness relate to financial independence? The most effective ways of achieving tax minimization, wealth accumulation, asset protection, and risk management lead to the highest level of financial independence.

Significance, as it relates to financial independence, may be expressed in many forms. Typically, clients aspire to achieve affluence in order to enjoy certain opportunities. Issues such as the following shape one's philosophy of wealth:

- The freedom to control all aspects of one's life
- Power and influence in society
- The ability to help others
- Personal or family financial security

- The ability to start, manage, control, or invest in business
- The time to pursue personal spiritual development
- The ability to help create breakthroughs for the benefit of society
- The ability to emerge as a leader among peers in responsible wealth management and deployment

(c) Family Legacy: Effectiveness and Significance

Effective family legacy planning generally refers to the efficient transfer of wealth between generations. This is accomplished by building a plan that ensures maximum efficiency in achieving stated inheritance objectives.

Significance at this level comes from passing value with values. The term *value* relates to the financial legacy—the sense of satisfaction and significance gained from an ability to help children and grandchildren secure a financial head start in life, the ability to contribute to the financial independence of succeeding generations.

The term *values* reflects the desire to transfer family values along with a financial legacy. Many people gain a tremendous sense of satisfaction from knowing they have transferred a strong base of positive values to heirs. Consider the following potential values that clients may wish to pass along to succeeding generations:

- Ethical values, such as honesty, justice, fairness
- Personal values, such as modesty, loyalty, faithfulness
- Emotional values, such as compassion, kindness, generosity
- Public values, such as good citizenship, community involvement, government service
- Economic values, such as financial responsibility, frugality, stewardship
- Spiritual values, such as inner spirituality, meditation, faith, religious commitment
- Work values, such as effort, punctuality, competence, professional achievement
- Physical values, such as health, relaxation, exercise
- Cultural values, such as music, visual arts, travel
- Relational values, such as family, friends, work associates
- Philanthropic values, such as contributions of time and money to care for others
- Recreational values, such as sports, leisure activity, hobbies, family vacations

- Educational values, such as study, self-improvement, academic achievement

(d) Social Capital Legacy: Effectiveness and Significance

Effective social capital planning derives from the manner and efficiency in which social capital is captured and how ultimately it is put to use through gifts or tax. Both, by the way, are necessary components of society as it exists today.

Many people gain a sense of significance from personally directing their social capital. They want to help shape the social, physical, or spiritual environment in which they live. They believe they will leave the world a better place by virtue of their contributions during their brief stay on earth. Others are content to benefit society through the payment of tax.

(e) Unpacking the Pyramid Levels

How do the three pyramid levels—financial independence, family legacy, and social capital legacy—interrelate? In many areas they overlap and intersect. It is important to recognize this and the potential for conflict.

For many people, net worth becomes a major component of self-worth. In fact, like it or not, money is a serious factor in keeping score in life. As a result, even the most grounded people may experience difficulty letting go of the resources they perceive they need for financial independence, even in the pursuit of significance at a higher level of the planning pyramid.

Most tax-effective strategies for establishing a family or social capital legacy also require the irrevocable separation of clients from their money. As a result, achieving a sense of significance at either of these two levels is accomplished only at the expense of the client's sense of significance regarding financial independence. These opposing forces can paralyze the planning process. Because the need for financial independence supercedes any desires regarding family legacy and social capital legacy, when this paralysis occurs, both advisors and their clients tend to err on the side of independence.

Understanding the relationship of effectiveness and significance at each level is essential to helping clients navigate their way up the pyramid of planning.

General Observation . . . on significance

For many, financial success is the primary focus earlier in one's work life. When financial success becomes a reality, the focus may shift to exploring a deeper sense of satisfaction and significance in life.

3.7 A BRIEF REVIEW

When confronted with financial and estate planning decisions, three intrinsic objectives must be met in priority order:

1. Financial independence—How will the decision affect the client's lifetime needs?
2. Family legacy—How will it affect inheritance for heirs?
3. Social capital legacy—How will it affect society through the application of tax or charitable gifts?

Clearly defined goals at each level will help achieve maximum results.

For the best result, effectiveness and significance must be maximized at each level of the planning pyramid. This will ensure consistency between planning decisions and the client's personal values.

The desired allocation of a client's estate among heirs, tax, and charity is the primary factor in determining the level of complexity required to accomplish estate planning goals. The higher the client's Planning Index, the more likely lifetime planning strategies will be necessary in order to accomplish client objectives.

Many lifetime planning strategies require an irrevocable application of planning resources. Planning resources are equal to total financial resources minus assets required for financial independence. Therefore, lifetime planning is controlled intrinsically by the client's self-confidence regarding financial independence.

POINTS TO PONDER

- Financial independence is achieved when clients have accumulated and preserved all they will ever need to maintain their desired lifestyle. A clear understanding of financial independence is the most important factor in effective lifetime planning.

- Family legacy is a predetermined portion of their estate that clients identify as appropriate to transfer to their heirs. Family legacy is the most significant factor in determining the required complexity of the estate plan.

- Social capital legacy is derived from that portion of the estate not required to maintain financial independence and not designated for family legacy. Specifying the desired allocation of social capital between charitable gifts and tax is essential in order to determine the appropriate level of complexity for a client's estate plan.

- Most people do not have a clear picture of what the three planning levels mean to them. As a result, they find it difficult to climb the pyramid of planning.
- Many individuals do not want to confront basic estate planning issues, such as their mortality, their philanthropic potential, or their children's ability—or inability—to manage inherited wealth. As a result, they procrastinate.
- For many people, net worth is a major component of how they measure their self-worth. Money is a serious factor in keeping score. As a result, even the most grounded people can have a difficult time letting go of wealth, even in the pursuit of significance at a higher level of the pyramid.
- A series of dilemmas exists within and between the levels of the pyramid. These dilemmas must be overcome, if planning is to reach a successful result.
- To build estate plans that reflect their clients' values, advisors must help clients traverse the pyramid of planning, seeking both effectiveness and significance at each level—financial independence, family legacy, and social capital legacy.

ASK A CLIENT TO TRY THIS

Many people aspire to achieve affluence so that they may enjoy special opportunities. Have the client rate how successful he or she has been in achieving each of the elements in Exhibit 3.3 on a scale from 1 to 4, with 1 being the least successful and 4 being the most successful.

A client's responses to these questions begin to shape his or her philosophy of wealth. Consider whether the client's views have encouraged or discouraged movement up the planning pyramid. Is there room for improvement?

---

1 2 3 4	The time and resources required to control all aspects of my life
1 2 3 4	Power and influence in society
1 2 3 4	The ability to help others
1 2 3 4	Personal and/or family financial security
1 2 3 4	The ability to start, manage, control, or invest in business
1 2 3 4	The time to pursue personal spiritual development
1 2 3 4	The ability to help create breakthroughs for the benefit of society
1 2 3 4	The ability to be seen as a leader among peers in responsible wealth management and deployment

---

Exhibit 3.3   Determining Achievements

1 2 3 4	Financial independence—Maintaining maximum access to financial resources, regardless of the impact on family wealth transfer
1 2 3 4	Tax-effectiveness—Transferring wealth from one generation to another, with a minimum of wealth lost to tax
1 2 3 4	Maximum inheritance—Maximizing the amount of wealth transferred from one generation to another, regardless of how much wealth is lost to tax
1 2 3 4	Social capital—Converting taxes into charitable gifts, regardless of how much wealth is transferred to heirs
1 2 3 4	Wealth maximization—Converting taxes into charitable gifts, but only after providing the desired inheritance for heirs

Exhibit 3.4   Client Planning Goals

ASK A CLIENT TO TRY THIS

Estate planning is generally motivated by one or more of the planning goals found in Exhibit 3.4. Have the client rate each on a scale from 1 to 4, with 1 being the least important and 4 being the most important.

Follow this exercise by asking the client to complete the following:

Based on the priorities you established, write a brief paragraph describing your motivation for planning. What is your focus for the planning process? Keep in mind, your motivation is neither right nor wrong. It is, simply, your motivation.

CHAPTER FOUR

Principle #2

Master the Concept of Social Capital

The concept of social capital redefines wealth and its potential impact on society. Most simply, social capital is one of two things: estate taxes clients will pay or charitable gifts they will make.

As more and more people become aware of their ability to direct their social capital voluntarily, many are deciding they have a *responsibility* to ensure the proper allocation of their financial *and* social capital, based on their values. They are able to do this with confidence only after they have secured lifetime financial independence. Once they have comfortably determined how much they will need for the rest of their lives, clients discover they then can choose how to distribute their wealth among the remaining three beneficiaries: their heirs, the IRS, and charity.

4.1 UNDERSTANDING THE CONCEPT

At the heart of the estate planning process, a fundamental shift is occurring in the way individuals and families view wealth. Social capital has added a new dynamic to the estate planning and asset distribution process. Increasingly, people who enter the process, along with their professional advisors, are beginning to realize that the "whole dollar" has value, not just that portion of a family's wealth that is used during life or passed on to heirs. What is left—the social capital—will pass on either as taxes or charitable gifts.

In order to understand the concept of *social capital*, it is important first to recognize that eventually we all will have to part with a portion of our wealth. The conscious distribution of that portion of one's wealth, either to the government or to charities, may be viewed as self-directed, or voluntary, social capital. Involuntary social capital is the mandatory redistribution of social capital that occurs when we fail to take responsibility for directing it and simply allow the government to do it for us. As we come to better understand this concept, it is clear that clients have distinct choices in how the assets they will not be allowed to keep ultimately will be distributed.

Despite the obvious difference in results achieved by those who voluntarily capture their social capital, self-directed social capital is far less prevalent than involuntary, government-directed social capital. The reality is that most families fail to recognize and capture the full value of their social capital. Consequently, vast sums are left to the government through the default plan, tax.

The concept of *values-based* planning has created a new set of planning objectives for clients: (1) to keep as much of what they earn as they *want*, (2) to pass on to heirs an amount they identify as *appropriate*, (3) *to control the distribution of all that is left*. As this section unfolds, it is important for advisors first to recognize the existence of social capital and then to place full value on that portion of a client's social capital that may be captured and directed through voluntary choice based on his or her values.

Anyone with assets or income possesses social capital. The question to keep in mind in working with clients is this: Are they using their social capital strategically to accomplish specific planning objectives at each level of the planning pyramid? As an advisor, are you helping your clients direct their social capital in a way that reflects their values?

General observation . . . on wealth maximization

Values-based planning results in optimum wealth transfer effectiveness and empowers clients to do the following:

1. Keep as much of what they earn as they want
2. Pass on to heirs an amount they identify as appropriate
3. Control the distribution of all that is left

4.2 SOCIAL CAPITAL: A NEW DEFINITION OF WEALTH

To fully understand the concept of social capital, we first must recognize that all citizens eventually will be forced to part with a portion of their wealth, whether voluntarily or involuntarily.

Voluntary social capital refers to the portion of estate distribution over which clients make a conscious decision to take responsibility. Consisting of either tax or philanthropic contributions, these *self-directed* dollars can create a lasting impact on society when directed in a manner consistent with the client's value system.

Involuntary social capital is extracted from clients under the default plan, tax. These *government-directed* dollars fall prey to the mandatory redistribution of wealth that occurs when clients fail to take personal responsibility for its ultimate allocation.

It is essential to understand the distinction between voluntary, conscious deployment of social capital (gift *or* tax), and involuntary, unconscious deployment of social capital (tax). Remember, the concept of voluntary versus involuntary social capital assumes a choice between gift and tax. It does not, however, dictate which is the *better* choice. That decision is purely a function of the client's personal values.

Failure to acknowledge the value and power of social capital, then, results in the loss of large portions of wealth to the government in the form of taxes. When advisors *do* acknowledge the value and power of social capital, they can then help clients *choose* how the income and assets they have earned over their lifetimes will be distributed. In facilitating the deliberate transfer of wealth to causes and organizations that are important to their clients, advisors deepen their relationships with clients and better serve their needs. A fundamental question is not *whether* one's clients will make gifts, but rather *to whom* they will make them—the IRS or charity.

As illustrated in Exhibit 4.1, total capital wealth consists of personal *financial* capital plus personal *social* capital. Simply stated, personal financial capital is that portion of what clients earn and own that they will be allowed to keep or pass on to heirs. Personal social capital is that portion of what they earn and own that they will *not* be allowed to keep.

Dividing total wealth into these two distinct categories provides a new way for many advisors and their clients to view financial resources. Many would hold that *income* plus *net worth* minus *tax* equals what is available for clients to keep or pass along. The concept of social capital suggests, however, that *tax* is just one part of the larger personal social capital category. It further suggests that clients have the capacity to control the distribution of a far greater amount of social capital than they may ever have realized.

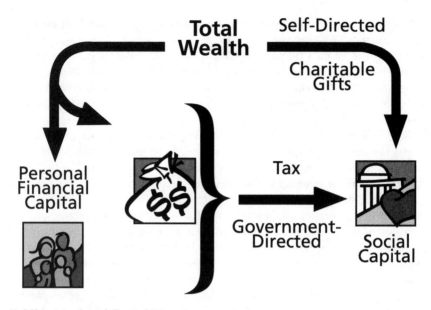

Exhibit 4.1   Social Capital Diagram

Fully understanding the concept of social capital allows clients to discover, likely for the first time, that they have a choice in how the financial resources they will not be allowed to keep ultimately will be distributed and used by society. Through a step-by-step, values-based process, the principles and strategies of social capital open the door to enormous opportunity for clients to redirect their wealth to organizations and causes that support their personal value systems.

Advisors whose clients do not wish to succumb to the default choice—that is, allowing the government to direct all or a portion of their social capital—must look for ways to help them capture and voluntarily direct their social capital. This requires specific financial modeling, investment management, and implementation of a combination of estate and charitable gift strategies. In short, it requires a commitment to values-based planning.

(a) The Role of Social Capital in Conventional Estate Planning

In planning an estate, many advisors compare expected plan results on a two-tiered basis. Using this approach, they place value only on those resources that benefit either (1) the client or (2) the client's heirs. This is the personal *financial* capital part of the dollar bill.

Not surprisingly, conventional planning favors strategies that produce the greatest benefit for clients and their heirs. Minimal, if any, value is placed on the client's personal *social* capital. Why? Because social capital too often is perceived as taxes alone. Therefore, the vast majority of advisors make little or no effort to maintain family control over these dollars. In this context, social capital is viewed only as something to reduce, rather than something to control.

Consider the positive impact redirecting those tax dollars might have on the results of a comprehensive estate plan. To do so requires attention to a third tier of planning: *self-directed social capital*. Here the objective is to maximize control over total financial resources, which includes both financial and social capital.

Using this approach, the advisor analyzes and compares strategies on the basis of the combined amount of personal financial and social capital generated. The emphasis shifts to strategies that provide the client with the greatest control over all resources and, consequently, the maximum potential influence. The process moves from a focus on tax and decreasing social capital toward a focus on increasing and controlling social capital through the use of charitable gifts.

(b) Self-Directed versus Government-Directed Social Capital: The Reality

As stated previously, tax is only one part of a larger category of wealth called social capital. Although clients do not have a choice about whether they will *create* social capital, they do have a choice about who will *direct* it. They can be either proactive and implement arrangements that will enable them to control their personal social capital through voluntary philanthropy, or they can do nothing, and let the government decide for them via involuntary philanthropy.

Consider how the government spends tax dollars. The chart depicted in Exhibit 4.2, taken from the 1999 IRS Form 1040 instruction booklet, illustrates how the government allocates social capital when individuals elect not to do so themselves.

Compare this to Exhibit 4.3, which illustrates how Americans chose to allocate their social capital through charitable gifts in the same year. The differences are startling and demonstrate an obvious disparity between how the government appropriates social capital dollars and the types of causes and organizations people in general select for voluntary support.

> **General observation . . . on social capital**
>
> Clients have no choice about whether they will create social capital. They can, however, choose to control where, ultimately, it goes.

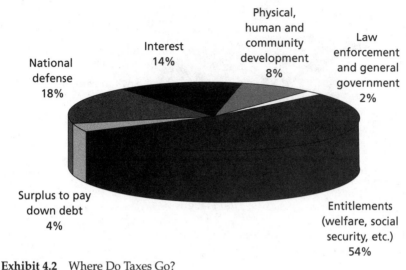

National
defense
18%

Interest
14%

Physical,
human and
community
development
8%

Law
enforcement
and general
government
2%

Surplus to pay
down debt
4%

Entitlements
(welfare, social
security, etc.)
54%

Exhibit 4.2   Where Do Taxes Go?
Source: 1999 IRS 1040 Instruction Booklet

(c) Dormant Social Capital: Finding the Potential

In order to maximize the value of planning and proactively move from being passive, involuntary participants to being active, voluntary participants in the process, clients must identify and harvest their dormant social capital.

Dormant social capital, which may be described as a future choice between gift and tax, is most easily identified in its default form—tax. Consider the following four major sources of dormant social capital:

1. Earned income (from employment)
2. Investment income (interest, dividends, rents, royalties)
3. Asset sales (capital gain tax paid on the sale of an appreciated asset for a profit)
4. Wealth transfer (estate and gift taxes paid on the transfer of assets to heirs)

(i) Earned income.   Earned income is the most common source of social capital and is the most frequently harvested. It also points to the inevitability of *creating* social capital. Unless people choose not to earn income, they will generate social capital by virtue of their productivity. Beginning with their very first jobs, clients establish a stream of social capital that flows from then on.

From the moment a client begins to earn income until the point at which taxes become inevitable (December 31, for most), the resultant social

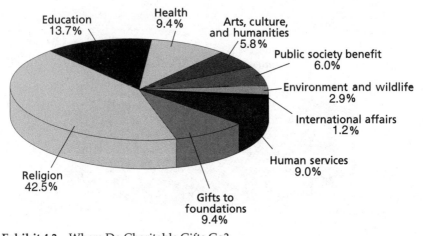

Exhibit 4.3 Where Do Charitable Gifts Go?
Source: Giving USA 1999: AAFRC Trust for Philanthropy

capital is dormant. During this hiatus, dormant social capital is available to be harvested, captured, and directed toward organizations and causes that support the client's personal value system.

(ii) Investment income.   At the core of a capitalist society is the opportunity to invest. Over time, investments produce income. Generally speaking, investment income takes the form of interest income (e.g., from a certificate of deposit), dividend income (e.g., from stock), rental income (e.g., income from real estate), or royalty income (e.g., from a book or movie).

Similar to earned income, the mere existence of investment income ensures that social capital is generated. A portion of this investment income is extracted as tax and put to use through our governmental system for the benefit of society.

(iii) Tax-exempt income.   It is interesting to note that one form of investment, municipal or tax-free bonds, is exempt from tax. On the surface, this investment seems to be an exception to the general rules of social capital. However, take a closer look.

Bonds are issued by corporations, cities, towns, and other governmental bodies as a means of borrowing from the general public. Each bond issued offers the investor a particular interest rate for a specified period of time. This interest is normally taxable.

Tax-exempt bonds enjoy an advantage because the interest paid on such bonds is exempt from federal tax and often state tax, as well. However, only organizations such as nonprofit corporations or municipalities may issue tax-exempt bonds. These organizations serve a charitable purpose or otherwise benefit society.

Because the interest paid is tax-exempt, the issuer of such bonds is able to offer a lower rate than that of taxable bonds, and still attract investors. The spread between the interest rate offered on tax-exempt bonds and taxable bonds is actually *social capital*. In fact, this is a form of charitable giving.

When clients purchase tax-exempt bonds from particular organizations, they are redirecting their tax dollars to that organization. They accept a lower interest rate in exchange for tax avoidance. They have converted a tax into a gift. In fact, if they consciously select bonds that support certain organizations or municipalities, they have exercised voluntary philanthropy.

(iv) Asset sale. Purchasing stock on the New York Stock Exchange, investing in a family business, or buying a second home all present the potential of a capital gain. When an investment asset is sold for more than its original cost, a capital gain is realized and social capital is harvested in the form of tax.

Unrealized capital gain, assets that have increased in value but have not yet been sold, represents a significant pool of dormant social capital. This form of social capital is quite possibly the most powerful, as the timing of its harvest is under the client's control.

(v) Wealth transfer. The final pool of dormant social capital results from the transfer tax system. Whether lifetime gifts or transfers at death, a client's ability to transfer assets to anyone other than his or her spouse is limited. During life, such transfers are limited to a one-time federal exemption, which will increase to $1 million per person and $2 million per married couple by the year 2006. In 2000, this exemption is $675,000 per person and $1,350,000 per couple plus $10,000 for each spouse each year to as many people as desired. Assets in excess of these amounts are taxed at rates ranging from 37 to 60 percent. As a matter of reference, the $10,000 annual exemption has an inflation-driven adjustment built into the tax code.

Any portion of the $675,000 exemption not used during life to shelter gifts is available at death. Therefore, if the entire exemption is unused, an individual may leave $675,000 of property without incurring a federal estate tax. Assets in excess of $675,000, left to someone other than a surviving spouse, are taxed at rates ranging from 37 to 60 percent. Therefore, in the year 2000, each *individual* has social capital to the extent his or her estate exceeds $675,000.

With proper planning, a married couple can leave $1,350,000, or $675,000 each, to heirs without incurring an estate tax. Therefore, if married clients have planned properly, they possess this form of dormant social capital if their combined estate exceeds $1,350,000.

In summary, by virtue of personal productivity, we all create and maintain a flow of social capital that continues for life. Despite this inevitable drain on the ability to accumulate wealth, many families manage to build sizable estates. What results is the creation of additional social capital through the payment of estate taxes.

General Observation ... on social capital potential

To avoid creating social capital dollars, one must avoid financial success.

(d) Evolution Toward Values-Based Planning: *From Success to Significance*

A new planning paradigm is emerging that facilitates a transition from conventional estate planning to client-centered, values-based planning.

(i) The old planning paradigm.   Conventional estate planning focuses on that portion of wealth clients will be allowed to keep—the portion left after taxes are paid. With this "50 percent plan," clients usually get to keep approximately 50 percent of the estate, while the other 50 percent is lost to taxes. The plan objectives are for clients (1) to keep as much of what they earn as they can and (2) to pass on to heirs as much of what they keep as they can.

This planning philosophy establishes two opposing sides to wealth—one positive and one negative. Historically, virtually all planning creativity applied by advisors has focused on reducing tax on the negative side and increasing the amount passing to heirs on the positive side. Not surprisingly, advisors have placed little if any value on the negative, tax side of the planning dollar.

(ii) An aging planning paradigm.   In order to preserve the estate for heirs, the "insured 50 percent plan" evolved. With this strategy, the client's total estate increases in size through the addition of a life insurance component, which is owned outside of the taxable estate. Objectives for clients under this alternative are (1) to keep as much of what they earn as they can, (2) to pass on to heirs as much of what they keep as they can, and (3) to replace what they cannot keep for the benefit of heirs.

Although net assets passing to heirs may increase, the fact remains that about the same total is lost to taxes. Therefore, control over distribution of a considerable portion of wealth is lost to the government. In essence, the tax has not gone away; clients and their advisors have simply found a more efficient way to pay it.

(iii) **A new, enlightened planning paradigm.** Values-based estate planning creates a new set of objectives for those clients who wish to achieve maximum control:

1. To keep as much of what they earn as they want
2. To pass on to heirs an amount they deem to be appropriate
3. To control the distribution of all that is left

With this "100 percent plan," advisors begin the process by recognizing and placing value on that portion of their clients' social capital that they can help "capture" and direct. Strategically, they start with the end in mind, helping clients control the distribution of their social capital, while achieving other family objectives.

Using this approach, the successful experience of developing a tax-effective estate plan is combined with the sense of satisfaction and significance gained through the conscious deployment of social capital. This values-based process allows the client to move beyond a position of financial success to one of greater effectiveness, coupled with a deeper sense of significance.

(e) Social Capital Planning Strategies: Harvesting the Client's Social Capital

Often clients wonder if they have the capacity to make significant charitable gifts. It is important to understand that the financial effectiveness of a particular charitable giving strategy can be an early motivation for capturing a client's social capital.

Sometimes social capital planning evolves through a process of enlightened self-interest. A client has a specific problem. Employing a charitable strategy can solve it. Tax benefits actually encourage the process by offering incentives for those who make the effort to plan and problem solve. This is precisely why these financial incentives exist. They afford an opportunity to experiment with social capital in a low-risk environment, where the government is even willing to provide a good deal of the working capital through tax incentives.

Social capital planning begins with a review of the clients' financial resources. What is the net worth? What types of assets do they have? Are assets liquid or illiquid? Are assets highly appreciated? What asset preferences do they have?

Next, what are their goals and objectives? Would they like more income? Would they like to increase asset diversification? Would they like to reduce income tax liability? Avoid a capital gain tax? Reduce estate tax liability? Would they like to make gifts to charity? Transfer assets to children?

Finally, advisors need to help clients identify their available social capital. Again, in this context, social capital is one of two things: taxes they will pay or charitable gifts they would like to make.

Once these areas have been carefully reviewed, the process shifts to problem solving. At this time, specific problems can be matched with specific charitable giving techniques and strategies that solve the problems.

(f) Ownership versus Influence and Control

Most people believe charitable giving results in lost control. This is a misconception. In reality, many gift strategies *increase* the client's control over the property contributed by removing burdensome layers of tax that have rendered the asset unproductive.

Take, for example, a charitable remainder trust (CRT). This strategy allows the client to avoid paying a capital gain on the sale of appreciated stock. This is accomplished by irrevocably transferring stock *ownership* to a qualified CRT before it is sold. Although ownership has been irrevocably changed, the client may act as trustee or retain the right to appoint the trustee. Consequently, the client maintains *control*. In fact, control is actually increased by (1) avoiding the capital gain tax, (2) earning a current income tax deduction, (3) avoiding estate taxes, and (4) deciding how the charitable gift will benefit others.

Maximum ownership results in maximum tax. For example, the costs of owning real estate include a property tax, income tax on rents, a capital gain tax if the client sells the property for a profit, and an estate tax if the client dies while owning the property. Maximum influence, on the other hand, is achieved by controlling more assets and owning less. The cost of maximum influence is maximum charitable gifts. For example, if the client owns real estate inside a CRT, taxes are reduced. However, all property remaining in the trust at the end of the trust term must be distributed to charity.

As a client moves from ownership to influence, income available for spending increases, taxes paid decrease, inheritance for heirs increases, and charitable gifts increase.

> ### General Observation ... on ownership versus control
>
> Maximum ownership results in maximum tax. Maximum control results in maximum charitable gifts.

4.3 A BRIEF REVIEW

A shift is occurring in the way individuals and their advisors view wealth. Social capital has added a new dynamic to the estate planning and asset distribution process. Increasingly, people who enter the process, along with their professional advisors, are realizing that the whole dollar has value, not just that portion of a family's wealth that is used during life or passed on to heirs. What is left—the social capital—will pass on either as taxes or charitable gifts. The concept of social capital and its intrinsic value to society are ideas rapidly coming of age.

POINTS TO PONDER

- The concept of *social capital* expands the definition of wealth, further complicating the planning formula. With increased awareness, many people are deciding they have a *responsibility* to ensure the proper allocation of their financial *and* social capital.

- The powerful tools of a values-based estate planning process can provide clients with an exhilarating opportunity to direct the portion of their wealth they cannot keep—their social capital—toward organizations and causes that will give them the highest level of personal satisfaction and significance.

- Advisors historically have placed no value on social capital. Therefore, plans have tended toward two objectives: (1) more for heirs, (2) less tax. The entire planning process has focused on financial capital to the exclusion of social capital.

- True values-based estate planning may be described as the creation of an estate plan in which the social capital outcome is a *strategic* motivation and where social capital planning tools are used to accomplish meaningful objectives.

- Very high net worth families often find it difficult to identify a motivation that is sufficient to drive the estate planning process. They have more than enough for themselves. Their children will have more than enough, even after taxes. For some, the only motivation that has the potential to drive the process is the ability to capture and direct social capital. Unless families of wealth come to realize this, they may not find estate planning to be meaningful or beneficial.

- The concept of voluntary versus involuntary philanthropy implies that clients have a choice between gift and tax. It does not, however, mandate which is the better choice. That decision is a function of their individual values.

- Philanthropy often evolves through a process of enlightened self-interest when a particular problem surfaces and a corresponding charitable solution is identified.

- Clients do not have a choice about whether they will *create* social capital. They do, however, have a choice about who will *direct* it.

- Many charitable gift strategies actually result in increased control over the property contributed by removing burdensome layers of tax that have, in the past, rendered the asset unproductive.

- Ultimately, clients allocate their estate among three beneficiaries of wealth: (1) their heirs, (2) tax (government-directed social capital), and (3) tax or charity (self-directed social capital). The manner in which clients choose to distribute wealth among these beneficiaries stands to have a profound impact for generations to come.

TRY THIS

Choose a well-established client relationship and estimate the client's social capital opportunity. Keep in mind, social capital is either a tax the client will pay or a gift he or she would like to make. Review the client's financial resources to determine if there is any social capital ripe for harvest. Does the client have concerns about any of the following:

- Selling appreciated securities?
- Selling appreciated real estate?
- Transferring a closely held business to heirs?
- Selling a closely held business to an employee stock ownership plan?
- Qualified stock options?
- Forced distributions from an IRA or profit-sharing plan?
- A need to increase current income from underperforming assets?
- A need to diversify investment assets?
- A need to balance the investment portfolio?

If one or more of these items applies, the client may have a current opportunity to harvest some social capital.

CHAPTER FIVE

Principle #3

Define the Family Financial Philosophy

Wills and trusts tell advisors, heirs, and others *how* estate assets will be distributed. The *Family Financial Philosophy* tells them *why*. This written mission statement clearly expresses the client's values and goals as they relate to financial resources.

Discussed in detail in Chapter 10, the triage phase of planning is used to establish the appropriateness of applying either a tactical or strategic planning process. When a strategic planning approach is selected, the Family Financial Philosophy will guide the planning process. When a tactical planning approach is selected, the process of developing a client's written financial philosophy generally is deferred.

In some cases, the advisor may never have the opportunity to engage in strategic planning with a particular client. In other cases, the opportunity may emerge only after a series of tactics have been employed successfully over time. Regardless of the approach selected, a fundamental principle of The Legacy Planning System is that appropriate recommendations are always supported by explicit objectives. This chapter illustrates how advisors can use a written Family Financial Philosophy as a tool for guiding the strategic planning process.

5.1 UNDERSTANDING THE CONCEPT

Strategies solve problems. Clear objectives lead to effective strategies. When it comes to planning an estate, it is important to start with the end in mind.

As previously stated, most people view estate planning as a process they *endure* rather than *enjoy*. They see it as a *responsibility* rather than an *opportunity*. In fact, as a society we do not like to plan. Nearly 7 out of 10 people die without a will. Of those who actually develop an estate plan, many spend less time considering their alternatives and developing objectives than they do planning family vacations. They probably even invest fewer dollars in the process. Unfortunately, the outcome generally reflects this lack of commitment.

Most people who enter the estate planning process have only a vague idea of what they want to accomplish. On top of that, they have an even less clear picture of what they *can* accomplish. If there is one overriding negative factor associated with estate planning, it perhaps is a sense of having little or no control over the process. This presents a tremendous obstacle.

Generally, clients find themselves acting as bystanders rather than participants—watching, listening, and waiting as advisors make recommendations that will affect them and their loved ones for the rest of their lives. These advisors may, in fact, know little about what really matters to them. Clients have little influence over what is happening because they don't understand the intricacies involved. Even the documents that are supposed to explain how the plan works often might as well be written in a foreign language.

Every advisor has his or her view of the world, based on individual past experience. Whether or not the advisor's perspective overshadows the client's perspective is a function of how well developed the client's objectives are.

Well-conceived objectives virtually ensure that plan design and implementation will follow with relative ease. If the process of thinking through and articulating objectives is not done correctly, or is skipped altogether, the planning will yield poor results. Furthermore, it will lead to an environment of considerable frustration.

Like most things in life, clients get out of estate planning what they are willing to put into the process. If they put the same energy and creativity into developing their estate plans as they do into building and preserving wealth, the return on investment will be just as great, if not greater. When objectives are clearly stated, the rest falls neatly into place.

5.2 LAYING A FOUNDATION THE VALUES-BASED WAY

The secret to effective planning is to lay a solid foundation. Advisors who employ values-based planning help clients develop written wealth mission statements that reflect their financial philosophy before they ever consider recommending specific strategies.

Once complete, the client's Family Financial Philosophy (FFP) mission statement guides every step of the planning process that follows. The FFP ensures that each strategy is judged for its consistency with client values and objectives, as well as its maximum effectiveness in the context of the overall plan.

> **General Observation . . . on underdeveloped objectives**
>
> Attempting to solve underdeveloped objectives will lead to planning paralysis.

5.3 ESTABLISHING OBJECTIVES WITH STRATEGIES: PUTTING THE CART BEFORE THE HORSE

By far, the most important part of the planning process is first to establish clear and concise objectives. It may be hard to imagine, but establishing objectives completes about 80 percent of the process. It also deserves, but rarely gets, 80 percent of the effort.

Most people enter the planning process unprepared and reluctantly, with only a vague idea about what they are trying to accomplish. Both individuals and professional advisors tend to focus on analyzing strategies first, solving problems before it is clear what the overriding objectives are. In short, they all too often put the proverbial planning cart before the horse.

Compounding this problem, many advisors are far more comfortable highlighting the benefits and features of a particular strategy than they are discussing core objectives with a client. They want to tell clients about the latest, greatest, and newest technique. They excitedly share the topic of discussion at the last seminar they attended—a new tax regulation, a new product, a new strategy. They are convinced their clients will benefit from whatever is the newest, fanciest strategy they have in their bag of tricks.

They may spend months, even years, putting one idea after another in front of their clients, more likely than not to little or no avail. Life insurance trusts. Family partnerships. Charitable remainder trusts. Sooner or later the square peg surely will find a square hole. Or perhaps it will be forced into a round one.

Many advisors continue to fire one idea after another at their clients. Eventually, the more strategies they ask clients to consider, the more confused clients become.

Sometimes clients may even be barraged by more than one advisor, each with different strategies and different objectives, each suggesting tools designed to solve problems that have not yet been clearly defined.

The typical client starts and stops the estate planning process about five times. Five times they begin the process, only to stop before it is complete. Why is that?

People start and stop the process for many reasons. Someone tries to sell them a product they don't want. They don't think it is necessary. They feel manipulated. Maybe they feel the process is running out of control. They become confused by the complexity of the strategies. While all of these factors may contribute to planning paralysis, evidence suggests that the main reason people stop the process is not because they don't understand what's going on but rather because they don't know exactly what they want to accomplish.

In reality, the frustration associated with planning has more to do with poor preparation than with difficulty solving the problems. Far too much time is spent attempting to resolve underdeveloped objectives.

Helping clients clearly state their goals and objectives in a written mission statement will eliminate wasted time and money. Furthermore, it will ensure that all specific strategies are consistent with client values and contribute positively to overall goals and objectives.

> ### General Observation . . . on establishing objectives
>
> Objectives lead to strategies. Strategies, with no clear objectives, lead only to confusion.

5.4 THE IMPACT OF PROFESSIONAL ADVISORS: IMPLIED VERSUS EXPLICIT NEEDS

Not surprisingly, advisors operate within their individual paradigms. A paradigm is like a pair of glasses through which we view the world. These glasses reflect every aspect of our personal and professional life experience. As Stephen Covey observed in his book *The Seven Habits of Highly Effective People*, "People do not see the world as it is, but as they are."

For the most part, estate planning professionals are far more comfortable discussing the technical aspects of a particular strategy than they are having an in-depth discussion about a client's values regarding wealth. Yet it is virtually impossible to plan without objectives. In fact, every competent advisor will seek to establish client objectives before planning. If a void exists where client objectives should otherwise be, what is the advisor likely to do? Supplement his or her best guess at the client's objectives, based on past experience.

Many estate plans seem to reflect remarkably similar objectives, often something like these:

- We want to maintain our financial security
- We want to reduce taxes
- We want to increase income
- We want to leave as much as possible to heirs
- We want to maintain flexibility and control

Each of these may be worthy, but do all clients *really* share this *same* set of objectives? Or, perhaps, do they readily adopt these common objectives because it is the easiest route to take, or simply because their advisors suggest them?

What likely occurs when a lawyer, accountant, insurance agent, and investment advisor each are asked to develop a solution for a specific planning problem? They come up with four different solutions—one each from the legal, accounting, insurance, and investment perspective. It makes perfect sense for advisors to focus advice around their particular areas of expertise, and each of the four responses may have merit and provide an adequate solution to the problem. The point is, certain experiences and biases will be reflected in the recommended solution.

For example, if a client's primary advisor is an insurance agent, it is far more likely that a plan will incorporate life insurance than if the primary advisor is a lawyer. Likewise, if the primary advisor is an attorney, it stands to reason the estate plan will reflect a legal perspective.

What if the primary advisor is an accountant who holds board positions for multiple charitable organizations? She personally has contributed time and money to these organizations for a number of years. Is she more likely to support, or even recommend, the use of charitable gifts to reduce income or estate tax burden?

5.5 THE MOST TRUSTED ADVISOR

Most families have one particular advisor whose opinion they almost always seek prior to making a major decision. This is their most trusted professional relationship. Keep in mind, this advisor has a paradigm through which he or she views the world. That paradigm invariably will influence professional recommendations. Advisors who see themselves as a most trusted advisor should take care that their views do not overshadow their clients' views in establishing plan objectives.

General Observation . . . on perspective

"People do not see the world as it is, but as they are."

Stephen Covey

5.6 THE FAMILY FINANCIAL PHILOSOPHY

The Family Financial Philosophy (FFP) is a written mission statement that defines financial independence, family legacy, and social capital legacy, all within the context of a client's expressed values and convictions regarding wealth. Used to its fullest potential, the FFP can effectively govern the estate planning process, guiding professional advisors as they recommend strategies that support only the stated goals and objectives.

Why does the written mission statement work so effectively?

- The FFP provides a context within which clients, their heirs, and their advisors can more fully understand their deepest values, beliefs, motivations, and goals regarding wealth.

- The process of creating an FFP stimulates clients to identify and examine the people and entities they hold in the highest esteem, leading to wealth transfer decisions that make sense to them.

- A will tells heirs—and the probate court—how assets will be distributed. The FFP tells them *why.*

- As a clear expression for heirs and others, the FFP can be a tool to help pass on personal values to succeeding generations.

- The FFP succinctly informs all advisors of the client's intentions, saving both time and money as they explore appropriate strategies to help clients achieve their goals.

- The FFP prescribes whether clients choose a tax legacy, allowing the government to control their social capital, or whether they choose to direct their social capital dollars toward charitable organizations.

- Perhaps most important, through the written FFP, the *client's* mission, values, goals, and dreams and the *client's* needs and desires unmistakably govern the planning process. The client is in full control. Right where he or she wants to be.

The FFP expands the discovery process of defining objectives. Whereas traditional objectives are limited to what clients want to accomplish, a financial philosophy goes to a deeper level and explains *why.*

Beneath a client's more obvious objectives, upon which the estate plan may have thus far been based, lies a series of issues closely tied to the client's *core values.* It is imperative that the client identify and address these issues *before* advisors develop a full-blown estate plan. As the Family Financial Philosophy unfolds, the client discovers and puts in writing all the issues and values that are of the greatest significance.

Developing a personal financial philosophy strengthens the client's convictions about the most effective or appropriate use of financial resources. Decisions in designing an estate plan will become more logical, sometimes even obvious, when made within the context of well-defined values. This heightens consistency between the client's priorities in life and how the most appropriate and satisfying uses of financial resources are determined.

Some planners have difficulty understanding the importance of the FFP. They may, in fact, be quick to suggest that clients skip this phase and move right into strategy development. However, upon receiving their first completed FFP, nearly all become enthusiastic supporters of this process. They find the mission statement provides a unique opportunity for the client to gain a sense of control. It actually empowers the client to move forward once and for all.

Advisors who integrate this technique into their practices have come to know that the FFP functions much like an operating manual for the client's financial goals and dreams. It is the business plan or road map that makes the planning journey effective and satisfying for both client and advisor.

5.7 THE DISCOVERY PROCESS: TRIAGE, INTERVIEWS, QUESTIONNAIRES, FINANCIAL DATA, GOAL PROFILES

In order to create estate plans that truly reflect clients' personal or family values, one must take clients through a process of discovery. Generally speaking, five methods will cover the ground required for a comprehensive, written Family Financial Philosophy. Planning triage is discussed in Chapter 10. The five methods are as follows:

- Planning triage
- Interviews
- Questionnaires
- Financial data gathering tools
- Goal profiles

(a) Interviews

Interviews help advisors gain perspective on past events and current circumstances that have shaped and are shaping the client's financial philosophy. Only by understanding the client's past and present can an advisor help shape a client's future. Information gained through the interview process is an important ingredient in developing a recipe for planning success.

(b) Questionnaires

Questionnaires help clients fully explore what they want to accomplish with their financial resources—and why. In completing a questionnaire, they begin to focus on facts that affect their values and beliefs regarding financial resources—how those resources were acquired, what they have done to build and preserve them, how much they will need for the future, and how they anticipate using them. A questionnaire is a useful tool in helping clients express how, ultimately, they will distribute their financial resources.

The questions are not necessarily easy to answer—nor should they be. They are designed to probe and to stimulate thought about what clients want to accomplish with their wealth. They facilitate in-depth dialogue among those who might play a role in the planning process. It is important to remember that in answering a questionnaire, the client makes no right or wrong choices. There are no right or wrong answers. There are only the client's answers!

Responses to a questionnaire will not magically produce an effective estate plan. In fact, this is just one step toward defining a personal Family Financial Philosophy. But it is critical to creating the document that will guide advisors and empower clients, as individuals or couples, to control the estate planning process.

(c) Financial Data Gathering Tools

Effective planning requires an appropriate context. The identification of a client's available financial resources is a major factor in establishing an accurate planning context. Furthermore, the specific attributes of a client's wealth provide essential clues in the identification of appropriate strategies.

(d) Goal Profiles

A profile of a client's key financial goals is critical to effective planning. Advisors should focus on three key financial goals in profiling a particular client. First, what portion of the client's resources is required to support financial independence? Second, what portion of the client's resources should be transferred to heirs? Third, how would the client like to allocate social capital between charitable gifts and taxes?

To properly facilitate planning, each goal should be established as a specific dollar amount or a percentage of available financial resources. These goals should then be related to values, preferences, and historical events that support their definition.

5.8 FROM DISCOVERY TO THE PHILOSOPHY

With the help of trusted advisors trained to use legacy planning tools, the client is enabled to define and write a Family Financial Philosophy—in essence, a personal wealth mission statement. The FFP further enables design of an estate plan that is consistent with everything the client has expressed in the mission statement.

(a) The Role of the Primary Advisor

In most situations, clients will want and need the assistance of at least one trusted advisor to help them develop a mission statement. It is important to have an impartial second or third party help negotiate the myriad issues involved, particularly so for married couples who may well have opposing perspectives that can lead to different priorities.

(b) Mission Statement Sections

General sections of the mission statement and the primary question answered with the pages of each include the following:

- Purpose—Why have I prepared this document?
- Legacy biography—What significant events from the past have helped shape my current financial philosophy?
- Source of wealth—What is the source of my wealth, or to what do I attribute my wealth?
- Responsibilities and obligations—To whom or what do I feel a responsibility or obligation with respect to the distribution of my wealth?
- Primary planning goals—What are my primary planning goals?
- Financial philosophy—What are my defining values regarding wealth?
- Financial independence—How do I define financial independence?
- Family legacy—How do I define an appropriate inheritance for heirs?
- Social capital legacy—How would I like to allocate my social capital between gift and tax?
- Acknowledgment—On what basis and to what extent can my advisors rely on the goals and objectives articulated in my financial philosophy?

5.9 ANNUAL REVIEW AND UPDATE

Clients understand the significance of a written mission statement. As a reflection of their financial philosophy, it should be reviewed each year to ensure nothing has changed. If nothing has changed, the mission statement remains as is. If, however, opinions, values, or circumstances have changed, and the mission statement no longer makes sense, it should be modified. The advisor should prepare a new version, indicating where appropriate changes have been made and referencing the version being replaced.

Through the mission statement, clients maintain control and advisors continue to nurture relationships that are solid and secure. It is incumbent upon the advisor to be sure the mission statement always accurately reflects the client's current views and opinions.

General Observation . . . on control

Clear objectives lead to maximum control.

5.10 A BRIEF REVIEW

Most people find estate planning quite difficult. There are many reasons for this, not the least of which is the fact that estate planning is hard work. Everything about it seems incredibly complex and hard to understand. It takes enormous time and patience. It deals with subjects many would rather avoid confronting. It's confusing and often frustrating. It often requires giving away financial resources—*forever*. And if all that weren't enough, it costs money—often a significant amount.

To help clients overcome these inherent obstacles and maximize the benefits of planning, the advisor should begin with a discovery process that ends with the development of a written mission statement. This Family Financial Philosophy expresses clients' core beliefs and values regarding the accumulation, preservation, use, and distribution of wealth. It clearly identifies the appropriate allocation of financial resources among heirs, tax, and charitable gifts. It establishes an appropriate level of planning complexity, and it identifies suitable planning strategies.

When planning decisions are based on the objectives set forth in the mission statement, planning strategies become readily apparent, and clients' estate plans are fully congruent with their value systems.

POINTS TO PONDER

- Many people have no idea what they can accomplish through the estate planning process. As a result, they lack the necessary perspective or context within which to identify their true objectives.

- Most professional advisors lack the necessary skills to motivate clients to develop clear, concise objectives.

- Many clients are not willing to pay their advisors to spend time to develop clear objectives. They think advisors should be able to establish adequate objectives without extensive review and discussion. Most of all, they just want to end the process.

- When it comes to subjective issues, many advisors use *implied* objectives as the basis for planning, rather than *explicit* objectives. Advisors should take care that clients' objectives—and the resulting plans—reflect client values rather than their own.

- Professional advisors usually are more comfortable discussing strategies than developing objectives.

- Different advisors have different agendas. Attorneys consider alternative strategies and draft documents. Insurance agents sell insurance. Planned giving officers generate gifts. Investment professionals sell investment opportunities. It is incumbent upon the advisor to take care that his or her agenda does not overshadow the client's agenda.

- The desire not to pay tax is *not* synonymous with the desire to give more to heirs. Such a misinterpretation may point down a path to which the client is not fully committed.

- Advisors often are not comfortable eliciting charitable objectives from clients who have minimal experience with philanthropy. Although they don't hesitate to fulfill the objectives of those clients who are experienced enough to open the discussion on their own, they are reluctant to enter this realm with the uninitiated.

- Given the opportunity to explore core values, most individuals will identify an appropriate role for philanthropy.

- A written financial philosophy will help clients, their heirs, and advisors more fully understand their values and beliefs regarding the accumulation, preservation, use, and distribution of their wealth.

ASK A CLIENT TO TRY THIS

Have the client take the time to review and complete a printed questionnaire. If the client is married, each partner should answer the questions individually and then discuss the answers with one another. Then have the client use the completed questionnaire(s) as the basis for articulating his or her (or their) Family Financial Philosophy.

The client then sends the completed questionnaire(s) back to you. You arrange a meeting to discuss the implications relative to the client's plan.

To get started, have your client(s) respond to the following preliminary questionnaire:

Take out a sheet of paper and write a brief answer to each of the following questions. If you are married, do this individually and then swap and review each other's answers. When you are done, send your responses to me with your completed questionnaire.

1. Why would I want to have a written mission statement?
2. How did I accumulate my wealth?
3. To whom do I feel a sense of responsibility or obligation regarding the distribution of my wealth?
4. Why am I planning my estate?
5. What does money mean to me?
6. What do I need from my money to maintain my financial independence?
7. If I could leave my heirs any amount of wealth, how much would I leave them, and why?
8. If I choose to control my social capital, to what organization(s) will I contribute? Why?
9. Can my advisors, heirs, and others with whom I choose to share my mission statement rely on it as a fair representation of my (our) values and opinions regarding wealth?

CHAPTER SIX

Principle #4

Quantify Financial Independence

The first level in the hierarchy of planning objectives requires that clients specify how much total wealth they will need to achieve and maintain financial independence for the rest of their lives. It is essential that they know how much they will need so that they can determine how much they will not need. Only if there is excess wealth will they have planning resources to apply to the other two levels of the pyramid—family legacy and social capital legacy.

6.1 UNDERSTANDING THE CONCEPT

Effective estate planning often requires the irrevocable separation of clients from their money. Therefore, securing the financial future of succeeding generations can be in direct opposition to basic instincts of financial self-preservation. The same holds true for any meaningful role philanthropy might play in the estate plan.

Whether clients climb the pyramid of planning during their lifetime depends on how they want to allocate their estate among heirs, tax, and charity.

Generally speaking, the larger the estate—and the larger the percentage clients wish to leave to heirs—the more likely they must take advantage of lifetime planning strategies. Lifetime planning requires a clear understanding about financial independence, the foundation upon which the estate planning process is built.

Unfortunately, the reality of wealth rarely has much to do with the perception of wealth. Regardless of how much wealth people have, most would assert that they do not have more than they need. This creates a dilemma between the basic human instinct of self-preservation and the desire to leave a legacy for heirs.

In order to maximize the benefits of planning, clients first must have a clear, concise picture of what they require to maintain financial independence. Their definition of financial independence will provide the confidence and freedom to apply planning resources toward strategies that accomplish their family and social capital legacy objectives. That confidence and freedom will enable them to climb to the top of the planning pyramid.

6.2 WEALTH TRANSFER PLANNING: GIVE IT AWAY EARLY

Estate planning can be complex and confusing for clients. However, the process really boils down to one simple directive—give it away and give it away early! Tax-effective estate planning generally requires the irrevocable separation of clients from their money—forever. The sooner that separation takes place, the more effective the planning will be.

Ironically, most people spend the first two-thirds of their lifetimes accumulating wealth, and when they finally reach retirement with a comfortable nest egg, planning advisors tell them they should give it all away! The annual gift exclusion, personal residence trust, grantor retained annuity trust, and charitable remainder trust are only a few of the strategies commonly recommended. Each of these requires an irrevocable transfer.

Unfortunately, giving everything away is contrary to most people's instinct of financial self-preservation. A client's desire to plan for heirs and charitable organizations is pitted directly against a desire to protect financial well-being. This may result in a constant tug-of-war between financial independence and the legacy clients want to leave their families and society. Not surprisingly, this dilemma all too often results in planning paralysis.

Climbing the pyramid of planning requires a clear definition of financial independence. Unfortunately, most people have only a vague idea of what is required to maintain financial independence and find it difficult to make planning decisions that require an irrevocable transfer during life. Consequently, they relegate themselves to planning strategies that neither require minimal lifetime transfers or are not implemented until death.

The most powerful of all planning tools is time. In fact, the biggest factor in the success of most planning strategies is time. Ultimately, because clients control their own time, they can determine the effectiveness of their own plan. The degree to which they succeed often depends on their confidence and knowledge regarding financial independence, and their willingness to allow time to work on their behalf.

General Observation . . . on estate planning

Tax-effective wealth transfer requires the irrevocable separation of clients from their money—forever. These transfers can be either irrevocably good or irrevocably bad!

6.3 PERCEPTION IS REALITY: WHAT DO CLIENTS NEED FROM THEIR WEALTH?

One of the greatest obstacles to effective planning is the gap that often exists between the perception of wealth and the reality of wealth. Some wealthy families may be convinced they will not have sufficient assets to cover the cost of long-term medical care when, in reality, they could easily afford to purchase the long-term care facility, never mind afford a room! Nevertheless, as we all know, *perception is reality.*

The importance of perception is easily demonstrated through the difference between the terms *cheap* and *thrifty*. *Cheap* is how we perceive others when they are conservative in deploying financial resources. *Thrifty* is how we perceive ourselves in the same situation.

Travel down any street in your community. Choose the largest and smallest house on the block. Chances are, the family living in the largest house does not feel much more financially secure than the family in the smallest house. Ironically, even the wealthiest of clients may harbor deep-rooted concerns that they may not have enough to achieve all their financial objectives and maintain their financial independence. This perception is diametrical to the reality that few families of wealth ever will consume their existing financial resources, never mind what they acquire in future growth and income.

According to many who study the wealthy, one common character trait of many affluent people is thriftiness or frugality. Many who have substantial sums of money attribute at least part of their wealth to living well within their means. They possess a certain cautiousness or reluctance to deploy assets—a cautiousness that may frustrate the estate planning process.

In order to maximize the benefits of planning, clients first must have a clear, concise picture of what they require to maintain financial independence. Once defined, financial independence provides the confidence to make gifts, either to heirs or charity.

6.4 DEFINING FINANCIAL INDEPENDENCE

As previously established, tax-effective wealth transfer planning generally requires the irrevocable separation of clients from their money, as early as possible. However, before they consider how to distribute their wealth, they must first decide what they need from their wealth. They must define their financial independence.

Financial independence results from the right combination of net annual income for personal consumption and a minimum resource base. The minimum resource base comprises all assets clients choose to own and control for the foreseeable future. The appropriate amount of income and minimum resource base that results in financial independence is a function of personal or family lifestyle, goals, and objectives.

Financial independence is a unique combination of consumption and preservation. Annually, clients consume a portion of their wealth in order to maintain their desired lifestyle. At the same time, they preserve their asset base in order to assure income in the future and cope with unexpected financial needs. As Exhibit 6.1 reflects, consumption is a descending need. The amount of capital required to meet consumption needs decreases with age. In other words, a married couple in their forties who spends $100,000 a year requires more capital than a couple in their eighties.

Unless consumed, the minimum resource base will increase as a result of normal inflation and investment performance. Therefore, clients may want to adjust their definition of an appropriate minimum resource base from time to time.

The minimum resource base is always composed of resources within the client's control and ownership, and, therefore, within the taxable estate. Income, on the other hand, can come from resources that are either inside or outside the taxable estate. From an estate planning perspective, resources outside the estate are most attractive because they are generally not subject to tax.

Establishing a definition of financial independence is similar to calculating income tax witholdings. In that scenario, the most desirable financial result is achieved when the amount of witholdings results in neither a payment nor a refund. If the client gets a refund, he or she overestimated the amount due and lost the opportunity to use those dollars throughout

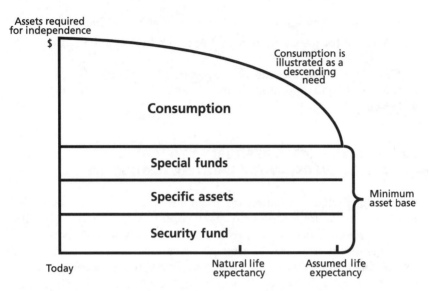

Exhibit 6.1   Defining Financial Independence

the year. If the client underestimates the taxes due, he or she ends up with a big bill at year end, and perhaps a penalty.

Caution clients to be realistic in developing financial independence assumptions. If they are too conservative, they will underestimate available planning resources and perhaps miss an opportunity. On the other hand, if they are too aggressive, they may overvalue their financial resources and prematurely consume them.

General Observation ... on financial independence

Define what clients need in order to determine what they don't need.

6.5 MAINTAINING LIFESTYLE: HOW MUCH INCOME DO CLIENTS WANT?

In order to determine what financial resources are needed to support a desired lifestyle, clients must do the following:

- Determine how much they currently spend, or how much they want to spend, to maintain their lifestyle
- Adjust this income goal to reflect the impact of inflation

- Determine how long they want the income to continue
- Account for the positive impact of future investment performance

This chapter describes the theory behind the concepts of financial independence. How to determine financial independence will be addressed in a later chapter.

6.6 PUTTING EXCESS RESOURCES TO WORK: THE CONVERSION TO PLANNING RESOURCES

By defining what is required to maintain financial independence, the Family Financial Philosophy creates the opportunity to put excess financial resources to work in order to accomplish planning objectives.

Remember that wealth transfer planning may be characterized as the irrevocable application of planning resources toward wealth transfer objectives consistent with clients' values. In the same context, then, philanthropy may be characterized as the irrevocable application of planning resources toward organizations and causes that perpetuate clients' values. In the latter, clients give away what they don't need specifically to charitable entities that support their values rather than to family members or other heirs.

Tax-effective planning—offensive planning—is about using planning resources to accomplish planning objectives. In effect, planning resources represent excess resources and may be determined by subtracting the client's financial independence goal from the total financial resources. A discussion on how to determine a client's financial independence appears later in this book. For now, suffice it to say the individual definition of financial independence is the determining factor in how much working capital the client has for planning.

Estate planning is the process of putting these excess resources to work to accomplish planning objectives at the second and third levels of the planning pyramid—family legacy and social capital legacy.

If a client has no excess resources, then any concern with complex estate distribution scenarios may yield only marginal benefits. On the other hand, if excess resources have been identified, the client may have the necessary working capital to accomplish meaningful results.

Again, many of the most powerful planning techniques available for preserving family wealth require an irrevocable transfer. That is, in order to protect their financial resources, clients must give them away, and give them away early. Once they have defined financial independence, it is easy to open up the proverbial money bag, because they know just how much they can afford to pour out without threatening their financial security.

> ### General Observation . . . on excess resources
>
> It is easier to identify excess wealth on someone else's balance sheet than on your own.

6.7 A BRIEF REVIEW

Clients must understand the relationship between financial independence and planning resources. The more conservative their definition of financial independence, the lower the amount of available planning resources. The more aggressive their definition of financial independence, the greater the likelihood of prematurely consuming assets.

The tax effectiveness of planning is generally enhanced when assets are irrevocably transferred outside the taxable estate. In fact, most effective lifetime planning strategies require the irrevocable transfer of planning resources. This is the place to begin. The ability to take advantage of such strategies is controlled by the financial independence goal.

If clients are unable to identify planning resources, this does not mean they won't benefit from planning. However, they will find it difficult to give up ownership of financial resources during their lifetime. This may reduce the effectiveness of the estate plan.

POINTS TO PONDER

- Regardless of how much wealth clients have (the reality), they may feel they need more (the perception). This incongruity can lead to planning paralysis.

- Because some families have so much wealth, they have never considered how much they really need.

- Most families are reluctant to define any portion of wealth as *excess*. Once they have excess wealth, they face a difficult question. What should we do with it? What is our responsibility?

- Family wealth transfer is the application of planning resources toward wealth transfer objectives. A clear definition of financial independence is required to establish the existence of planning resources. Determine precisely what clients need in order to establish what they don't need.

- Philanthropy may be characterized as the application of planning resources toward organizations and causes that perpetuate the client's personal value system.

- Once financial independence is defined, the next step is to determine how financially independent the client wants to be. Few people are comfortable being just 100 percent financially independent. Most aim for 120 percent or more!

ASK A CLIENT TO TRY THIS

- Have the client establish how much he or she spends annually.
- Have the client make a list of all the assets he or she does not presently have but would like to have.
- Walk a client through the process described later in this book that will quantify financial independence.

CHAPTER SEVEN

Principle #5

Identify an Appropriate Family Legacy

M ost people want to leave some part of their estate to family members or others who are important to them. Because passing "value without values" can be detrimental to heirs, it is important to examine issues related to inheritance and specify an appropriate amount for each heir.

7.1 UNDERSTANDING THE CONCEPT

Clients often establish objectives regarding how much tax they are willing to pay yet rarely establish specific objectives regarding how much to leave heirs. Instead, heirs usually get what is left after taxes and other expenses are paid.

Whether expressed in dollars or percentages, in order for an estate plan to be most effective, the amount that will go to heirs must be specific. The difficult question is this: How does one determine how much?

Family legacy is a predefined inheritance identified as appropriate for transfer to each individual heir. It is important to remember that in most cases, the heirs have a primary responsibility to create and maintain their own economic and social capital. Generally, clients will want to provide supplemental wealth to the extent it is necessary and appropriate, an amount only the client can determine.

In order to determine the appropriateness of a specific inheritance, clients need to identify specific assets or lifestyle attributes they would like their heirs to enjoy as a result of receiving an inheritance. Parallel to establishing their own financial independence, they should consider two specific areas of inheritance: (1) minimum resource base and (2) lifetime income available for spending.

Many people are concerned that a financial legacy has the potential to cause more problems than it solves. Success has been defined as that point where opportunity meets preparedness. In order to ensure that the legacy clients leave behind has a positive impact on heirs, they should take the time to identify an appropriate amount and then prepare their heirs for the opportunity.

(a) What Do Heirs Normally Get from the Estate?

In most cases, heirs get what is left. The amount of the inheritance typically is an outcome of how much tax is paid. How much tax is paid typically is an outcome of planning. However, what heirs receive *rarely* is an outcome of planning. In other words, clients often establish objectives regarding how much tax they are willing to pay yet rarely establish specific objectives regarding how much to leave heirs. Instead, heirs get what is left after taxes and other expenses are paid.

Even when objectives regarding inheritance are established, more often than not they are fairly generic, such as, "I want my heirs to have as much as possible." Although this type of general objective may demonstrate good intentions, it frustrates the planning process. How much *is* "as much as possible"? Clients could use all their assets to purchase life insurance and perhaps provide heirs with an inheritance that totals two, three, or four times their own current estate. Is this what they mean? More important, is this what they truly want?

After defining financial independence, the most difficult and most important step is to define specifically the inheritance clients want their heirs to receive. Whether expressed in dollar amounts or percentages, the numbers *must be specific*. But how do clients determine what is appropriate?

7.2 INHERITANCE: HOW MUCH IS ENOUGH?

Many families of wealth are concerned about leaving a huge financial legacy for their heirs. In fact, the popular press has covered this subject for more than 10 years.

An article entitled "Should You Leave It All to Your Children?" (*Fortune*, September 1986) recounted interviews with 30 multimillionaires. More than one-half intended to leave 50 percent or more of their wealth to charity. Why? One common reason was that they had serious concerns about the short- and long-term effects that leaving large sums of inherited wealth might have on their offspring.

Investor Warren Buffet, already worth billions of dollars at the time, put it this way: "Parents should leave children enough money so that they would feel they could do anything, but not so much that they could do nothing."

This is a telling statement regarding the concept of *appropriate inheritance*. It points out that the act of determining an appropriate inheritance requires careful consideration. What is appropriate for one is not necessarily appropriate for another. Fair is *not* necessarily equal, and equal is *not* always fair.

A more recent article, "You're on Your Own, Kid!" (*Forbes*, May 1997), took another look at the subject of inherited wealth. In this article, Home Depot chairman Bernard Marcus, worth some $850 million at the time, lamented that inheritance can be "a terrible burden for some." He decided, "If my kids want to get rich, they'll have to work for it." Reflecting on his stepfather's decision in the same article, Michael Morris commented, "This is a tough business. I work 70 to 80 hours a week. I really don't know that I would have pushed this hard. I am happy that I have my own company. I am glad that I had the incentive." At that time, Morris was pursuing a successful career as an investment banker in Atlanta.

Relative to ensuring their heirs' financial independence, clients can make meaningful contributions in two areas: (1) increasing their minimum resource base and (2) providing supplemental income.

Once they have contributed an appropriate amount to their heirs' financial independence, many people want to consider how they might contribute to the second level of their heirs' pyramid, or family legacy. Do they want to make bequests to grandchildren? This can reduce pressure that their own children may feel about providing an appropriate inheritance for their children.

Finally, many clients have an opportunity to help their children construct the social capital portion of their pyramid. Private foundations, support organizations, and donor-advised funds are some of the tools available for transferring social capital to the next generation.

Keep in mind, inherited wealth affects an ambitious overachiever differently than a spendthrift ne'er-do-well. The simple reality is, no two people are the same. Therefore, each individual's needs and unique circumstances must be carefully considered. As clients construct pyramids for the next generation, it is important to heed the fact that one size might not fit all. Clients will want to consider how much they *want* to contribute to heirs' pyramids. Then they will want to consider how much they *should* contribute. Most will want to ensure that their contribution does not undermine or overshadow their heirs' contribution to building their own pyramid.

General Observation . . . on inheritance

Family wealth transfer is about building pyramids for succeeding generations. Clients must take care to leave room for their heirs' own contributions.

7.3 ESTABLISHING A SPECIFIC INHERITANCE OBJECTIVE: THE FAMILY LEGACY

Family legacy is a predefined inheritance amount that clients identify as appropriate for transfer to each heir. There is no right or wrong amount. The appropriateness of a specific inheritance is a function of the individual person and his or her specific situation. It may be $10 million in one case and zero in another. It may be all of the estate or a small fraction. Every answer is correct, as long as it is determined through a conscious thought process. As Michael Bloomberg said, "I have no intention of cutting them out; the question is how much to give them so as not to hurt them."

Although establishing specific inheritance objectives sounds good in theory, putting it into practice is difficult. Many people, when asked how much inheritance they would like to leave heirs, respond with a blank stare or perhaps a comment such as, "As much as possible, of course." Or "How could I possibly know? They are too young at this point." In general, people tend not to deal with this question because it is difficult to know how and where to begin.

Many clients need to be reminded that their heirs have the primary responsibility to create and maintain their own economic and social capital. For most people, the inheritance goal will be to provide supplemental wealth to the extent they feel it is necessary, possible, and appropriate.

General Observation . . . on passing values with value

Leaving no money but passing values to heirs is acceptable. They likely will manage their lives very well.

Leaving money and passing values to heirs is usually a positive situation. They just may change the world.

Leaving money to heirs who have poorly developed values is asking for trouble.

7.4 EQUATING LIFESTYLES: KEEPING THE FAMILY LEGACY IN CLEAR FOCUS

Many people are concerned about the values their heirs possess. Clients who want to know how their heirs will treat an inheritance need only take a close look at how heirs currently manage their money. It is a revealing indicator of how they will handle inherited wealth.

One important advantage of establishing specific inheritance objectives is that it forces clients to compare their lifestyle with that of their heirs. This provides an opportunity to compare values regarding wealth.

Heirs do not always have values that are directly in line with those of their parents, nor do they always have opposing values. However, clients should recognize that money means different things to different people. One should caution clients not to apply their personal standards to others, not even to their own offspring.

> **General Observation . . . on heirs and managing money**
>
> A word of caution to clients: Your heirs will manage your money the way they manage their money, not the way you manage your money.

7.5 TEACH CHILDREN WELL: PREPARING HEIRS TO RECEIVE THEIR INHERITANCE

Many people worry that their heirs may not have the necessary skills to manage their inheritance without outside intervention. Is inheritance a good thing or a bad thing? When should heirs be informed regarding family wealth and their potential inheritance? If they learn of an inheritance too early, will that knowledge adversely affect their initiative as self-sufficient adults? If they are told at a later date, will the surprise adversely affect their ability to maximize the advantages of inherited wealth? The answers to these questions generally have to do with how well clients prepare their heirs for the responsibilities of wealth.

When should clients inform heirs of their potential inheritance?

The answer to this question is a function of financial maturity. Generally speaking, children tend to overestimate or underestimate their parents' wealth by a wide margin. They rarely guess correctly.

The difficulty arises from the fact that everyone is different. Clients are the best judges about when it is best to talk with their children about these issues. They should follow three basic rules.

First, they should teach their children about the responsible use and management of wealth.

Second, they should clarify their thoughts before dropping the bomb. Rather than simply laying their financial statement on the table, they should give their heirs a copy of their written Family Financial Philosophy. This will help the heirs better understand what money means to their parents and what expectations the parents may have regarding inheritance issues.

Third, clients should not ask their children for advice with respect to their estate plan. Doing so puts them in an impossible position. It is unreasonable to expect heirs to be impartial. Assure clients that their heirs will respect their decisions.

(a) Preparing Heirs to Manage Inherited Wealth

Most children have only minimal experience in successful money management. Yet the habits they develop as young adults are likely to continue for a lifetime.

Heirs can learn how to manage money from a variety of strategies. Some involve placing assets under their control as early as possible. Many parents utilize the gift tax exclusion to place assets under the control of heirs during their lifetime, when they can provide advice and monitor performance. The annual gift tax exclusion allows transfer of cash or assets to heirs, free of both gift and estate tax. In 2000, this exclusion is $10,000 per donee.

Another idea is to establish a brokerage account for each potential heir. Once established, parents might send each a note, indicating the account has been established and outlining their expectations. For example:

> I have established this account on your behalf. It is my desire that you invest these assets toward an objective at least five years from today. Suitable objectives might include a new home, tuition for children, or retirement savings. If you have not yet funded an individual retirement account, and you are eligible to take a deduction, I suggest you use a portion of this gift for that purpose. If you would like some advice, please don't hesitate to call.

Another method is the time-tested gift-of-thirds approach. The client makes a gift to each heir, with the following instructions:

> It is my wish that you spend one-third any way you like, invest one-third for your future, and give one-third to charity. When you have completed this task, please write a report for me on what you did, and why.

Charitable giving provides an interesting opportunity to experience the responsible and effective management of wealth. Some families establish charitable foundations to create a quasi-business setting in which heirs are given the responsibility to manage money for someone else. Placing heirs in a fiduciary capacity, where they must share the responsibility with siblings or other board members, provides a unique perspective on wealth management.

Should heirs receive their inheritance outright, in trust, or over time? It is important for clients to consider whether their heirs have the capacity to manage an inheritance. Although it is impossible to "reach up from the grave," it is possible to anticipate certain problems.

Trusts can be used to control the way in which heirs receive their inheritance. Consider the following examples of possible arrangements:

- Income and principal are paid at the discretion of an independent trustee.
- Income is distributed annually, with principal distribution at the discretion of an independent trustee.
- One-third is distributed at age 35, one-third at 40, and the remainder at age 45.
- Income and principal are distributed as requested by the beneficiary.

(b) Incentive Trusts—The "Magic Carrot"

Some families use the transfer of wealth as a perpetual incentive for achievement of preferred milestones. Incentive trusts are designed to increase the likelihood of heirs accomplishing milestones consistent with family values. Consider the following hypothetical trust provisions and corresponding values:

Trust provision. "Each heir shall receive an annual distribution equal to his or her earned income reported for federal income tax purposes in the prior year."

Corresponding values. Personal initiative, hard work, personal achievement.

Trust provision. "Each heir shall receive an annual distribution equal to two times the total charitable contributions reported in his or her federal income tax return from the previous year."

Corresponding values. Philanthropy, generosity, gratitude.

Trust provision. "Each heir shall receive an annual distribution equal to $50 for each hour of documented volunteer service to others."

Corresponding values. Volunteerism, selflessness, service to others.

Trust provision. "Each heir shall receive the distribution indicated upon achieving the following milestones: (1) master's degree, $50,000; (2) doctorate, $100,000; (3) Pulitzer Prize, $200,000; (4) Nobel Prize, $500,000."

Corresponding values. Education, intellectual accomplishment, service.

Trust provision. "Each heir shall receive the distribution indicated upon achieving the following milestones: (1) state senator, $50,000; (2) governor, $200,000; (3) U.S. congressman or senator, $500,000; (4) president of the United States, $1,000,000."

Corresponding values. Political activism, leadership, service to others.

This method of using financial incentive to motivate heirs is sometimes referred to as *financial parenting.* It provides an opportunity for heirs to carry on the values that were important to their parents by virtue of the legacy their parents left for them.

7.6 A BRIEF REVIEW

Start with the end in mind when considering the distribution of a client's estate. Tax savings are a measure of effectiveness—not a goal. Family legacy, on the other hand, is a predetermined amount deemed appropriate for transfer to heirs. This is a goal. The most effective estate planning process begins with a specific family legacy in mind and incorporates strategies to achieve the desired result.

When it comes to wealth transfer, it is important to remember that passing value without values can be detrimental. When wealth is transferred, especially at a young age, it has a tremendous impact on the person who receives it. Clients should take care that the amount they leave heirs is appropriate, specific, predetermined, and in keeping with their value system.

POINTS TO PONDER

- Few families have any concept of what *appropriate inheritance* means. As a result, they tend to err on the side of leaving too much, rather than too little.

- Heirs will spend their inheritance the way they have always spent their money. Parents should not expect that their heirs will follow the parents' spending example.

- Leaving no money but passing values to heirs is acceptable. They will manage their lives well. Leaving money and passing values to heirs also is fine. They can change the world. Leaving money to heirs who have poorly developed values is asking for trouble.

- Legacy planning is about constructing a planning pyramid for each heir: financial independence, family legacy, and social capital legacy. Clients should be careful to leave room within each level for their heirs' own contributions.

- Inherited wealth is best used to supplement the economic and social capital of succeeding generations, not to eliminate the need for it.

- Heirs who are prepared to receive their legacy will grow into financial maturity.

- Incentive trusts teach and motivate heirs in perpetuity.

ASK A CLIENT TO TRY THIS

This exercise encourages clients to evaluate how successful they have been in transferring their values to children or other heirs. Have the client rate each of the values seen in the following exhibit on a scale from 1 to 4, with 1 being the least successful and 4 being the most successful.

---

1 2 3 4 *Ethical values,* such as honesty, justice, fairness
1 2 3 4 *Personal values,* such as modesty, loyalty, faithfulness
1 2 3 4 *Emotional values,* such as compassion, kindness, generosity
1 2 3 4 *Public values,* such as good citizenship, community involvement, government service
1 2 3 4 *Economic values,* such as financial responsibility, frugality, stewardship
1 2 3 4 *Financial values,* such as material possessions, independence, social standing
1 2 3 4 *Spiritual values,* such as inner spirituality, faith, religious commitment
1 2 3 4 *Work values,* such as effort, punctuality, competence, professional achievement
1 2 3 4 *Physical values,* such as health, relaxation, quiet time alone, exercise
1 2 3 4 *Cultural values,* such as music, visual arts, travel
1 2 3 4 *Relational values,* such as family, friends, work associates
1 2 3 4 *Philanthropic values,* such as contributions of time and money to care for others
1 2 3 4 *Recreational values,* such as sports, leisure activity, hobbies, family vacations
1 2 3 4 *Educational values,* such as study, self-improvement, academic achievement
1 2 3 4 *Other* (please specify).

Exhibit 7.1 Determining Values That Have Been Passed on to Children

Then have the client consider those areas where he or she rated his or her progress 1 or 2 but would like to improve.

---

1 2 3 4   Actively discuss the importance of specific values
1 2 3 4   Demonstrate deeply held values in how we lead our lives
1 2 3 4   Establish a family mission statement
1 2 3 4   Involve our children in our charitable giving and volunteering
1 2 3 4   Establish a family foundation
1 2 3 4   Become involved in a religious place of worship
1 2 3 4   Encourage our children to work, to learn the meaning of money
1 2 3 4   Involve children in a family business

Exhibit 7.2   Ranking Methods for Handing on Values

This next exercise demonstrates that there are numerous ways to transfer one's values to children and other heirs. Have the client rank the methods for transferring family values seen in Exhibit 7.2 on a scale from 1 to 4, with 1 being the least helpful and 4 being the most helpful.

Now have the client consider his or her responses to these ideas. Could one or more of these strategies be used to enhance progress in transferring values to heirs?

CHAPTER EIGHT

Principle #6

Maximize the Social Capital Legacy

Will the clients' ultimate social capital legacy be in the form of taxes or charitable gifts? They can choose! Decisions regarding the distribution of excess wealth become relatively easy when they are values-driven.

8.1 UNDERSTANDING THE CONCEPT

For families fortunate enough to make it through the first two levels in the planning pyramid—financial independence and family legacy—the last area of concern is their social capital legacy.

The question is whether it will be in the form of tax or charitable gifts. That decision is a reflection of their value system.

Most people have participated in checkbook philanthropy. They respond with an immediate gift when organizations ask for contributions. Far fewer have participated in philanthropy at a level that requires greater thought and planning.

As the amount of their available social capital grows, some clients may want to focus on strategic philanthropy and defining a mission for those dollars. If they wish to direct their social capital through philanthropy, they will consider either (1) specific organizations they know will help fulfill their personal mission or (2) general social categories they would like to address, such as education, health, human services, the arts, and so on. With the latter, they may want to begin researching what specific organizations best suit their interests and their desire to make a difference in society.

Keep in mind that it is not necessarily easy to give money away, but it is perhaps one of the most rewarding things anyone can do. Advisors can do a great service to clients by helping them distribute their social capital dollars thoughtfully and well.

8.2 THE SOCIAL CAPITAL LEGACY: HARNESSING THE POWER

Most people have never made a truly significant gift. Therefore, they have never experienced firsthand the joy it brings. At the same time, most people believe they lack the necessary resources to make significant contributions. Giving to charitable organizations plays a minor role in their lives. Although they may pull out the checkbook when asked, they have never given much thought to whether they could do substantially more.

Strategic philanthropy is giving based on a plan or mission—a predetermined act with an expected outcome. Advisors are in a unique position to help clients make a number of decisions that will shape their philanthropic mission.

Will their philanthropy be focused? If so, what will the focus be? Should they provide broad support for multiple organizations they believe to be worthy, or should they limit their support to a few, in order to maximize the potential impact? What types of organizations will they support? What fields will benefit from their generosity—health care, education, religion, human rights, humanitarian relief, medical research, the environment?

Clients also must decide on a delivery method. Should they give directly to the recipient organization, establish a foundation, or use a conduit such as a community foundation? If they establish a foundation, how will they arrange the governance process? Will their children or other heirs be involved? What about their grandchildren or in-laws?

They also must decide how to measure results. Is their philanthropy producing the impact they expected? Have the gifts they made been used in accordance with their intentions?

As clients make gifts that are in tune with their well-articulated mission statement, they and their families undoubtedly will find the process of philanthropy rewarding and compelling. As Percy Ross said, "He who gives while he lives also knows where it goes." Strategic philanthropy gives clients the opportunity to participate directly in the good work their gifts make possible.

General Observation . . . on lifetime giving

"He who gives while he lives also knows where it goes."

Percy Ross

8.3 FAMILY PHILANTHROPY: PASSING VALUE WITH VALUES

Wealthy families often express concern that their children may not possess the financial and social skills necessary to successfully manage wealth. They fear their children may, in fact, be adversely affected by a significant inheritance.

Some families of wealth are troubled by their belief that the world in which they are bringing up their children embodies a value system inconsistent with their own. Still other families experience a loss of family unity as their children forge into the world to make their own way.

The charitable organizations or causes clients choose to support help define their personal values and beliefs. Unfortunately, most of them do not involve their children in the charitable giving process. In fact, most families experience only checkbook philanthropy. In response to a solicitation, most assess their cash position and make a contribution, if they are able.

A significant amount of literature suggests that it is important for parents to instill in their children a positive self-image and a high sense of self-esteem. Philanthropy provides an opportunity for children to gain *a sense of satisfaction and significance through helping others.*

This sense of satisfaction can be derived from a simple good deed, like shoveling an elderly neighbor's driveway and refusing payment. It can be achieved by providing financial support for a particular project, collecting toys for poor children at Christmas, or volunteering to serve turkey at a homeless shelter on Thanksgiving. The resulting sense of satisfaction will stay with most families for life.

With today's live coverage of news events, one can hardly avoid society's problems—hunger, children shooting children, armed robbery, drugs, teenage pregnancy, illiteracy, domestic violence, warring nations. Providing philanthropic support to address these and other pressing social issues reinforces core values and exposes children to positive behavior and role models who share those values.

Benefits derived from making charitable gifts increase significantly when the entire family is involved in the decision-making process. The shared experience of family philanthropy provides an opportunity to explore financial issues in a context that reflects family values, teaches the responsible use of money, and enhances family unity. What better way is there for clients to show their children what is important to them than to share information and the experience of supporting organizations and causes that help others?

Family philanthropy involves adult and minor children, grandchildren, and other heirs in the charitable giving process. Whether making an annual gift as a family, establishing a private foundation, or serving as volunteers, the result can be positive for any family. The experience of shared philanthropy uses actions, not just words, to teach children about what is important and worthy of financial support. What organizations do their parents care about? Why? How do they decide which organizations or causes to support?

At the core of family philanthropy is the process of family interaction. Every family has its own dynamics. Participating in the charitable decision-making process enhances communication skills and elevates confidence. Consider just a few potential outcomes:

- Parents and children interacting on a peer level
- Family "adventures" and shared experiences
- Cooperation and conflict resolution
- Program research and joint project initiation

Asking children or grandchildren what they would do regarding a gift situation may bring surprising answers. Asking children to research possible funding opportunities can lead to new possibilities for growth and confidence-building.

It is clear that many people are deeply concerned about maintaining—or perhaps regaining—a sense of family unity. There was a time when it was uncommon for children to move further away than the next town. Today, it seems uncommon for children to stay close to home. Families are faced with an inevitable loss of unity as children move to other parts of the country and the world to build their own lives.

In some situations, our daily lives are so busy we may experience difficulty functioning closely as a family unit. Limited time spent together is not as significant as the lack of opportunity to function as a family unit, interacting with each other through the process of making family decisions. A number of families have found that philanthropy offers a positive way to enhance and maintain family unity.

(a) Creating a Foundation to Support the Family Business

In some cases, proximity has little to do with the loss of family unity. Consider the family that owns and operates a closely held business. As might be expected, a significant part of family life tends to revolve around the business. Because it is not uncommon that some children will be actively involved with the business and some will not, those children outside the family business may feel disenfranchised or outside the loop. Over time, this can lead to a significant loss of family unity.

A number of families have found that a foundation can provide a solution to this problem. For example, consider the family with two daughters—one in the business, one not in the business.

This scenario can result in considerable tension, as the child outside the business struggles to find her place in the family. A possible solution is to establish a family foundation, perhaps with the same or a similar name as the corporation. For example, if the corporation is XYZ Inc., the name XYZ Foundation could be used. In some situations, it may be more appropriate to use the family name or something completely unrelated.

The daughter who is not involved with the business would be given an opportunity to serve in a leadership position within XYZ Foundation. This gives her the chance to experience a governance process involving other family members.

There are a variety of ways the family corporation can be used to fund the XYZ Foundation. This is appropriate, as the business is precisely what caused the family disunity in the first place. Over time, the philanthropic work done by XYZ Foundation in the community will indirectly benefit XYZ Corporation, as it is recognized for its efforts. More important, each daughter has an opportunity to play a leadership role in the family, contribute to the family's economic success, and achieve a sense of significance through personal accomplishment.

(b) Charitable Support Foundation

The charitable support foundation is fast becoming a philanthropic tool of choice for many families. This is especially true for those who are willing to reduce modestly the control and flexibility offered by establishing a private foundation and who want maximum tax benefits, simplicity, and cost effectiveness. Similar to a private foundation, the support foundation is a separate entity. It is called a support foundation because its sole purpose is to provide support for a specific charitable organization, group of specific organizations, or a broad class of organizations. As a result, the support foundation is given public charity status, which affords its donors favorable tax treatment.

Unlike the private foundation, the donor who establishes the support foundation may not have unilateral control over distributions. However, with careful planning and proper design, it is quite easy to balance the needs of the donor with the requirements for qualification.

One primary advantage of the support organization is the ability to avoid the prohibitions against self-dealing and excess business holdings that pertain to private foundations. This creates an opportunity to utilize the support foundation as a tool for transferring a family business to children and to take advantage of other charitable planning strategies.

(c) The Donor-Advised Fund

Donor-advised funds, offered by a variety of charitable organizations, can provide an attractive alternative to a private foundation or support foundation. A gift to a donor-advised fund can be thought of as a special type of restricted gift. The restriction provides the donor with the right to "advise" the charity with regard to the deployment of fund assets within the charity itself or regarding the distribution of fund assets to other charities.

Many specialized organizations such as community foundations offer the advantage of grant-making expertise. In recent years, community foundations have refined their services in this area, helping donors deploy their philanthropic assets more strategically.

(d) Annual Family Gifts

Many families lack the interest or financial resources to warrant the use of a foundation, support organization, or donor-advised fund. These families can achieve a similar sense of satisfaction from making an annual family gift.

8.4 INTERGENERATIONAL DILUTION OF FAMILY WEALTH: MAINTAINING THE FOCUS

When wealth is transferred from one generation to another, invariably its focus becomes diluted. Typically, a portion is lost to tax. The balance is divided among the heirs, perhaps spread across the country or even the world. When an estate is divided among multiple beneficiaries, the concentration of family wealth is reduced. Even if this phenomenon is only temporary, the fact remains that the family takes one large step backward before it can move forward again.

Social capital provides an interesting opportunity to minimize the dilution of family wealth. Many families have taken advantage of their social capital dollars to fund entities that will continue in perpetuity. A private family foundation, supporting organization, gift fund, or donor-advised fund each offers this possibility to some degree.

Because charitable dollars are not reduced by tax and are not subject to the rule against perpetuities, it is possible for the assets to maintain their value and actually increase over time. Over several generations, applying this approach can capture tremendous amounts of wealth, resulting in an increased focus for its use. Dilution of family wealth not only can be halted, but can be reversed.

8.5 A BRIEF REVIEW

In order to maximize a social capital legacy, clients first must recognize their ability to control and direct their social capital. In order to maximize the impact of their social capital, they then must distribute their social capital through a process of strategic philanthropy.

By harnessing the power of their social capital, families gain an important opportunity to engage in family philanthropy. Whether using a private family foundation, charitable support foundation, donor-advised fund, or annual gifts, advisors can provide clients with meaningful opportunities to complement the obvious benefits associated with charitable giving. Families have much to gain from joining together in the process of family philanthropy—shared experiences; family adventures; and parents, children, and even grandchildren interacting as peers. For many clients, the simple satisfaction that they derive from being involved in worthwhile projects is sufficient reward.

The dilution of family wealth as it is transferred from one generation to the next is of great concern to wealthy clients. However, once social capital evolves into a strategic component of a client's overall wealth transfer and management plan, significant opportunities emerge for maintaining the focus of family wealth from one generation to the next. Foundations and other charitable strategies offer unique opportunities to perpetuate wealth from one generation to the next while alleviating the dilution of tax.

POINTS TO PONDER

- Social capital awareness is created when families can measure the relative impact of a specific gift strategy within the parameters of their well-defined objectives.

- Benefits derived from making charitable gifts can be increased significantly by involving the entire family in the decision-making process.

- The shared experience of family philanthropy provides an opportunity to explore financial issues in a context that reflects family values and teaches the responsible use of money.

ASK A CLIENT TO TRY THIS

Have the client complete the following social capital exercises:

1. Determine what you will do with your social capital. How will you maximize the efficiency of these dollars? Remember that the job is not done once you capture your social capital. The job is done only when the dollars are put to work effectively.
2. Before you make your next gift to charity, have a family meeting and ask your children, grandchildren, or other heirs for their input. Consider having them research a specific project for potential funding.
3. Take a child or another heir on a site visit to a charitable organization you have supported in the past and would like to support in the future. Explain why you have made gifts in the past and how your gifts were made. Ask him or her for advice about how to allocate your next gift. Then make the gift.

CHAPTER NINE

Principle #7

Build a Virtual Planning Team

The ideal estate planning team is multidisciplinary, with each advisor bringing one or more unique abilities to the table. Using the values and objectives expressed in the Family Financial Philosophy as a guide, the client's planning "dream team" works synergistically to recommend the best possible strategies and plan design to fulfill the client's mission.

9.1 UNDERSTANDING THE CONCEPT

The *virtual corporation* model works well in the estate planning environment. A virtual planning team is brought together for one purpose—to design an estate plan that achieves the client's expressed goals and objectives. The ideal team is multidisciplinary, with each advisor serving a different function and bringing a unique competency to the mix.

The team gives each strategy idea full consideration, regardless of which advisor makes the suggestion. The advisory team members must reach consensus on the validity of any idea before they present it to the client. They achieve consensus by using the client's Family Financial Philosophy mission statement as their guide.

A team may be large or small. But the most important thing to remember is that the *client* is the team leader. The client is at the center of, and in total control of, the planning process. If at any time the client feels he or she has lost control, the makeup of the team should be reevaluated and necessary adjustments made.

A highly effective planning team, with the client in the center of the process, leads to both excellence and trust. Each advisor brings a core competency to the effort, creating a best-of-everything planning team. No single advisor can achieve this. The professionals experience a sense of co-destiny and trust each other in the shared goal of helping the client achieve his or her highest planning aspirations.

9.2 THE CONVENTIONAL PLANNING PROCESS

Generally, people have more than one professional advisor. Typically, these advisors compete for the client's love and affection, each wanting to control the planning process. Each advisor likely has a different opinion of what the client is trying to accomplish. Not surprisingly, that opinion usually is based on the advisor's perspective, not the client's.

Consider a planning team with four advisors—an attorney, an insurance agent, an investment manager, and an accountant. Given the identical planning problem to solve, each typically would come up with a different solution. Each also would have a different perspective on what the client is trying to achieve.

In reality, most people enter the planning process unsure about what they can accomplish. In fact, far too little time is spent in developing clear and concise objectives. Instead, the process quickly moves into reviewing techniques and strategies in an attempt to solve problems that have not yet been clearly identified.

At the end of what is often a long, drawn-out, uncoordinated process, the client is asked to decide which option will work the best. Ironically, clients are forced to make the decisions they hire their advisors to make on their behalf. Yet, in many cases, the clients are least qualified to make the decisions.

9.3 THE VIRTUAL PLANNING PROCESS: WORKING WITH A TEAM OF PROFESSIONAL ADVISORS

In the virtual planning environment, advisors function as a team. They respect each other's ideas. They understand that they must reach consensus prior to presenting any idea to the client for consideration.

A multidisciplinary team is the most advantageous. This team may, at any given time in the process, require the expertise of an attorney, accountant, life insurance agent, investment manager, development professional, financial planner, trust officer, independent gift planner, and perhaps even the client's heirs. Regardless of how few or how many team members are needed, the group shares a common goal. That one goal is to work synergistically to provide the client with a plan that meets his or her specific objectives. In the virtual planning process, members of the planning team fit together like the pieces of a puzzle.

Virtual planning advisory teams are less permanent and less formal than typical teams of the past. They band together to meet a specific market opportunity—to solve a client's particular planning needs. Although they may choose to work together as a team after this experience, for all intents and purposes, their job is done when the plan is done, and their paths may never cross again.

The very best advisors rely on other advisors. Each trusts that the unique abilities of the others will contribute toward the best possible outcome. The client's advisors further trust each other in their desire and ability to accomplish client goals and objectives.

9.4 UNIQUE ABILITIES: THE BUILDING BLOCKS OF A SUCCESSFUL PLANNING TEAM

Dan Sullivan, founder and president of The Strategic Coach, Inc., addresses his concept of *unique ability* in the ongoing training of successful entrepreneurs. The following discussion is adapted from Sullivan's work.

Organizing the right team of advisors can be a significant challenge. Personalities can clash. Services often overlap and sometimes conflict. As successful professionals and businesspeople, one thing is certain—estate-planning advisors are rarely at a loss for opinions!

With these and other considerations in mind, how can clients construct an estate planning *dream team*? The answer is to align the right combination of unique abilities in order to achieve unique teamwork. The key is to focus on the necessary skills rather than on a combination of particular people.

According to Sullivan, a unique ability is a one-of-a-kind, extraordinary skill that improves continually and cannot be taught, copied, or replaced. Everyone has a unique ability. Consistently using one's unique ability invariably leads to success.

The quality of estate planning results will mirror the quality of the unique abilities assembled to achieve them. In building a planning team, it is critical to identify and combine unique abilities for maximum effectiveness.

The team, then, becomes an organized group of unique abilities working on the client's behalf. Progress in planning comes from applying those abilities to clearly established objectives. Because the team is assembled in terms of unique abilities rather than particular individuals, its members constantly reinforce each other's strengths and talents.

> **General Observation . . . on building a planning team**
>
> "Combine *Unique Abilities* for maximum effectiveness and extraordinary results."
>
> Dan Sullivan

9.5 BUILD THE PLANNING TEAM

The following three steps are necessary in order to assemble an effective virtual planning team:

1. Protect and reinforce important existing relationships
2. Identify the unique abilities offered by existing advisors
3. Identify the unique abilities necessary to complete the planning team

(a) Protect and Reinforce Important Existing Relationships

Most affluent clients have a difficult time establishing new advisory relationships. Many find this so difficult that they would rather maintain a dysfunctional relationship than go through the agony of establishing a new relationship. Taking this into consideration, advisors should pay particular attention to existing advisor relationships, and immediately diagnose their importance.

An advisor can play a role on a client's virtual planning team in one of two capacities: relationship or technical competency. Any advisor that is essential to the client's decision-making process has an important role on the team, regardless of technical competency. Likewise, any advisor that contributes a necessary technical competency has an important role on the team, regardless of the depth of relationship.

As clients' needs for advisory services evolve over time, they sometimes find themselves with relationships that add little technical competency yet offer substantial consultative value. Unfortunately, new advisors often discount the importance of existing advisory relationships by focusing their attention exclusively on an advisor's limited technical competency. This oversight can lead to unnecessary confrontation.

As existing advisors consciously or unconsciously watch their technical competency diminish relative to the client's needs, they establish defensive strategies designed to protect their advisory relationships. This defensive posturing can be extremely detrimental to effective planning.

Effective planning requires a process and mind-set that places equal value on relationship and technical competency. A team made up of members who fill both roles will instill confidence in the client and lead to results.

(b) Establish Required Unique Abilities

In order to create a virtual planning team, advisors should begin by identifying a complete spectrum of ideal unique abilities. Following is a sample list.

- The ability to understand and interpret a client's goals, dreams, and desires and reduce them to a written mission statement
- The ability to instill confidence in client decisions based on past relationship, experience, and performance
- The ability to initiate creative planning strategies that address specific planning objectives
- The ability to design and draft state-of-the-art legal documents
- The ability to understand and take full advantage of available tax laws, regulations, and strategies
- The ability to design, execute, and manage investment strategies that enhance a client's estate plan
- The ability to design, execute, and manage insurance strategies that enhance a client's estate plan
- The ability to design a financial model that accurately reflects how a client's plan will function today, over time, and at life expectancy
- The ability to design creative charitable planning strategies that convert tax into self-directed social capital
- The ability to identify and manage a virtual planning team toward a specific set of objectives, within a desired time frame
- The ability to help clients explore and implement philanthropic strategies that reflect their values, interests, goals, and unique perspectives

9.6 INVESTMENT VERSUS EXPENSE: PAYING ADVISORS

It should come as no surprise that most people have an aversion to paying large fees to advisors. In fact, many believe the cost of establishing an estate plan is outrageous. This perspective often is based on negative past experience. When the planning process lacks clarity and focus, time and money are wasted.

(a) The Impact of Advisor Bias

Advanced estate planning often requires the involvement of multiple advisors. As previously discussed, each advisor possesses his or her unique perspective. Because clients sometimes perceive this unique perspective as advisor bias, they waste considerable time jumping from one advisor to another, seeking second and third opinions. Each new advisor adds an additional level of complexity and expense.

(b) The Impact of Vague or Unclear Objectives

When clients lack clarity and focus they tend to exacerbate the cost of planning through indecision. As planning paralysis slowly sets in, bills accumulate without a corresponding benefit. One possibility after another is explored, yet nothing is implemented. When combined with multiple advisors, the planning process spins out of control. Hours mount and bills accumulate.

(c) The Impact of Compensation

Whenever possible, hourly compensation should be avoided. This form of compensation tends to diminish the relative value of an advisor's services as the advisor becomes more skilled. Measuring time and effort alone, the more proficient the advisor becomes at solving client problems, the less he or she is paid. Quite simply, this is because providing the service takes less time. The historical solution to this problem has been to increase the hourly rate. However, once an advisor hits the hourly rate ceiling for any given marketplace, compensation is forever limited by the number of hours in a day.

(d) The Virtual Planning Process Solution

The virtual planning process provides a simple solution to the historical problems associated with fees. All planning recommendations are guided by the client's written financial philosophy. This establishes a clear foundation for each planning decision.

A team that combines unique abilities with clear goals and objectives both eliminates planning paralysis and increases effectiveness. This collapses the time required to move the process forward and promotes immediate results.

Fees are based on results, not hourly rates. With this approach, the client and advisor define the desired result together. The advisor then commits to a flat fee for providing that result. The fee is based on the value of the result, not the time required to articulate or deliver the solution. Wherever possible, fees should be stated as a percentage of the benefit to be gained. In the most effective planning, each advisor is viewed as an investment rather than a cost.

9.7 A BRIEF REVIEW

The virtual planning process is built on the fundamental premise that effective planning requires a combination of unique abilities. Guided by the written Family Financial Philosophy, a multidisciplinary team of planning professionals will develop a plan based on client values and desired outcomes. Advisor bias is eliminated and return on investment is maximized as results are delivered within an appropriate time frame. Fees are based on expected and realized planning results.

POINTS TO PONDER

- In the past, professional advisors have competed for the love and affection of the client, each wanting to be the single, most trusted advisor. This desire for control, coupled with a lack of collaboration, generally results in a limited perspective and biased results.

- Developing an effective values-based estate plan requires the talents of a multidisciplinary team of advisors with unique abilities.

- Most clients view professional advisors as an expense rather than an investment. As a result, they focus on minimizing expenses, rather than maximizing benefits.

- Effective planning yields a return that more than justifies the investment.

ASK A CLIENT TO TRY THIS

Have the client make a list of all current advisors. Next, have the client review the list of unique abilities in this chapter. Based on the client's knowledge of each advisor, match each with his or her unique ability. If the unique ability is not on the list, have the client describe the unique ability in a single sentence, as simply as possible. Given the related nature of the unique abilities, some advisors may possess more than one. In most cases, however, one will be dominant.

Now review the list of desired unique abilities from this chapter. Does the current estate planning team include the necessary unique abilities to maximize planning results? Has the client associated each required unique ability with a specific advisor? Has the client associated all unique abilities with a single advisor? Which unique abilities must be added to get the job done? Which of these unique abilities can you perform?

PART II

The Legacy Planning System: A Methodology for Overcoming Planning Obstacles

CHAPTER TEN

The Legacy
Planning System

10.1 UNDERSTANDING THE CONCEPT

One of the most important steps in initiating an estate plan is the creation of an appropriate planning context. Essentially, a planning context is the integrative structure that enables the client to identify the beginning, middle, and end of the process. Each step is situated within the appropriate context.

Clients become frustrated when they cannot measure progress. Because estate planning is largely a conceptual process, clients often lose track of their progress, or become confused. Complex strategies and technical jargon make things even worse.

The Legacy Planning System is based on the premise that maximum results can be achieved when two objectives are met. First, the results of the client's current plan must be in perfect alignment with the client's current goals at each level of the planning pyramid—financial independence, family legacy, and social capital legacy. Second, each outcome must be supported by clearly articulated, written values.

The Legacy Planning System has three parts: *discovery, analysis,* and *documentation.* The Legacy Planning System uses three key tools to bring planning results into perfect alignment with client objectives: (1) a *written Family Financial Philosophy,* (2) the *current legacy blueprint,* and (3) the *Legacy Positive Focus.* Chapter 10 reviews the steps outlined in Exhibit 10.1.

(a) The Discovery Process

In most planning scenarios, the process of gathering client data is relegated to a minor role, and in some cases it is virtually ignored. In The Legacy Planning System, data gathering is elevated to a new level. In

THE LEGACY PLANNING SYSTEM™

DISCOVERY	ANALYSIS OF CONTENT	DOCUMENTATION
TRIAGE	Due-diligence ▲ Suitability ▲ Strategic vs. Tactical	FEASIBILITY
THE LEGACY INTERVIEW	Family Background ▲ Growing Up ▲ The Present ▲ The Future	THE LEGACY BIOGRAPHY
THE LEGACY QUESTIONNAIRE	Values ▲ Goals ▲ Philosophy ▲ Preferences ▲ Attitudes	PLANNING AFFIRMATIONS
THE LEGACY GOAL PROFILE	Financial Independence Goal ▲ Family Legacy Goal ▲ Social Capital Legacy Goal	HIERARCHY OF PLANNING OBJECTIVES

THE CURRENT LEGACY BLUEPRINT

- ▲ Inventory of Financial Resources
- ▲ Financial Independence Status
- ▲ Family Legacy Status
- ▲ Social Capital Legacy Status
- ▲ Available Planning Resources

SUCCESS FACTORS
Financial ▲ Family ▲ Social

THE FAMILY FINANCIAL PHILOSOPHY
- ▲ Purpose
- ▲ Source of Wealth
- ▲ Legacy Biography
- ▲ Responsibilities & Obligations
- ▲ Primary Planning Goals
- ▲ Financial Philososphy
- ▲ Financial Independence
- ▲ Family Legacy
- ▲ Social Capital Legacy
- ▲ Acknowledgment

THE LEGACY POSITIVE FOCUS

Exhibit 10.1   The Legacy Planning System Diagram

fact, the discovery process is the most important step. It allows both client and advisor to fully understand the client's planning values in a whole new way.

The discovery process focuses on self-awareness. The client looks into the past, explores the evolution of values, and identifies important lessons learned. The client examines how those values have shaped the unique financial philosophy that has become the framework for appropriate planning decisions today. The process further provides an opportunity to evaluate the consequences of past planning decisions and develop specific new planning goals that are in line with personal values. Finally, it creates an opportunity for the client to consider what is truly important from a personal standpoint and to plan for the future, based on those priorities.

The advisor's role is one of archeologist. The task is to uncover the client's past experiences and reconstruct them in order to understand the present and the client's dreams for the future. In the manner of an archeologist, each artifact is treated with great care and respect.

In the discovery process, the advisor uses five methods to assist clients in exploring and understanding how the past, present, and future have shaped their values: (1) planning triage, (2) the legacy interview, (3) the legacy questionnaire, (4) the legacy goal profile, and (5) the current legacy blueprint. Each method helps clarify objectives and develop goals. Each method incorporates a variety of tools and techniques designed to facilitate the process and provide the necessary structure.

All methods are utilized to some degree in each planning case. However, the depth to which they are applied depends on the advisor's personal style and the specific facts and circumstances of each case. The actual order in which the methods are used may vary from case to case.

(b) Analysis of Content

Whereas discovery is designed to uncover information, analysis is designed to organize, understand, and substantiate the information by placing it within an appropriate planning context.

It is important for advisors to be aware that analysis does not refer to qualitative judgments with respect to the information obtained through discovery. Rather, the advisor simply organizes the information and repeats it back to the client for evaluation and confirmation.

In the analysis phase, the advisor carefully records each level of analysis in order to provide the client with clear, unambiguous feedback. Each step builds upon the previous steps, allowing the client to track progress and trace each decision to its origin. For example, once the client has completed the legacy questionnaire, the first level of analysis is to present the client with an opportunity to evaluate his or her initital responses. This is accomplished by converting each questionnaire response into a written affirmation. The affirmation is a first person statement that reflects the advisor's interpretation of the client's response.

(c) Documentation

Each discovery method uses a unique process for reporting the information gathered in discovery and substantiated through analysis. In the documentation phase, the advisor transforms the wealth of information obtained into a practical format designed to support planning.

Each level of discovery results in a single document that plays an integral part in future planning decisions. *Planning triage* determines results in a feasibility study that establishes the scope of the engagement. The *legacy interview* results in the *legacy biography*, outlining important experiences from the client's past. The *questionnaire* is documented by converting the legacy questionnaire results into a list of planning affirmations that detail the client's goals, values, preferences, and attitudes toward 39 distinct planning areas. The *legacy goal profile* is documented through the hierarchy of planning objectives, which outlines the client's financial goals at each level of the planning pyramid—financial independence, family legacy, and social capital legacy. Finally, the *current legacy blueprint* outlines the results under the client's current plan.

(d) The Family Financial Philosophy

Once each level of discovery has been properly documented, the next step is for the advisor to prepare a draft of the client's Family Financial Philosophy. The FFP is derived from three of the aforementioned documents: the legacy biography, the list of planning affirmations, and the legacy goal profile. The legacy biography provides information about the client's unique past, present, and future. The planning affirmations detail the client's goals in 39 planning areas. The legacy goal profile provides specific financial goals for financial independence, family legacy, and social capital legacy.

(e) The Current Legacy Blueprint

The legacy blueprint illustrates the client's present status with regard to financial independence, family legacy, and social capital legacy. Furthermore, it identifies the current organization of estate assets and income, and the flow of assets through the current estate plan.

The legacy blueprint clearly establishes the impact of existing wealth transfer strategies upon financial independence, family legacy, and social capital legacy.

(f) The Legacy Positive Focus

The final stage of The Legacy Planning System identifies gaps between the client's current plan and the ideal goals and objectives as expressed in the Family Financial Philosophy. If possible, the advisor should begin by identifying any areas where the current legacy blueprint is consistent with the FFP mission statement, in order to reinforce confidence regarding what the client already has accomplished.

Ultimately, the Legacy Positive Focus becomes the driving force behind future planning decisions. Each decision is associated with the elimination of a specific inconsistency, one that has been substantiated by both the client and the advisor.

It is important to stress that most advisors begin where The Legacy Planning System leaves off. They tend to start with a perceived or assumed list of observations. Once assumptions are made, many advisors waste considerable time and resources constructing plans on shaky or nonexistent foundations. The Legacy Planning System constructs the foundation out of steel-reinforced concrete. As a result, future planning decisions are decisive and effective.

10.2 PLANNING TRIAGE

Planning triage is the initial step in the discovery process. The term *triage* is derived from military medical vernacular and refers to a process of priority allocation of limited medical resources based upon the severity of illness and potential benefit from treatment. The goal is to identify and treat patients quickly who will gain the maximum benefit from the smallest amount of available resources.

Because advisors are working with limited time and resources, it is essential to prioritize prospects quickly. Planning triage addresses three specific issues: due diligence, client-advisor suitability, and the establishment of either a strategic or tactical planning focus.

It is important to note that planning triage is in and of itself a valuable service for clients. Depending upon the size and scope of the case, an advisor may need to charge a triage fee to justify the time and effort associated with evaluating the client's situation.

(a) Due Diligence

Due diligence is the process whereby clients establish the credibility of an advisor. This step is often taken for granted by advisors. Essentially, conducting due diligence refers to review of the entire package presented by an advisor. It covers everything from references, education, credentials, marketing materials, published materials, and office space, even to an advisor's personal appearance.

Client references are one of the most critical elements of due diligence. Successful people like to be associated with other successful people. An advisor should be prepared to provide a list of references at this stage of the planning process.

(b) Client Suitability

Assuming an advisor makes it past due diligence, the next level of triage is client-advisor suitability. The advisor should begin by considering whether the prospect is likable. After all, life is too short to be around miserable people!

The advisor must determine if the prospect qualifies to be a client. Can the advisor provide sufficient value for the prospect to justify minimum compensation standards? Does the prospect perceive sufficient value from a potential relationship to justify paying the advisor's minimum compensation?

In order for this level of suitability to be established, obviously the advisor first must define a minimum compensation standard. Whether specifying a minimum net worth, or minimum fee, setting a minimum client standard is a fundamental part of establishing credibility.

In order to determine client suitability, an advisor may need to gather preliminary data. In practice, an advisor begins the discovery process during the triage phase of planning. However, for the most part, the effort is limited to the accumulation of data. Detailed analysis is deferred until the prospect has engaged the advisor.

Gathering preliminary data is helpful for two reasons. First, after an initial review of a client's financial resources and current planning documents, advisors are in a better position to establish the value of their services. The most effective way for advisors to establish the value of their services is to identify the value of those services in specific dollar amounts.

Advisors should always remember that clients reward financial benefits with financial benefits. In other words, the more clearly advisors establish the positive financial results they can provide for clients, the more likely a client will agree with a proposed compensation schedule.

Advisors should be careful not to overdo this preliminary phase of analysis. The goal is to exert minimal effort in order to identify the benefits of a future relationship. Advisors who provide too much value for too little compensation to clients during this preliminary phase may find it difficult to justify their minimum compensation standards later. To that end, in most cases, clients should be provided only a summary of potential benefits, and perhaps a list of possible strategies. In those cases where significant effort is required to effectively diagnose the financial repercussions of a case, a triage fee should be charged.

After establishing financial benefits, the second reason advisors may want to gather preliminary data is to establish a philosophical basis for a relationship. Although this will be less significant in justifying an advisor's compensation, in many cases, it is the final factor associated with securing the relationship.

The level to which an advisor should go to establish a philosophical link with a prospective client depends upon the size and scope of the case. In a routine case, an advisor may want to have the prospect complete a legacy questionnaire in order to get a quick overview of where the client stands relative to key planning issues.

In more complicated cases, an advisor may want to incorporate both the legacy interview and legacy questionnaire into the triage phase of planning. Here again, advisors should limit their effort to the discovery phase, leaving analysis and documentation for later. The legacy interview and legacy questionnaire are being used at this point purely as tools for establishing client suitability.

(c) Establishing a Strategic or Tactical Planning Focus

The final step in planning triage is to establish if the case will be tactical or strategic in nature. A tactical plan is designed to address a specific planning issue, whereas a strategic plan is composed of numerous tactical strategies organized in a systematic way to accomplish broader planning objectives.

Many prospects need assistance in reaching the conclusion that they want to enter a strategic planning process. In other words, it is easier to get them focused on single, specific issues than on broad strategic planning. Recognizing this reality, the final step in planning triage allows an advisor to determine whether a prospect is prepared for strategic planning, or must first address tactical planning issues.

In some cases, tactical problem solving may be the preferred approach with a particular prospect or situation:

- A prospect may have a problem that is time sensitive—for example, the impending sale of a closely held business.

- A prospect may be so focused on a specific problem that it is impossible to move beyond that issue—for example, reallocating his or her investment portfolio in light of a recent market drop.

- A prospect may want the advisor to prove the value of his or her services before engaging in comprehensive planning. This is much easier to accomplish when dealing with a specific issue. It is also less costly if the prospect is not satisfied with the advisor's services.

- A prospect may be interested only in a specific issue at this point in time—for example, tax-effective management of incentive stock options.

- Exhibit 10.2 illustrates an interesting correlation in the relationship between estate size and the choice between tactical or strategic planning. Generally speaking, estates between $3,000,000 and $50,000,000 are best suited for strategic planning. Those with estates below $3,000,000 tend to have more tactical needs and may perceive strategic planning as overkill. Those with estates above $50,000,000 typically prefer a tactical approach initially, and tend to warm to strategic planning only after initial success.

Whatever the reason, the goal is to engage the prospect in a process that leads ultimately to a long-term client relationship. In some situations, an advisor may find that a client must first deal with a number of tactical issues before engaging in a strategic planning process. Some prospects may never enter a strategic planning process at all. The point is, advisors must find people they want to do business with, and then make it easy for their clients to do business with them.

(d) Feasibility Study

Planning triage is documented with a feasibility study. The actual level of detail provided will vary from one client to the next, based on complexity and whether the advisor charged a triage fee. At a minimum, the feasibility study should summarize the conclusions of the triage process, quantify specific financial benefits, and associate the benefits with the cost of additional planning.

The advisor should include appropriate disclosures regarding all potential compensation, including planning fees, commissions, overrides, and referral fees. Finally, the feasibility study should include a letter of engagement that outlines and details the services to be rendered and the scope of the contract.

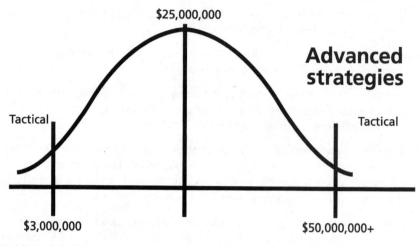

Exhibit 10.2   The Wealth Curve

10.3 THE LEGACY INTERVIEW

The next major step in the discovery process is the legacy interview, a process whereby an advisor interviews a client, asking open-ended questions that lead to the accumulation of significant issues from the client's past. A formal interview process is often limited to larger cases. Nevertheless, this step may be used to enhance the planning affirmations established when processing the legacy questionnaire.

The most effective values-driven process combines the use of questionnaires and face-to-face interviews. From these two information sources, the planning advisor elicits patterns and themes with respect to individual or family history, values, and beliefs.

The interview content should cover the following subject areas:

- Family background
- Growing up
- The present
- The future

Once the interview is complete, a transcript of the interview is prepared. The transcript is used as the primary tool for analyzing and understanding the significance of the information gathered through the interview process.

The legacy biography is the final step in the legacy interview process. At this juncture, key paragraphs and phrases are organized as a chronological biography, outlining significant historical events that played a role in shaping the client's financial philosophy.

Refer to Chapter 12, "The Legacy Interview," for a complete discussion of the legacy interview process.

10.4 THE LEGACY QUESTIONNAIRE

The third discovery method utilizes the legacy questionnaire. At this point, the client is provided with a multiple-choice questionnaire and asked to select the response that best reflects the client's perspective on that issue. Each question deals with a specific planning issue and falls into one of five basic categories:

- Values
- Goals
- Philosophy
- Preferences
- Attitudes

The goal of the questionnaire is to identify and refine the client's perspective with respect to 39 specific planning areas. Couples complete the questionnaire separately, allowing advisors to evaluate similarities and differences in their responses. The completed questionnaires are then reviewed, with each client response converted into an affirmation statement. Each affirmation statement represents a response to the questionnaire, stated in first person. The client is then taken through a series of steps to adjust, refine, and ultimately adopt a personal affirmation list.

The advisor documents the legacy questionnaire through the creation of planning affirmations. These statements are called planning affirmations because they represent the individual or couple client perspective with regard to the 39 key planning areas.

When working with couples, an additional step is associated with reconciling differences of opinion and creating joint planning affirmations. The final documentation is a joint list of planning affirmations.

Chapter 13, "The Legacy Questionnaire," discusses the legacy questionnaire process in detail.

10.5 THE LEGACY GOAL PROFILE

Using the next method of discovery, the advisor helps clients define their unique hierarchy of planning objectives—specific dollar amounts for financial independence, family legacy, and social capital legacy. This is accomplished by processing the legacy goal profile. These three financial goals are essential to developing a client mission statement that will facilitate the planning process:

- Financial independence goal
- Family legacy goal
- Social capital legacy goal

See Chapters 14 and 15 for a complete discussion of the legacy goal profile process.

10.6 THE CURRENT LEGACY BLUEPRINT

The final step in the discovery process is creating the current legacy blueprint. This step focuses on gathering all available information with respect to the client's current financial position and all existing planning documents. The greater the detail, the greater the benefit. At this point, the advisor analyzes the following aspects of a client's current financial position:

- Financial resources
- Financial independence status
- Family legacy status
- Social capital legacy status
- Available planning resources

Chapter 16, "The Legacy Blueprint," discusses the blueprint process in detail.

10.7 THE FAMILY FINANCIAL PHILOSOPHY

The next step in The Legacy Planning System is the creation of a written Family Financial Philosophy, or FFP. This personal, written wealth mission statement clearly expresses the appropriate uses of wealth in view of the client's values.

The legacy biography, planning affirmations, and hierarchy of planning objectives provide the basis for a client's Family Financial Philosophy. The biography provides a family perspective entirely unique from one client to another. The planning affirmations define the client's financial philosophy. The hierarchy of planning objectives defines the client's key financial goals in specific financial terms.

Like a business plan, the Family Financial Philosophy guides clients toward achieving their highest goals and objectives. The FFP reveals true client motivation and objectives regarding all aspects of wealth. Used to its fullest potential, it effectively governs the estate planning process for all advisors on the planning team. The team recommends strategies only if they support the client's stated goals and objectives. Consequently, there is a strong likelihood the client will act on the recommendations.

See Chapter 17, "Drafting the Family Financial Philosophy," for a complete discussion of the Family Financial Philosophy and its preparation.

10.8 THE LEGACY POSITIVE FOCUS

The final step in The Legacy Planning System is to identify consistencies and inconsistencies between the client's current estate plan and the FFP mission statement. Advisors should make a list of each consistency and inconsistency, restating the relevant part of the mission statement and stating the result under the current plan. The inconsistencies will be readily apparent.

The Legacy Positive Focus is the final step in The Legacy Planning System. Using the completed Family Financial Philosophy as a guide, this important step accomplishes two things. First, it recognizes the positive aspects of the current plan, reinforcing the value of past efforts. Second, it creates a positive framework for the task by clearly identifying areas that require further progress. Those areas form the basis for the client's planning objectives.

CHAPTER ELEVEN

Wealth Optimization and Design

11.1 UNDERSTANDING THE CONCEPT

Estate planning is a process, not an event. It must be managed continuously over time, with each step building on the last. To be effective, the entire process must be completely integrated. Wealth optimization is an integrative structure that helps the client understand, and the advisor manage over time, the relationships between and among financial independence, family legacy, and social capital legacy.

A central component of legacy planning, wealth optimization is managed within the scope and boundaries of the client's values as defined in the written Family Financial Philosophy. Therefore, the process begins with specific goals for financial independence, family legacy, and social capital legacy. See Exhibit 11.1, wherein each respective group of goals is represented by a circle in a Venn diagram. These goals are critical, because they define the size and relationship of a client's desired optimization circles.

Once each goal is defined, strategies that have a positive impact on the client's goals in one or more goal areas are identified. Maximum advantage is gained where a single strategy has a positive effect on all three goals.

In selecting suitable strategies for a particular client, the advisor must take into consideration the client's *strategy risk tolerance, complexity threshold*, and *cost-benefit assessment*. Strategy risk tolerance refers to how aggressive the client is willing to be in accomplishing specific goals and objectives. Complexity threshold refers to the maximum amount of complexity the client is willing to endure in accomplishing the goals and objectives. Cost-benefit assessment determines whether the client perceives

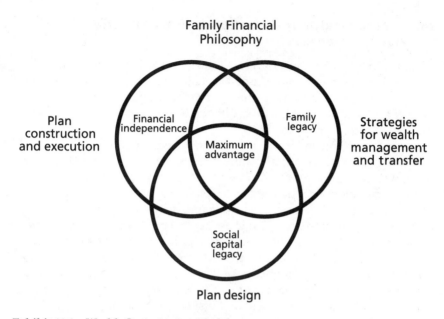

Exhibit 11.1   Wealth Optimization Model

sufficient value from a particular strategy to warrant the cost, risk, and complexity.

Once the required strategies have been identified and optimized, they are combined into a wealth design plan. The purpose of this step is to make sure the strategies work as effectively together as they do independently, by eliminating competing strategies and unnecessary overlap.

The final step is plan construction and execution, during which the client's advisors draft legal documents, design and acquire financial tools, and implement strategies. The result of this step is a wealth design plan that optimizes the client's current goals for financial independence, family legacy, and social capital legacy within the client's strategy risk tolerance and complexity threshold.

Once complete, the wealth optimization and design plan is evaluated annually, or even more frequently if circumstances dictate. During each evaluation, goals are updated, existing strategies are optimized, plan construction is evaluated, and new strategies are implemented. The wealth optimization and design process results in constant planning innovation and the complete integration of financial resources, financial goals, and family values.

(a) Placing Wealth Optimization within a Traditional Planning Context

The process of wealth optimization allows an advisor to define and integrate a client's financial independence goal, family legacy goal, and social capital legacy goal. Because a single profession typically has dominated each of the three areas, it has been difficult to create effective coordination and a synergistic environment.

Financial independence is a function of effective *financial planning*. Generally speaking, financial planning focuses on three goals: (1) creating a lifestyle, (2) insuring against unexpected contingencies, and (3) achieving financial independence. Financial planning addresses topics such as personal savings, investment management, debt management, cash-flow management, insurance planning, retirement planning, education planning, and income tax planning. Although estate planning and social capital planning may be discussed, most advisors who specialize in financial planning have limited knowledge in these two areas. Traditionally, financial planning has been dominated by the financial services industry, with a significant focus on investment and insurance planning.

Family legacy planning refers to *estate planning*, usually with a focus on wealth preservation and transfer. The primary goal is to establish a plan that ensures that financial resources are transferred to whom the client wants, when the client wants, the way in which the client wants, and at the lowest possible cost.

Estate planning techniques may be defensive or offensive. Defensive techniques govern the transfer of assets. Offensive techniques are designed to reduce costs. Lawyers dominate the estate planning industry. Because lawyers are not trained in the area of financial planning, issues related to that discipline often are not addressed effectively in the estate planning process.

Social capital legacy refers to the field of *charitable gift planning*. Charitable planning focuses on converting taxes into charitable contributions. Historically, this industry has been dominated by professionals who represent larger charitable organizations, although financial advisors and lawyers have become actively involved in recent years.

A focus on wealth optimization creates synergy among all three goal areas. Advisors help clients improve planning results by utilizing strategies that have a positive impact in more than one goal area. Maximum advantage is gained where a strategy or combination of strategies helps a client achieve the goals in all three areas.

Advisors who use the wealth optimization approach are among an elite group who have become proficient in each area of planning. They provide optimal service to their clients by taking full advantage of the overlapping synergy that exists among financial independence, family legacy, and social capital legacy.

(b) The Family Financial Philosophy: Defining the Size and Relationship of the Client's Three Circles

Before wealth optimization can be achieved, clear definitions of financial independence, family legacy, and social capital legacy must be developed. These three definitions establish the focus for future planning.

The client's written Family Financial Philosophy articulates the goals for financial independence, family legacy, and social capital legacy. It also ensures that each goal is consistent with the client's values, beliefs, attitudes, and preferences. Therefore, preparing the client's FFP is the first step toward achieving wealth optimization.

As one prepares the FFP, it is essential to specify in monetary terms a financial objective for each goal. Advisors should view each goal as a separate bucket that must be filled with the amount of cash resources required to meet the client's goal in that area. See Chapters 14 and 15 for a complete discussion of establishing financial goals.

(c) The Evolution of Financial Goals, Objectives, Values, Attitudes, and Preferences

Although the size of the three goal circles will vary from one client to the next, all three are always present. However, at any given point in time, one or more of these areas may not show up on the client's "radar screen." In other words, the issues related to each goal area are always present but not always on a conscious level. The purpose of defining each goal area specifically is to establish magnitude and interest at a given point in time.

The wealth optimization process illustrates how a client's priorities, goals, values, preferences, and attitudes change over time. By managing the various relationships among financial independence, family legacy, and social capital legacy, harmony is maintained between the changing priorities of the client's goals and the results of the current plan.

For most clients, financial independence is the first area of planning significance. As illustrated by Phase 1 in Exhibit 11.2, the accumulation and management of financial resources dominates the client's early financial world. At this point, family legacy and social capital legacy are not even recognized.

Over time, as the client accumulates resources and approaches financial independence, family legacy begins to surface as a planning issue, as illustrated in Phase 2 of Exhibit 11.2. The initial venture into family legacy planning often is focused on defensive planning strategies designed to protect the family in the event of a premature death. However, as financial independence is attained and clients gain knowledge about the potential of estate taxes, the nature of planning turns more aggressive. At this point, the importance of estate planning is acknowledged and the focus of planning shifts.

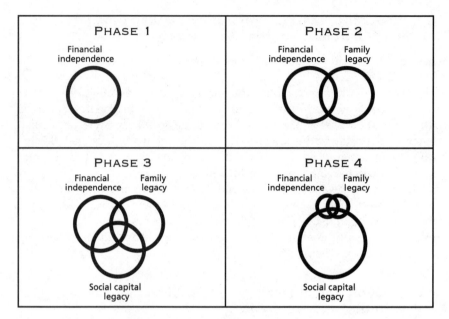

Exhibit 11.2   The Evolution of Wealth Optimization

Another transition in the evolution of wealth optimization occurs when the concept of paying estate taxes changes from a mere possibility to a reality. Phase 3 of Exhibit 11.2 illustrates a situation where social capital legacy planning enters the client's radar screen. Prior to this point, many clients see charitable gifts as conflicting with financial independence and family legacy. However, when a client's financial resources reach a level whereupon estate taxes become inevitable, the idea of converting taxes into charitable contributions begins to make a great deal of sense. At this point, charitable gifts become a desirable alternative to tax.

For many wealthy families, the final phase of wealth optimization occurs when financial resources are so substantial that they dwarf the client's goals for financial independence and family legacy. Clients who achieve financial success of this magnitude often find charitable giving, or social capital planning, as the only reasonable focus for future planning, as illustrated in Phase 4 of Exhibit 11.2.

Although the evolution shown in Exhibit 11.2 is the most common, variations are possible. For example, clients born into wealthy families may have different experiences. In such a case, resources accumulated by previous generations may already have fulfilled the client's goals for financial independence and family legacy. Many of the wealthiest families also have provided for their descendents' social capital legacy through family foundations or other family charities.

Advisors should keep in mind that the wealth optimization circles provide a snapshot of a particular client's goals at a given point in time. Regardless of how a client defines the size of the circles on a given day, this definition is certain to change in the future.

11.2 OPTIMIZING STRATEGIES

Once the size of a client's wealth optimization circles has been defined, strategies that support each goal area must be identified. In selecting strategies that optimize a client's plan, advisors must consider the client's strategy risk tolerance, complexity threshold, and cost-benefit assessment. In addition, advisors must select strategies or combinations of strategies that are consistent with the client's goals in each of the three goal areas. This is referred to as achieving maximum advantage.

(a) Strategy Risk Tolerance

In evaluating and selecting strategies for a particular client, an advisor must take the client's strategy risk tolerance into consideration. Strategy risk tolerance refers to the risk associated with implementing a particular strategy.

Here an advisor must be concerned with the following factors:

(i) Legality. The first consideration regarding strategy risk tolerance is legality. Generally speaking, strategies fall into one of three categories: (1) clearly legal, (2) clearly illegal, and (3) neither clearly legal nor clearly illegal. Many advanced planning strategies fall into this third, gray area. No law or regulation explicitly states that the particular strategy cannot be done, and none explicitly states that it can be done. The answer is a matter of opinion and interpretation.

For the most part, those responsible for regulating the tax laws argue that if the law does not say it is legal, then it must be illegal. Alternatively, many advisors argue that if it does not say it is illegal, then it is legal. This difference of perspective is the source of significant potential risk associated with advanced strategies. Selecting an appropriate wealth optimization strategy requires an advisor who can assess a client's tolerance associated with the risk of a tax audit or other legal challenge.

(ii) Irrevocability. The second factor in assessing a client's strategy risk tolerance is irrevocability. As previously stated, many tax-effective wealth transfer strategies require an irrevocable transfer. These transfers will be either irrevocably good or irrevocably bad. Because most clients prefer to avoid irrevocably bad decisions, every irrevocable decision is treated with an enhanced amount of scrutiny and skepticism.

For younger clients, the risk of irrevocability is exacerbated. The younger the client, the longer he or she will have to live with the consequences of each decision. It also is more difficult to predict the future impact of current decisions. As a result, younger clients tend to have a lower tolerance for irrevocability than do older clients.

(iii) Investment risk tolerance.   Competent investment advisors recognize the importance of assessing a client's investment risk tolerance. When evaluating a particular wealth optimization strategy, an advisor must evaluate whether it requires an investment strategy that is beyond the client's investment risk tolerance.

(b) Complexity Threshold

In estate planning, the quality of results achieved often is in direct proportion to the level of complexity associated with the plan. Therefore, a client's tolerance for complexity is a major factor in selecting appropriate strategies. What level of complexity is a client willing to endure in accomplishing the desired objectives? An advisor must determine a client's complexity threshold in order to select strategies that optimize the plan.

(c) Cost-Benefit Assessment

Cost-benefit assessment is the final step in selecting suitable strategies for a client. Here, the advisor must assess whether a client perceives sufficient benefit from a particular strategy to justify its cost, risk, and complexity.

11.3 ACHIEVING MAXIMUM ADVANTAGE

Wealth optimization is achieved when selected strategies have a positive impact on more than one goal area. As depicted in Exhibit 11.3 (which displays a sample client's wealth optimization model), maximum advantage is achieved when a strategy has a positive impact on all three goal areas.

For example, assume the client wants to sell an appreciated asset. Although many possible strategies are available for accomplishing this objective, a standard charitable remainder unitrust (SCRUT) in combination with a wealth replacement trust (WRT) results in maximum advantage.

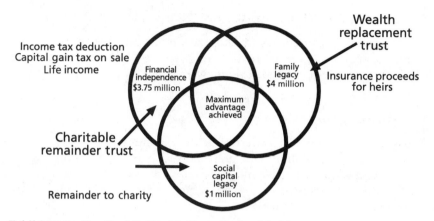

Income tax deduction
Capital gain tax on sale
Life income

Financial
independence
$3.75 million

Family
legacy
$4 million

Wealth
replacement
trust

Insurance proceeds
for heirs

Maximum
advantage
achieved

Charitable
remainder trust

Social
capital
legacy
$1 million

Remainder to charity

Exhibit 11.3 The Gould's Wealth Optimization Model

(a) Hypothetical Situation

(This case study is fictitious in circumstance and characters.)

Dr. Robert Gould is a partner in a successful family practice. His wife, Joan, is also a physician. Bob and Joan are both age 60 and preparing for retirement. Over the years, the Goulds have accumulated $5 million of financial resources. Included among their assets is a medical office building with a current fair market value of $500,000. Joan purchased it 15 years ago. Bob's family practice is the sole tenant in the building. With Bob's impending retirement, his partners would like to purchase the building.

Joan originally purchased the building as an investment for $250,000 and has invested an additional $45,000 in improvements. However, taking advantage of straight-line depreciation, the Goulds have reduced their cost basis to $50,000. As a result, if they were to sell the property today, they would incur a capital gain of $450,000, resulting in a capital gain tax of $112,500 (i.e., $450,000 × 20% capital gain rate = $112,000).

(b) The Challenge

Over the years, the Goulds have been active with a number of charitable organizations, including the hospital where they both practice medicine. They wish to explore strategies that will allow them to maintain control over their assets, while enabling them to make sizable gifts to various nonprofits. However, they want to be sure such gifts will not adversely affect their children's inheritance.

(c) Current Wealth Optimization Circles

Working with their financial advisor, the Goulds established their financial independence ($3.75 million), family legacy ($4 million), and social capital legacy ($1 million) goals. Refer to Exhibit 11.3.

(d) Strategy Objectives

The Goulds are primarily concerned about maintaining their financial independence ($3.75 million) and protecting their intended family legacy ($4 million). Assuming these initial two objectives can be accomplished, the Goulds are interested in converting tax into charitable contributions wherever possible ($1 million).

(e) Wealth Optimization Strategy

To accomplish their objectives, their financial advisor recommended the Goulds implement a standard charitable remainder unitrust. The advisor indicated that because a SCRUT is tax-exempt, this strategy would allow them to sell their building without incurring a capital gain tax at the time of sale. As a result, the Goulds would be able to maximize their long-term income.

To ensure that the gift of the office building to the SCRUT will not reduce their children's inheritance, their advisor suggested the Goulds implement an irrevocable life insurance trust to complement the SCRUT. This technique, often referred to as a wealth replacement trust, will provide tax-free cash to the children, offsetting the assets passing to charity. As a result, the Goulds, their children, and one of their favorite charities all win.

(f) Maximum Advantage Achieved

This strategy produces maximum advantage for the Goulds by creating a positive impact on their goals for financial independence, family legacy, and social capital legacy. Reducing ordinary income taxes, through the resulting charitable income tax deduction, enhances financial independence. Selling the building through a SCRUT averts the loss of capital through the payment of a capital gain tax, resulting in increased income, thereby enhancing financial independence.

Using a charitable remainder trust enables the Goulds to fulfill their social capital objectives by generating a future charitable gift of $1,000,000. Finally, by incorporating the wealth replacement trust, they are able to protect their family legacy goal.

11.4 DESIGNING THE WEALTH OPTIMIZATION PLAN

Once appropriate wealth optimization strategies have been selected, they must be combined into a wealth optimization plan to assure proper coordination. The objective is to identify possible conflicts between strategies, as well as unexpected synergies.

In evaluating a wealth optimization plan, an advisor should evaluate whether the plan accomplishes the client's goals within acceptable levels of risk and complexity. This underscores the importance of defining the client's goals for financial independence, family legacy, and social capital legacy in specific financial terms. Unless specifically defined, optimization cannot be achieved.

11.5 PLAN CONSTRUCTION AND EXECUTION

Once the design phase of wealth optimization is complete, the mechanisms must actually be constructed. At this point, legal documents must be prepared, financial tools implemented, and administrative protocols established.

11.6 MAINTAINING WEALTH OPTIMIZATION

Wealth optimization can be measured only as a snapshot of a client's current situation at a given point in time. Because the client's definitions of financial independence, family legacy, and social capital legacy are fluid, the model is constantly evolving. Once a client wealth optimization model is established, the advisor should reevaluate the client model annually, or more frequently if circumstances indicate a need to do so.

As a client's model appropriately changes over time, existing strategies may need to be adapted and new strategies may be necessary in order to optimize the results. Furthermore, as strategies are modified and new strategies are added, advisors should update the client's wealth optimization plan to eliminate conflicts and identify synergistic potential.

CHAPTER TWELVE

The Legacy Interview

12.1 UNDERSTANDING THE CONCEPT

When an advisor meets a prospective client for the first time, it is similar to walking into a three-act play at the end of the second act. Advisors often have little or no idea what the client's play is about. They are forced to recreate the first two acts in order to put the rest of the play into context. Unfortunately, when they do this, the acts are apt to be more a reflection of their own past experience than of the client's.

Advisors tend to make quick assumptions based on their personal and professional experience with people who exhibit similar circumstances. Consider these statements:

"If you've seen one business owner, you've seen them all."

"All children are the same."

"Having three children always yields a similar experience."

Common sense and practical experience tell us nothing is further from the truth. No two people, and no two families are the same. Therefore, it follows that no two clients are the same. Clients are a direct reflection of their unique past experiences. The circumstances they have encountered, mistakes they have made, and successes they have achieved are all factors that contribute to their unique story.

The interview process covers a wide range of topical areas. Generally, the advisor will touch upon family origin, growing up as a child, adult experiences—past, present, and future. In each area, the advisor will unpack the client's life experiences and relate them to the planning process at hand.

The interview is documented through a written transcript that is refined into a unique legacy biography. This written legacy biography tells the client's story and identifies significant experiences that have helped shape the client's current financial philosophy.

12.2 DISCOVERING THE CLIENT'S PAST, PRESENT, AND FUTURE

(a) Conducting the Interview

The interview is the suggested initial step in the discovery process because most clients have a high level of confidence in talking about their personal lives. Therefore, it is the easiest place to overcome procrastination and move forward. The interview should not be an intimidating process, but should feel similar to a thoughtful conversation with a good friend.

The intent of the interview is to capture the client's story. As with every other step in legacy planning, the advisor and client must establish a common expectation of what the interview process involves and the purpose of each individual step. In other words, it is essential to understand why the advisor wants to conduct an interview in the first place.

A typical interview will take one to four hours, depending on the particular client. When working with couples, the advisor should interview spouses together. This will put the clients at ease and allow the advisor to gain a sense of how they communicate and make decisions. It also will help eliminate conflict by ensuring that both spouses have a common experience and participate in the same conversations.

An advisor should never make value judgments about anything a client says and should be careful to keep in mind who is being interviewed. When the client is talking, the client is in control. When the advisor is talking, the client is merely waiting to talk.

In order to probe areas of interest further, the advisor should simply say, "Tell me more about that." Advisors should pay close attention to the client's emotional state while responding to each question. Often the way someone says something is more important than what is said.

Throughout the interview, advisors should watch for and ask about dilemmas the client has faced. It is important to observe mixed and sometimes conflicting emotions, ideas, and activities and the strategies clients pursued to deal with life dilemmas.

(b) Recording the Interview

Advisors should audiotape the interview. Recording allows the advisor to focus on the conversation and maintain eye contact, ensuring that the flow of the interview is not disrupted. More important, it captures all the details for future reference.

Clients may initially be hesitant about having the interview recorded. The advisor should be prepared with clear reasons for taping the interview, reassuring the client with statements such as these:

- Recording the interview will allow me to devote my complete attention to the conversation.

- Taking notes makes it difficult to have an effective dialogue, as each time I pause to take a note, I miss what is being said.

- During a conversation, it is often difficult to determine what is important and what is not. The tape provides an opportunity to review the content of our conversation to make sure valuable information is not missed.

- I will gladly provide an unedited copy of the transcript for your review.

- I would be happy to return the original tapes to you once the transcript has been prepared.

If the client absolutely declines a recorded session, the advisor must decide either to move on to the next prospective client or proceed without a tape recording. In making this decision, the advisor should consider that the client's refusal might indicate a lack of trust. If this is the case, it must be addressed. Unless overcome, lack of trust generally results in an ineffective planning process. The advisor should confront the issue directly with the client and be prepared to move on to the next prospect if not satisfied with the response.

In some cases, the client's objection to a taped interview will be unrelated to the advisor. Regardless of the client's rationale, if he or she refuses to participate in a recorded interview and the advisor wishes to continue the relationship, an alternative approach must be identified.

(c) An Alternative to Taping

One alternative to taping the interview is to have an assistant or a business associate participate in the interview and take notes. With this approach, the advisor must pay careful attention to how the person taking notes filters what he or she hears. Unless a stenographer is used, it is highly unlikely a person taking notes will capture everything that is said in the interview. How will the note-taker choose what to write? Whose perspectives will be taken into consideration in deciding what is relevant and what is not?

12.3 THE INTERVIEW CONTENT

The interview is a semiorganized conversation aimed at learning what the advisor needs to know in order to help clients define and accomplish their legacy. The key is to ask questions that give clients a chance to tell where they have come from and where they hope to go. Simply inviting them to "tell me a bit more" gives them that rare opportunity to tell someone who is truly interested those significant details they hardly ever get a chance to recount. Advisors should dwell a while longer on any topic that has an emotional undertone or appears to be an important benchmark or turning point.

(a) Schematic Overview of Interview Questions

Advisors should keep in the forefront this simple schematic overview of the interview topics. The goal of the interview is to elicit as many details as are relevant for understanding the clients' past, present, and future.

(i) Growing up. Here the advisor seeks to better understand the key people, ideas, emotions, and events that surrounded and shaped the construction of the legacy pyramid for the family in which the client(s) grew up. The purpose is to unearth all those people, ideas, emotions, and events that left a mark—positive or negative—on the clients' lives.

Sample questions and topics might include these:

- Tell me about your family. Who are they, and where are they from originally?
- How is your family distributed throughout the United States? The world?
- Did you grow up near your extended family?
- Is there anything unusual or unique about your family origins?
- What is the single most important factor that defines your family origins?

(ii) Adult past. Here the interview focuses on key people, ideas, emotions, and events that surrounded and shaped the construction of the client's financial philosophy. What events left marks on the client's life?

Sample questions and topics might include the following:

Marriage and family
- When were you married?
- How many children do you have and when were they born?

Business and professional life
- Business/professional background.
- Education.

Earliest work experiences

- When you were starting out, did you have any business, professional or financial goals you wanted to achieve, and if so, what were they?
- Have your goals changed over the years, and if so, how are they different now?
- Describe your business or career history. Sketch your business activity from its beginnings to the present.

(iii) Present. Here the advisor seeks to learn about key people, ideas, emotions, and events that surround and shape the current configuration of the client's financial philosophy and that are leaving a mark presently on the client's life.

Sample questions under the topic of *family* might include these:

- Tell me about your children.
- What do they do for a living?
- Where do they live?
- Do they have families of their own?
- What things do they like to do?
- Where do they go on vacation?

(iv) Future. Here the interview focuses on key people, ideas, emotions, and events that will surround and shape the reconfiguration of the client's financial philosophy and that the client hopes will mark his or her life and legacy.

Sample questions under the topic of *financial dreams and goals* might include the following:

- If money were no object, what is the one thing you would most like to do?
- What are your financial goals for the future?
- How do you see your financial situation changing in the future?
- What is your first financial priority for the future?

12.4 DOCUMENTING THE LEGACY INTERVIEW

(a) The Interview Transcript

Once the interview is complete, a transcript should be prepared directly from the audiotapes. The transcript should be typed in similar fashion to a legal deposition, with each comment identified with the initials of the party who is speaking. For example:

ADVISOR: Where did you grow up?

CLIENT: I grew up in rural Texas in a small town with a population of about 2,000. My grandparents lived there as well.

This phase is essential and should not be skipped. The written transcript will reveal more information than can possibly be imagined. It is not unusual upon review of an interview transcript to find a substantial amount of new information. In other words, the person conducting the interview almost always learns as much, if not more, from reading the transcript than from conducting the interview.

The rough transcript should be edited to refine the wording and grammar. The advisor should review the transcript to be sure the intent of each comment has been appropriately captured. Some grammatical corrections may be made; however, make them sparingly. It is best to use the client's own words and phraseology.

Interview transcripts often include personal information over which clients generally wish to maintain a fair degree of control. Ideally, someone on the advisor's immediate staff should prepare the transcript. At a minimum, the advisor should select someone who has a high degree of integrity and is accustomed to working with sensitive information.

The manner in which the advisor intends to handle the preparation of the transcript should be communicated to the client prior to the interview. Attention to such details will instill confidence and enhance open dialogue and communication.

(b) Identifying Key Quotes and Paragraphs

Once the transcript has been edited and reviewed by both the client and advisor for accuracy, key quotes and paragraphs should be identified. The purpose of this step is to capture information that can be used in the preparation of the client's Family Financial Philosophy mission statement.

The advisor should ask the client to review the transcript and indicate which sections and paragraphs are particularly significant. At the same time, the advisor should review the transcript and identify which sections and paragraphs are significant. When the client and advisor have completed this task, it is time to compare notes.

Always remember that if the client thinks something is important, it is important. The advisor should ask the client to explain the significance of any paragraph or quote that is marked as significant yet has no apparent significance. Perspective is a very subtle thing. The advisor should make no assumptions about what is important and what isn't important to the client.

In considering which are key elements, the advisor should remember to follow the emotion. What parts of the interview sparked the greatest emotion? When was the client most animated?

In carefully reviewing the interview transcript, the advisor will find the client has written major sections of the mission statement already, in the form of interview responses.

(c) The Legacy Biography: Documenting the Interview

The advisor should document the interview with a written legacy biography. The legacy biography is a distillation of the paragraphs and quotes identified by the advisor and client as important or reflective of the client's financial philosophy.

12.5 INTERVIEWING THE AFFLUENT: A GUIDE TO ASKING THE RIGHT QUESTIONS

A comprehensive list of the types of questions that advisors may want to ask when interviewing clients may be found in Appendix C.

CHAPTER THIRTEEN

The Legacy Questionnaire

13.1 UNDERSTANDING THE CONCEPT

This phase of legacy planning provides the advisor with a unique opportunity to help the client shape financial objectives around family values. Focusing on the relationship between family values and financial resources, the advisor utilizes questionnaires to clarify and refine the client's position in critical planning areas.

Using a questionnaire designed specifically for this purpose, the content in this segment of discovery is divided into 39 topical areas. These 39 areas are divided into four primary sections: (1) general questions regarding wealth and family values, (2) questions related to financial independence, (3) questions related to family legacy, and (4) questions related to social capital legacy. See Appendix A: The Legacy Questionnaire.

The process is documented by developing a list of *planning affirmations.* Each affirmation is a first-person statement reflecting the client's answer to a specific question in the questionnaire. They are considered planning affirmations because each one documents the client's values and beliefs in relation to a particular area of planning or a specific objective.

One of the most difficult tasks in helping clients construct an estate plan around values is finding out precisely what those values are. Clients and advisors alike often are at a loss as to where to begin the conversation. No effective precedent exists for having a discussion about how family values pertain to financial resources. Yet, one way or another, every significant financial decision hinges on those family values.

Furthermore, many advisors have a difficult time motivating clients to complete data forms and other tools that require client initiation and follow-through. In fact, many have trouble convincing clients to sit through an interview to gather personal data. The reasons are threefold:

1. In an effort to motivate clients to engage in estate planning, advisors inadvertently discount the significance of gathering data by oversimplifying the process. In doing so, they imply that it is not an

important step. Unfortunately, clients are not likely to complete a voluntary homework assignment.

2. Questions are in the wrong format. Effective planning requires both objective and subjective information. Advisors who attempt to gather objective information through lengthy questionnaires often overwhelm the client. Advisors who attempt to gather subjective information through open-ended questions are providing only a vague context for the client.

3. Advisors dwell on the superficial and avoid the controversial. Asking questions can be an intimidating process for both clients and advisors. Estate planning covers a variety of personal issues that are laden with emotion. Many advisors are not comfortable with this invasion of a client's personal life, and therefore limit the discussion to superficial issues. As a result, advisors often fail to identify key planning issues.

13.2 DISCOVERING VALUES, BELIEFS, ATTITUDES, PREFERENCES, AND PRIORITIES

(a) Using Questionnaires

Questionnaires are fast emerging as the tool of choice for enabling clients to develop an instructive list of planning objectives that accurately reflects their values. Recognizing that advisors have a difficult time gathering information from clients and that most people have a difficult time expressing their values, a multiple-choice approach is preferable. Not just any multiple-choice questionnaire will do. It must be one where every answer is correct. All the client must do is select the answers that best fit his or her situation.

This approach has been successfully used for a number of years in the investment management field in an effort to establish risk tolerance for potential investment clients. Each question has several potential responses from which to choose. Consider this example:

Question Category: Wealth Accumulation
People accumulate their wealth in many ways. What is the source of your wealth? *Check all that apply.*

- ☐ Inheritance
- ☐ Gifts from living individuals
- ☐ Spouse

☐ Building or growing a personal or family business

☐ Employment earnings

☐ Successful investment

☐ Other (please specify)

Although it is not necessarily easy to choose between options, a full range is presented. The response to this question provides the advisor with insight regarding the client's view of how family financial resources have been accumulated.

The primary consideration is in establishing consistency with the client's values, beliefs, preferences, attitudes, and priorities. When asking a question of this type, it is neither possible nor practical to offer every possible response. However, it is quite easy—and effective—to cover the range of possibilities. A space for elaboration in the form of comments will fill in the gaps naturally and comfortably.

(b) Working with Couples

Over the years, couples have a tendency to develop a pattern for making financial decisions. Typically, one spouse dominates as the decision maker. Although this lopsided approach may work effectively in more routine financial matters, it very often leads to planning paralysis. Effective estate planning requires numerous values-based decisions. When one spouse's values are ignored, the process almost certainly produces less-than-satisfactory results.

A multiple-choice format offers a significant advantage when working with couples. By presenting a limited set of possible answers, advisors can quickly compare how a husband and wife respond to the same question. Once the advisor has identified the underlying differences of opinion between spouses, these can be addressed and reconciled before they become paralyzing issues.

Advisors should emphasize several points when setting the stage for completion of a questionnaire:

- Tell clients not to spend too much time analyzing the questions; their first, instinctive reactions are generally the best.
- Have the client(s) sign the questionnaire(s) when complete.
- Remind clients that their answers are not etched in stone; they merely provide a guide for future conversations.
- Instruct couples to complete questionnaires independently of each other. A primary objective is to identify differing perspectives and opinions. Spouses should review and sign each other's questionnaire.

- Ask clients to leave "problem" questions blank. When appropriate, the advisor can revisit a question with a client and address specific obstacles or concerns.

(c) Questionnaire Content

The purpose of the questionnaire is to provide clients with a tool that quickly and effectively summarizes how they feel about key planning areas. The questionnaire should have at least one question for each of the 39 value topics outlined in Exhibit 13.1.

(d) Understanding the Relationship between Questions

It is absolutely essential that each question address only one subject. If the question covers more than one subject, advisors may have a difficult time interpreting what the client means by the answer. Advisors will find it helpful to look at combinations of various questions. Consider the following question in relation to the question asked earlier in the chapter (i.e., What is the souce of your wealth?).

Question Category: Attributions of Success
To what or whom do you attribute your wealth? *Check all that apply.*

- ☐ Personal initiative
- ☐ Unexpected good fortune/luck
- ☐ Assistance from a Higher Power
- ☐ Supportive environment provided by spouse
- ☐ Financial success of parents or other ancestors
- ☐ Financial success of spouse
- ☐ Teamwork/partnership with spouse
- ☐ Teamwork/partnership with other(s) than spouse
- ☐ Other (please specify)

Advisors may find the distinction between the two questions insignificant. However, upon close review, the distinction becomes clear. The first asks about the sources of wealth. This is a matter of fact that most clients can quickly answer. The second question, on the other hand, requires the client to evaluate and make judgments about *why* the wealth has been accumulated. The combination of these two answers can be quite informative.

1. Wealth accumulation
2. Attributions of success
3. Personal values
4. Senses of obligation
5. Planning goal priorities
6. Current estate allocation
7. Ideal estate allocation
8. Factors that may influence planning
9. State of financial independence
10. Opportunities created by money
11. Definition of financial independence: $ _____
12. Excess assets: $_____
13. Thoughts on ownership and control
14. Conservation of assets for heirs
15. Ideal inheritance
16. Philosophy to impart to heirs—financial stewardship
17. Perspective on talking about money and stewardship
18. Best time to reveal potential inheritance
19. Assessing heirs' stewardship capabilities
20. Balance between inheriting and acquiring
21. Equality versus fairness
22. Perspective on lifetime transfer to heirs
23. Perspective on transfer to grandchildren
24. Transferring values to heirs
25. Wealth preservation versus heirs' feelings
26. Gift versus tax
27. Perspective on charitable gift transfer through estate plan
28. Level of volunteerism—time, talents, resources
29. Perspective on charitable gift transfer during lifetime
30. Satisfaction and effectiveness of current contributions
31. Perspective on current and future levels of giving
32. Perspective on family foundations
33. Perspective on shared philanthropy
34. Philanthropic interests
35. Preferences for philanthropic recognition
36. Allocation of $1 million of social capital
37. Uses of the Family Financial Philosophy
38. Opportunities provided by wealth
39. Expectations of estate planning

Exhibit 13.1 Questionnaire Value Topics

If a client selects *inheritance* for the first question and *financial success of parents or other ancestors* for the second, the client apparently recognizes and comfortably attributes financial success to the efforts of ancestors. Alternatively, if a client selects *inheritance* for the first question and *personal initiative* for the second, a very different picture emerges. The client clearly acknowledges ancestors as a source of wealth but attributes some aspect of the wealth to personal initiative. On the surface, this may seem inconsistent. However, what if the client inherited $5,000 from a grandparent in 1970 and invested those funds in Berkshire Hathaway? Today, the client would be a multimillionaire. Taken in this context, the answers seem reasonable.

To emphasize this point, what if the client's brother had inherited a similar sum of money in 1970 but invested poorly and lost it all? Now the client's responses not only appear reasonable but make a great deal of sense.

Without question, the manner in which a person or family has accumulated wealth will have an impact on the manner in which it will be distributed. From the self-made wealth holder to the child born with the proverbial silver spoon, different circumstances in life create differing client attitudes toward inherited wealth. Whereas one person may feel that inherited wealth provides a disincentive for personal achievement, another may consider inherited wealth a matter of family history and pride. This one factor can be of considerable importance in creating an effective estate plan.

A client who selects *personal initiative* may not be highly motivated to structure an estate plan that focuses on heirs. Such a client might prefer to take a more proactive approach, such as establishing a values-based trust to benefit heirs, timing distribution of assets and income to coincide with certain events or accomplishments. For example, the trust could make distributions to heirs as a reward for their achieving milestones such as college or graduate school graduation. It might provide low- or zero-interest loans to heirs interested in starting their own businesses. The possibilities are limited only by a client's imagination.

It is important to remember that broad generalizations can be dangerous. In some cases, clients who have worked hard to accumulate wealth may want to ease the burden for succeeding generations. They want their heirs to avoid experiencing the hardships they faced during their lifetime. For this reason, it is always important to acknowledge a client's response to a particular question but clarify its meaning from the client's perspective. Also, pay close attention to any written comments that might provide a clue. Do not assume that you know what the client means by a specific comment. Always ask him or her.

(e) Clues Offered by Certain Assets

Certain assets can provide clues that help the advisor make judgment calls and clarify hidden meanings. For example, when a closely held family business has contributed to wealth accumulation, the chemistry of the situation may be important. Often the existence of a family business creates a deep-rooted desire to perpetuate the lifestyle represented by the business for succeeding generations. This is particularly true where the business is second or third generation.

In the situation where a closely held nonfamily business has contributed to the accumulation of wealth, particular attention should be given to those nonfamily members who have made a significant contribution to the business.

Personal or family businesses often are a source of wealth. In many cases, the founder has a strong emotional attachment to the business, its management, and its employees. This can be a considerable obstacle when it makes sense to sell it or prepare for business succession.

When other family members are involved, additional family concerns regarding leadership and governance may surface. Issues related to family dynamics are likely to be present in those situations where several family members work together in a business. Sometime these dynamics are positive and sometimes they are negative, but they invariably exist.

(f) Establishing Planning Priorities

One advantage of using questionnaires is the ability to establish priorities or rankings. This is an effective technique for helping clients reconcile planning dilemmas. Consider the following question:

Question Category: Planning Goal Priorities
There are many goals for financial and estate planning, among them the following. Rank all four goals in order of importance to you, where 1 = most important and 4 = least important.

- ☐ To ensure lifetime financial independence
- ☐ To maximize inheritance for heirs
- ☐ To minimize estate tax
- ☐ To make charitable contributions

Asking clients to rank all choices forces them to reconcile planning dilemmas. They must choose which statement ranks first, which second, and so on. Placing dilemmas in such a context helps clients focus on priorities and planning dilemmas.

(g) Assessing a Client's Knowledge and Awareness

The value of a particular planning solution is established in relation to the problem that it will solve. In other words, a client must consciously acknowledge a problem before it is appropriate to consider a solution.

Unfortunately, advisors often have a difficult time identifying the level of awareness a client has with respect to the results of the current plan. The following question provides a simple way to diagnose a client's awareness.

Question Category: Current Estate Allocation

If your estate were distributed to your beneficiaries (excluding your spouse, if applicable), give your best estimate of how it would be allocated among the following, assuming you did no additional planning and your estate were settled as it exists today.

      _____% Taxes

      _____% Children, stepchildren, grandchildren, and step-
               grandchildren

      _____% Other heirs

      _____% Charitable and philanthropic giving

      _____% Other (please specify) _____

100% Total

(h) Addressing Controversial Topics

Every advisor eventually runs into the issue of equality in estate distributions. The premise that fair is not always equal and equal is not always fair has confounded clients for years. Further complicating this problem is the reality that spouses often disagree over this fundamental issue. Questionnaires are invaluable for gathering a client's initial reaction to difficult issues such as this. By having each spouse answer the same question independently, advisors quickly identify potential planning obstacles. Consider the following question:

Question Category: Equality versus Fairness

What is your opinion about leaving each child the same amount of inheritance? *Check the answer that most closely reflects your view.*

☐ Regardless of his or her individual circumstances or needs, each child should receive an equal share of my estate.

☐ Because of his or her different circumstances or needs, each child should receive a different share of my estate.

(i) Transforming Intangible Concepts into Tangible Actions

Although questionnaires most commonly are used to gather information, a properly designed question also can educate a client by presenting a range of action-oriented solutions. The following question introduces the concept of family values by presenting a client with a range of possible future activities.

Question Category: Transferring Values to Heirs
There are numerous ways to transfer your family financial values to children and other heirs. *Check the three that are most important to you.*
   I prefer to

☐ Actively discuss the importance of specific financial values

☐ Demonstrate values in how I lead my daily life

☐ Establish a family mission statement

☐ Involve children in charitable giving and volunteering

☐ Establish or use an existing family foundation or other family charity

☐ Become involved as a family in a spiritual community

☐ Encourage children to work, in order to learn the meaning of money

☐ Involve children in the family business

☐ Hold regular family meetings

☐ Use rites of passage and family celebrations

(j) Overcoming Emotional Barriers

Clients often have emotional barriers with respect to using charitable giving strategies in their estate plans. As a result, advisors find it difficult to have meaningful conversations about the possible planning solutions that charitable giving affords. As soon as the subject is introduced, the client tunes out, changes the subject, or dismisses the subject altogether. This typically results from the misguided belief that charitable giving is in opposition to a client's goals for financial independence and family legacy. This perceived dilemma prevents the client from absorbing the information, virtually eliminating an entire category of planning solutions.

   The following question illustrates how a questionnaire can introduce the concept of charitable giving within an appropriate context. The question eliminates the emotional barrier to charitable giving by converting the planning dilemma into a planning opportunity.

Question Category: Gift versus Tax
Taking into account all of the taxes you have paid over your lifetime (income, capital gain, excise, property, and so on), if you were required to give estate assets away and your only choices were government and charitable purposes, how would you like to see your estate allocated?

Government _____%
Charitable purposes _____%

13.3 ANALYSIS OF CONTENT

Although simply reviewing a client's responses to a well-organized questionnaire may be helpful, a few additional steps are recommended.

(a) Affirmation Statements

When a client has completed the questionnaire, the advisor should review each response. Following this initial review, the advisor should provide the client with an opportunity to review the responses for accuracy. Simply having the client look at the questions and responses again can accomplish this, but it is preferable to use a different format. This will prevent the client from feeling his or her efforts are redundant. Also, it will provide a different way to evaluate the underlying issues.

Converting each client response into a planning affirmation is an effective method for affirming client responses. Consider the example that follows:

Sample Question
Which statement most closely reflects your definition of financial independence? *Check one box only.*

☐ I have no clear picture of whether I am financially independent.
☐ I am not yet financially independent.
☐ I am financially independent but have no excess wealth.
☐ My present assets and income exceed what I need for financial independence.

Affirmative Statement
"I have no clear picture of whether I am financially independent."

The affirmation or *I* statement forces the client to take ownership. Unlike the response to the questionnaire, the statement is intended to represent the client's words. To emphasize this point, the statements are presented in quotation marks.

(b) Clarification of Affirmations

In the next step, the advisor presents the affirmations to the client for confirmation and clarification. When working with a couple, the advisor should have each spouse review his or her respective list independently. Each spouse should be instructed to mark each statement with an *A* (agree), *D* (disagree), or *U* (unsure). When complete, spouses can review each other's responses if they wish.

The purpose of this step is to provide the client with a chance to see how the advisor has interpreted the responses. Additionally, it provides an opportunity for the client to view the information in a slightly different format. Advisors should always emphasize that any answer may be changed at any time, for any reason. The way in which the client answers the questions is far less important than his or her level of commitment to the answers.

When complete, the client should return the completed affirmation statements to the advisor for review.

(c) Individual Areas of Conflict

Once the client has reviewed the affirmation statements, the advisor should identify individual areas of conflict or confusion. Although the affirmations state nearly the same thing as the questionnaire responses, many clients indicate disagreement with or uncertainty about their answers when they are viewed as affirmative statements.

When the advisor receives the completed affirmation statements from the client, if no statement is marked *D* or *U*, then the advisor should proceed to planning affirmations.

If either spouse has marked any statement with *D* or *U*, the advisor should ask the client to review that question again and indicate the appropriate response. If the client is unable to reconcile the conflict or confusion alone, a phone call or an appointment to review the issues and help resolve the problem may be in order.

(d) Reconciliation of Differences

When working with couples, advisors must help reconcile differences in philosophy. To limit the number of variables, this should be done only when each spouse has made a commitment to his or her respective list of affirmations.

The advisor should review both spouses' agreed-upon affirmations lists and identify areas in which they have answered the same question differently. These differences in philosophy form the basis for the next meeting between the advisor and client.

The objective is to present each difference to the client for resolution. The advisor's obligation is to bring the issue to the surface. The client's obligation is to resolve the issue. During this process, advisors should always remember they are impartial third parties. An advisor should never take sides or express a third opinion, even when invited to do so.

13.4 PLANNING AFFIRMATIONS: DOCUMENTING THE LEGACY QUESTIONNAIRE

This step concludes the questionnaire segment. The final result of this step is to produce a joint list of affirmations that both spouses adopt as representative of their combined viewpoint. This list of affirmations is referred to as *planning affirmations* because it forms the basis for drafting the client's Family Financial Philosophy mission statement.

When the list of planning affirmations is complete, the client signs and returns it to the advisor as final confirmation and acceptance of the list.

CHAPTER FOURTEEN

The Legacy Goal Profile

Financial Independence

14.1 FINANCIAL INDEPENDENCE GOAL: UNDERSTANDING THE CONCEPT

It should be clear by now that a client's first and most basic planning objective is to identify how much wealth is required to achieve and maintain lifetime *financial independence.* Simply stated, clients have achieved financial independence when they have accumulated and preserved all they would ever need to maintain a desired lifestyle. Generally expressed as a unique combination of annual income and a minimum resource base, financial independence answers the question "What do I want from my wealth for the rest of my life?"

The financial independence goal should be stated as the net amount of cash resources in today's dollars that is required to support the client's definition of financial independence. Clearly defining financial independence at this point in the planning process is essential in order to draft the client's Family Financial Philosophy mission statement.

Tax-effective wealth transfer planning generally requires the irrevocable separation of clients from their money, as early as possible. Before they consider how to distribute their wealth, clients must first decide how much they need from their wealth.

Financial independence results from the right combination of net annual income for personal consumption along with a minimum resource base. The minimum resource base is made up of all those assets over which clients choose to maintain ownership and control well into the future. The appropriate amount of income and minimum resource base comprising financial independence is a function of personal or family lifestyle, goals, and objectives.

Financial independence further is a unique combination of consumption and preservation. Annually, clients consume a portion of their wealth in order to maintain their desired lifestyle. At the same time, they preserve their asset base in order to ensure income in the future and cope with unexpected financial needs. As explained in Chapter 6, consumption is a descending need; the amount of capital required to meet consumption needs decreases with age. In other words, a married couple in their forties spending $100,000 a year typically requires more capital than a couple who are in their eighties.

Unless consumed, the minimum resource base will increase as a result of normal inflation and investment performance. Therefore, clients should review and adjust their definition of an appropriate minimum resource base from time to time.

The minimum resource base is always composed of resources within a client's control and ownership, and, therefore, within the taxable estate. Income, on the other hand, can come from resources that are either inside or outside the taxable estate. From an estate planning perspective, resources outside the estate are most attractive because they generally are not subject to tax.

Establishing a definition of financial independence is similar to calculating income tax withholdings. The best financial result is achieved when the amount of withholdings results in neither a payment nor a refund. Clients who get a refund have overestimated the amount due and lost the opportunity to use those dollars throughout the year. If they have underestimated the taxes due, they end up with a big bill at year's end, perhaps even a penalty.

It is important that clients be realistic in developing financial independence assumptions. If they are too conservative, they will underestimate available planning resources and perhaps miss a potential opportunity. On the other hand, if they are too aggressive, they may overvalue their financial resources and prematurely consume them.

14.2 MAINTAINING LIFESTYLE: HOW MUCH INCOME DO CLIENTS WANT?

The following four steps will determine the financial resources needed to support a client's desired lifestyle:

1. Determine how much the client currently spends, or how much the client wants to spend, to maintain his or her lifestyle.
2. Adjust this income goal to reflect the impact of inflation.

3. Determine how long he or she wants the income to continue.

4. Account for the positive impact of future investment performance.

(a) The Budget

One can easily derive the appropriate level of net annual income needed to maintain financial independence from a budget. Clients who already have budgets are ahead of the game. It is important to note that the purpose of a budget is not to limit spending. That is only the case when a budget establishes that clients are spending beyond their financial capacity, or, in other words, enjoying a lifestyle beyond their means.

In many cases, a written budget provides the peace of mind that clients may need to allow themselves to increase spending. A budget can actually help clients enjoy their financial resources more, by establishing a freedom to spend.

At this point, the definition of required annual income is limited to items of personal consumption. Gifts to heirs and charity and the acquisition of additional assets, such as a new home, will be handled separately from this step in the process.

(b) The Budget Alternative

There is a simple, alternative way to estimate how much clients spend each year. Determine gross income from the last income tax return. Subtract taxes paid, gifts to charity, and gifts to heirs. Now estimate how much income was invested directly in various investment accounts. Also, estimate how much investment income was automatically reinvested in existing investment accounts. Subtract the total of these two numbers, and the result should approximate annual consumption.

$$\text{consumption} = \text{gross income} - \text{income tax} - \text{gifts to heirs} - \text{gifts to charity} - \text{reinvestment} - \text{savings}$$

(c) Adjusting Lifestyle for Inflation

Once a client's annual consumption has been identified, consider the effect normal inflation will have on this goal. To account for inflation, increase the client's annual income goal by an inflation factor. Most people use a factor of somewhere between 3 and 7 percent. For example, if the client's goal is $100,000 this year, an inflation factor of 3 percent would call for an income goal of $103,000 next year, or $100,000 × (1 + inflation factor). The higher the inflation factor, the more conservative the estimate will be. In other words, the higher the inflation factor, the greater the likelihood the client will retain more wealth than is required to maintain the desired lifestyle.

(d) How Long Will the Client Need This Income?

How long the client will need this stream of income is anyone's guess. Most people take into consideration normal life expectancy and then add or subtract years based on their personal health and family history. The longer the term, the greater the amount of wealth required, and hence the more conservative the estimate.

14.3 DETERMINING THE REQUIRED ASSET BASE

What financial resource base is required to support the client's desired future income stream? Two methods may be used for establishing the required asset base: an income-based model and a consumption-based model.

(a) Income Model

With an income-based model, the goal is to identify the maximum annual income that can be consumed while adjusting for inflation and without reducing principal. Using this approach, total expected investment return is used to establish the financial resources required to support the client's desired lifestyle. Generally speaking, total return includes income, realized capital gains, and unrealized growth. Once this figure is established, it must be adjusted for inflation and income taxes.

> appropriate rate of consumption = total investment return
> − income tax assumption − inflation assumption

To continue the previous example, assume a total expected investment return of 8 percent, less taxes at 40 percent (3.2 percent), and inflation of 3 percent. Using these assumptions, the appropriate rate of consumption is 1.8 percent.

> total return (8%) − tax (3.2%) − inflation (3%)
> = appropriate rate of consumption (1.8%)

Under this scenario, if the client wants an after-tax income stream of $150,000 increasing at 3 percent each year, he or she must have financial resources of $8,333,333 earning a pretax return of at least 8 percent. This will ensure that the resource base increases by 3 percent each year, thereby ensuring that income will increase by 3 percent each year, offsetting the impact of inflation. By the end of year 25, financial resources will have increased to $16,939,957.

The formula for estimating the required resource base using this method is as follows:

$$\text{required resource base} =$$
$$\text{after-tax income goal} \div \text{appropriate rate of consumption, or}$$

$$\$150,000 \div 1.8\% = \$8,333,333$$

The higher the appropriate rate of consumption and the lower the income goal, the lower the required resource base. The lower the appropriate rate of consumption and the higher the income goal, the larger the required resource base.

For example, with 4 percent as the appropriate rate of consumption, the results change dramatically.

$$\text{required resource base} =$$
$$\text{after-tax income goal} \div \text{appropriate rate of consumption, or}$$

$$\$150,000 \div 4\% = \$3,750,000$$

To summarize, at ages 65 and below, this model generally produces a reasonable estimate of required assets. In addition, it pretty much eliminates the possibility of clients outliving their financial resources.

On the other hand, at ages 65 and over, this model tends to overestimate significantly the resource base required to maintain independence. It does so because the model does not account for the consumption of principal. This is an understandable strategy at younger ages, yet it often leads to a less effective estate plan at older ages by retaining financial resources in the estate too long. Remember that estate planning is about separating clients from their money, as early as possible. The more they identify as excess wealth, the more they can accomplish through planning.

(b) The Consumption Model

Under the consumption model, the need for income is projected for a specific period. Most people begin with natural life expectancy, and then add a cushion. Couples typically use joint life expectancy as the base. Again, health and family history also are relevant considerations. Once an appropriate term of years is established, one estimates the resource base required to support the desired level of income.

Let's assume the appropriate term is 25 years. Without taking into account inflation, the desired income stream of $150,000 for 25 years equals $3,750,000, or $150,000 × 25. However, if $150,000 is adjusted for 3 percent inflation each year for 25 years, total required capital increases to $5,468,890. This is referred to as adjusting the client's purchasing power.

One final step is necessary to estimate the required resource base. Because the client does not need all of the income in the first year, one must take into consideration the investment return that is earned on the excess financial resources. Completing the example, if one assumes the client can earn 4.8 percent after taxes on investment assets, the total required capital decreases to $3,069,916. This is referred to as the *present value*. Therefore, under the consumption model, if the client's lifestyle requires an annual after-tax income of $150,000 for a period of 25 years, adjusted for 3 percent inflation, the client would need $3,069,916 of cash earning 4.8 percent after taxes, or 8.0 percent gross return minus 3.2 percent tax.

(c) Comparison of Income and Consumption Models

The primary advantage of the income model is the certainty of maintaining the client's investment principal. The primary disadvantage of this model is that it generally results in overexposure to estate tax. At older ages, it tends to overestimate the resources required to maintain the desired lifestyle. Using the income model, and assuming 3 percent annual inflation, the original financial resources of $8,333,333 would have grown to $16,939,957 by the end of year 25.

Under the consumption-based model, clients retain only those resources required to support the desired lifestyle to life expectancy. This is the primary advantage of the model. It minimizes estate tax exposure by freeing up resources to accomplish other objectives. The primary disadvantage is that it minimizes financial resources at life expectancy. Clients who are too aggressive or unrealistic with assumptions could prematurely consume their resource base.

Because the income model does not take into consideration life expectancy, the resource base required does not change at older ages. As a result, the required resource base tends to be overstated at older ages. Consider the comparison in Exhibit 14.1.

Joint Age	LE/LE +10	Income Model	Consumption Model	Difference
40/40	49/59 yrs	$3,333,333	$2,883,900	$ 449,433
50/50	39/49 yrs	3,333,333	2,667,925	665,408
60/60	29/39 yrs	3,333,333	2,380,125	953,208
70/70	20/30 yrs	3,333,333	2,040,108	1,293,225
80/80	13/23 yrs	3,333,333	1,707,732	1,625,601
90/90	7/17 yrs	3,333,333	1,364,542	1,968,791

Exhibit 14.1   Required Resource Base: Income Model versus Consumption Model

Based on $100,000 of annual income, 9% pretax investment return, 3% inflation, and 33% tax. LE = life expectancy; LE + 10 = normal life expectancy plus 10 years.

In this comparison, natural life expectancy is increased by 10 years. This increases the resource base required under the consumption model, making it more conservative. Even with this conservative approach at older ages, the income model has the effect of overstating the required resources between 40 and 70 percent.

The best model undoubtedly is somewhere in between. At younger ages, either model will produce a reasonable estimate. At older ages, the consumption-based model with reasonably conservative assumptions is favored. The results are far more realistic.

Generally, conservative means

- High after-tax income assumption
- High inflation assumption
- High income tax rate assumption
- High life expectancy assumption
- Low investment assumption

In the example, if the after-tax investment assumption changes to 4.5 percent (from 4.8 percent), the inflation assumption to 4 percent (from 3 percent), and the term to 30 years (from 25), the required financial resources increase to $4,201,302 from $3,069,916. Hence, the assumptions are more conservative. Nevertheless, even after the adjustment, the consumption model still produces a figure that is significantly below the $8,333,333 established under the income model.

For the purpose of the ongoing example, extend life expectancy by 5 additional years to 30 and assume after-tax investment return of 4.8 percent and inflation rate of 3 percent. This changes the resource base required to support life income from $3,069,916 to $3,539,855.

The next two sections discuss the minimum resource base. Regardless of which method is used to determine the financial resources that are required to support life income needs, the minimum resource base provides an additional level of financial security.

14.4 ESTABLISHING THE MINIMUM RESOURCE BASE

In calculating the amount of property required to meet and maintain financial independence, the client's minimum resource base must be determined. This is the combination of specific assets that the client wishes to maintain as part of the estate and a series of special purpose funds to supplement the desired life income. The minimum resource base comprises those assets over which the client intends to maintain ownership for the foreseeable future.

(a) Specific Assets

The term *specific assets* refers to those assets the client presently owns and intends to own in the future, such as a primary residence or second home, personal property, antiques, and collectibles. For the purpose of determining financial independence, the client should not rely on these assets for providing either liquidity or income.

In the continuing example, assume specific assets identified have a total value of $1 million, comprised of a primary residence valued at $650,000 and personal property valued at $350,000.

(b) Special Purpose Funds

Similar to the specific assets, special purpose funds supplement the client's lifestyle. These cash resources are not required to support life income, but rather they are designated to offset unexpected contingencies.

(c) Petty Cash Fund

A petty cash fund holds the amount of cash the client needs in a checkbook to enjoy a sense of financial freedom.

(d) Investment Opportunity Fund

Liquid assets have become a symbol of financial independence. Many people wish to have adequate liquid assets on hand to take advantage of an unexpected investment opportunity. If a client already has had a fair share of opportunities, this fund may be of little concern. Here the focus is the "opportunity cost" of not maintaining a significant amount of liquid assets, with the accompanying fear that the client may miss investment opportunities, like the stock tip of a lifetime, a unique parcel of real estate, or public auction of property. It is important to establish how much money the client wants available to take advantage of unexpected opportunities.

(e) Emergency Fund

How much cash is readily available for emergencies? Could the client withstand unexpected medical expenses or other uninsured loss? What if a family member needs immediate financial assistance? How much would the client like to have set aside for this type of situation?

(f) Business Opportunity Fund

If an irresistible business opportunity presents itself, is the client in a position to invest? Perhaps the client must act immediately in order to take advantage of a chance to expand an existing business. Or a child wants to start a business, and the client wants to help out. Many clients want resources available for this type of situation.

(g) Vacation Fund

In addition to the amount included in the life income goal, what amount should be set aside to supplement the ability to take all the vacations the client might plan over time? Some clients may want to be able to take their entire family on vacations through the years. A vacation fund provides for these special opportunities.

(h) Education Fund

How much should be made available to enhance the client's personal education? Is there an advanced degree or professional training that might be desirable at some point? Maybe the client wants to try culinary school or fine arts study or something totally new, to expand avocations. A special fund can make these things possible.

(i) Asset Acquisition Fund

What assets would the client like to acquire? What about that dream house? A new vacation home? A luxury sports car? A swimming pool? Diamond jewelry? Artwork? What are all the things the client may want but does not yet have?

(j) Special Funds Summary

Once the client has considered each of these accounts and decided on a proper amount of funding, total the results. Depending on the purpose of the fund, this amount either will be maintained as a contingency fund or will be consumed.

Continuing with the earlier example, assume the desired minimum resource base is $1.5 million. In other words, in addition to financial resources securing income, the client would like to retain specific assets valued at $1 million and special funds totaling $500,000. When combined with the income goal established previously, under the consumption model (i.e., $3,589,855), total financial resources required to maintain financial independence become $5,089,855.

14.5 SETTING GOALS FOR INDEPENDENCE: THE SECURITY FUND

At this point, the formula has established the amount of capital required to support the client's desired level of life income; it has also established the desired minimum resource base as a combination of specific assets the client intends to own for the foreseeable future plus a series of special purpose funds. The question now becomes this: Just how independent does the client want to be?

In this hypothetical case, financial independence has been defined as $5,039,855 (in other words, $1.5 million minimum resource base plus $3,539,855 life income). This number reflects the client's personal definition of financial independence. Even though this method of calculating financial independence is reasonably conservative, most people want to exceed their own definition by a certain percentage. The question is, by how much? For example, assume the final goal is 120 percent. Once the financial independence percentage goal is established, the definition of financial independence is adjusted to reflect the desired financial independence goal. The following formula achieves this.

resources required for financial independence goal = financial independence definition × financial independence goal %

In our example, the numbers look like this.

$$\$6,047,826 = \$5,039,855 \times 120\%$$

Based on a goal of 120 percent, the resources required for financial independence increase from $5,039,855 to $6,047,826. The goal then is to maintain access to this amount of resources.

As indicated in Exhibit 14.2, four components make up the financial independence goal. The bottom three create a safety zone that supports lifetime income.

(a) Resources inside or outside the Estate

Keep in mind that income may come from sources inside or outside the estate. Only the minimum resource base is composed of income and assets that must remain in the estate. By definition, this is the portion of the financial resources a client intends to own forever. All things being equal, the lower the minimum resource base relative to total financial resources, the greater the planning opportunities.

From an estate planning perspective, resources outside the estate are preferred over resources inside the estate. This is because financial resources outside the estate generally are not subject to estate tax.

The most versatile financial resources are outside the taxable estate and provide income when needed. These assets contribute to a client's financial independence yet are effective for estate tax purposes.

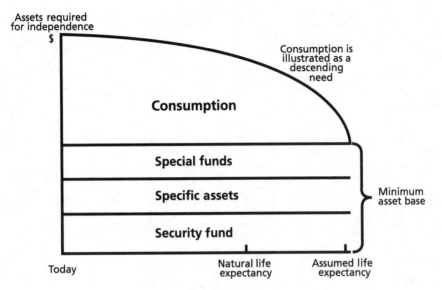

Exhibit 14.2   Components of the Financial Independence Goal

(b) Maintaining Financial Independence

But how does this model perform over time? What if the client lives longer than expected? Exhibit 14.3 illustrates how the model becomes more conservative with every step.

Each of the following scenarios is based on these assumptions:

- Natural life expectancy of 25 years
- Pretax investment assumption of 8 percent
- Marginal income tax rate of 33 percent
- Annual income goal of $150,000
- Annual inflation factor of 3 percent

(i) Scenario one.   This scenario is based on the resources required to support the desired life income ($2,895,665), that is, the exact amount of money required to support the income objective for the specified 25-year term. In this case, the fund reaches zero by the end of year 25 (age 90). This is obviously the most aggressive definition of financial independence. If the client lives beyond normal life expectancy and the assumptions are correct, the client will outlive his or her resources.

(ii) Scenario two.   This scenario illustrates the impact of the security fund, increasing the base definition of financial independence from

		Scenario 1			Scenario 2			Scenario 3		
Year	Age	Beginning Value	Income	Ending Value	Beginning Value	Income	Ending Value	Beginning Value	Income	Ending Value
1	65	$2,895,665	$150,000	$2,745,665	$3,903,636	$150,000	$3,753,636	$4,310,682	$150,000	$4,160,682
2	66	2,892,833	154,500	2,738,333	3,954,831	154,500	3,800,331	4,383,695	154,500	4,229,195
3	67	2,885,107	159,135	2,725,972	4,004,029	159,135	3,844,894	4,455,879	159,135	4,296,744
4	68	2,872,084	163,909	2,708,175	4,050,980	163,909	3,887,071	4,527,050	163,909	4,363,141
5	69	2,853,334	168,826	2,684,507	4,095,418	168,826	3,926,592	4,597,005	168,826	4,428,179
6	70	2,828,397	173,891	2,654,506	4,137,057	173,891	3,963,166	4,665,529	173,891	4,491,638
7	71	2,796,787	179,108	2,617,679	4,175,591	179,108	3,996,484	4,732,390	179,108	4,553,282
8	72	2,757,987	184,481	2,573,506	4,210,695	184,481	4,026,214	4,797,338	184,481	4,612,857
9	73	2,711,446	190,016	2,521,430	4,242,019	190,016	4,052,004	4,860,106	190,016	4,670,091
10	74	2,656,579	195,716	2,460,863	4,269,191	195,716	4,073,475	4,920,407	195,716	4,724,691
11	75	2,592,765	201,587	2,391,178	4,291,813	201,587	4,090,226	4,977,935	201,587	4,776,347
12	76	2,519,345	207,635	2,311,710	4,309,462	207,635	4,101,827	5,032,360	207,635	4,824,725
13	77	2,435,617	213,864	2,221,753	4,321,685	213,864	4,107,821	5,083,330	213,864	4,869,466
14	78	2,340,839	220,280	2,120,559	4,328,000	220,280	4,107,720	5,130,469	220,280	4,910,189
15	79	2,234,221	226,888	2,007,333	4,327,894	226,888	4,101,005	5,173,375	226,888	4,946,487
16	80	2,114,926	233,695	1,881,231	4,320,819	233,695	4,087,124	5,211,618	233,695	4,977,923
17	81	1,982,065	240,706	1,741,359	4,306,194	240,706	4,065,488	5,244,740	240,706	5,004,034
18	82	1,834,696	247,927	1,586,768	4,283,398	247,927	4,035,471	5,272,250	247,927	5,024,323
19	83	1,671,819	255,365	1,416,454	4,251,772	255,365	3,996,407	5,293,627	255,365	5,038,262
20	84	1,492,376	263,026	1,229,350	4,210,614	263,026	3,947,588	5,308,313	263,026	5,045,287
21	85	1,295,243	270,917	1,024,327	4,159,179	270,917	3,888,263	5,315,714	270,917	5,044,797
22	86	1,079,231	279,044	800,186	4,096,673	279,044	3,817,629	5,315,199	279,044	5,036,154
23	87	843,076	287,416	555,661	4,022,254	287,416	3,734,839	5,306,092	287,416	5,018,677
24	88	585,444	296,038	289,406	3,935,026	296,038	3,638,988	5,287,678	296,038	4,991,640
25	89	304,919	304,919	—	3,834,038	304,919	3,529,119	5,259,192	304,919	4,954,273
26	90				3,718,279	314,067	3,404,213	5,219,822	314,067	4,905,755
27	91				3,586,678	323,489	3,263,190	5,168,703	323,489	4,845,215
28	92				3,438,097	333,193	3,104,903	5,104,918	333,193	4,771,725
29	93				3,271,326	343,189	2,928,137	5,027,489	343,189	4,684,300
30	94				3,085,085	353,485	2,731,600	4,935,379	353,485	4,581,894
31	95				2,878,014	364,089	2,513,925	4,827,483	364,089	4,463,394
32	96				2,648,671	375,012	2,273,659	4,702,632	375,012	4,327,620
33	97				2,395,527	386,262	2,009,265	4,559,580	386,262	4,173,318
34	98				2,116,961	397,850	1,719,111	4,397,008	397,850	3,999,157
35	99				1,811,256	409,786	1,401,470	4,213,512	409,786	3,803,726
36	100				1,476,589	422,079	1,054,509	4,007,606	422,079	3,585,527

Exhibit 14.3   Financial Independence over Time

Each scenario is based on an investment assumption of 5.4%, a tax rate of 33%, and an inflation rate of 3.0%.

$2,895,665 to $3,903,636. As a result of this increase, $3,529,119 of financial resources remains at normal life expectancy and $1,054,509 at the end of year 36, age 100.

(iii) Scenario three. This scenario builds on scenario 2 by extending the anticipated life expectancy from 25 years to 30 years. This produces a corresponding increase in the definition of financial independence to $4,310,682. As a result of this increase, $4,954,273 of financial resources remains at normal life expectancy and $3,585,527 at the end of year 36, age 100.

This is obviously the most conservative of the three models. At first glance, scenario 3 might appear to be the clear winner. Yet, if the assumptions are correct, the client has overstated the requirements for financial independence by a wide margin, and perhaps missed a planning opportunity today.

(c) Financial Independence and Planning Resources Summarized

It is essential that clients understand the relationship between financial independence and planning resources. The more conservative their definition of financial independence, the lower the amount of available planning resources. The more aggressive their definition of financial independence, the greater the likelihood of prematurely consuming assets.

The tax-effectiveness of planning is generally enhanced when assets are irrevocably transferred outside the taxable estate. The ability to take advantage of such strategies is controlled by the financial independence goal.

14.6 A BRIEF REVIEW

As advisors enter the planning process with clients, it is important first to define how much is required from financial resources for lifetime independence, so that the client can see what might be available for accomplishing other planning objectives. Remember the formula:

planning resources = total financial resources
+ discounted future income − taxes − discounts
− financial independence goal

Most effective lifetime planning strategies require the irrevocable transfer of planning resources. This is the place to begin.

If the advisor cannot identify planning resources, it does not mean the client won't benefit from planning. However, it will be difficult for the client to give up ownership of financial resources during his or her lifetime. This may reduce the overall effectiveness of the estate plan.

CHAPTER FIFTEEN

The Legacy Goal Profile
Family and Social Capital Legacy Goals

15.1 THE LEGACY GOAL PROFILE: FAMILY LEGACY GOAL

Helping clients establish an appropriate family legacy is one of the most difficult tasks advisors face in developing an estate plan. One particularly complicating factor is the need to determine what portion of an heir's financial independence should result from personal initiative and what portion should or might come from inheritance. In other words, what is an appropriate inheritance?

Complicating matters even further, in estate planning, fair is not always equal and equal is not always fair. With this in mind, many parents wrestle with the decision to provide each heir with the same inheritance amount, regardless of unique circumstances and needs, or an amount that reflects each heir's unique circumstances and needs.

With careful consideration, some will choose an objective to supplement the ability of each heir to accomplish the goal of becoming financially independent on his or her own. It is important to remember that only the client can determine what is meant by an appropriate inheritance. The appropriate amount is strictly a reflection of the client's or couple's personal values.

The following formula is helpful in determining how much to provide each heir:

$$\text{appropriate inheritance} =$$
$$\text{heir's financial independence goal}$$
$$- \text{current financial resources} - \text{future contribution from heirs}$$
$$- \text{future investment performance},$$

whereby

- *Financial independence* equals the total financial resources required to secure financial independence for the life of a specific heir.

- *Current financial resources* equals the existing financial resources of each specific heir.

- *Future contribution from heirs* equals the amount of additional financial resources to be added through the personal initiative of heirs. Generally, this relates to income from employment or building and growing a business.

- *Future investment performance* equals the anticipated earnings on total financial resources.

The ultimate question is this: How much room would clients like to leave for heirs to contribute to their *own* financial independence? Do clients want merely to supplement heirs' financial independence, or do they want to make their heirs financially independent?

If clients decide to build the entire planning pyramid for their heirs, including financial independence and family and social capital legacies, they will want to be sure their heirs have other interests to challenge their time and abilities.

(a) Identify Each Potential Heir

The first step in defining an appropriate inheritance is to identify all potential heirs. It is helpful to divide heirs into appropriate categories based on relationship, such as children, grandchildren, siblings, parents, and so on. This makes it easier to total appropriate inheritance across categories of heirs. It may be worthwhile to develop a family tree to assist in this purpose.

(b) Estimate Financial Independence for Heirs

In order to determine the appropriateness of a specific inheritance, the numbers need to be expressed in tangible terms. In other words, clients need to identify specific assets or lifestyle attributes they would like their heirs to enjoy as a result of receiving an inheritance. Similar to helping clients define their own financial independence, advisors should consider two specific areas of family legacy: (1) minimum resource base and (2) lifetime income available for consumption.

(i) The minimum resource base. Helping a client establish an appropriate family legacy includes the same basic steps as defining financial independence. In essence, the advisor is defining a financial independence goal for each individual heir and then establishing what contribution the parents or grandparents want to make toward achieving that goal.

The advisor should begin with the minimum resource base. As discussed in Chapter 14, the minimum resource base is a combination of specific assets and a series of special purpose funds.

1) Specific Assets   The first step is to identify specific assets that clients would like each individual heir to have. These are not assets clients are willing to provide as inheritance but rather assets necessary to attain the lifestyle they wish to see their heirs enjoy. This is a good place for clients to reflect on their own definition of financial independence. Perhaps they would like to see their heirs in a position similar to their own? Perhaps they would like to see them in an improved position?

Advisors should emphasize to their clients that the list of assets developed will be hypothetical. These are ideals that clients would like to see, and they may not even be attainable. The point behind this exercise is to help the client establish a goal. Refer to Exhibit 15.1.

2) Special Purpose Funds   Similar to the specific assets previously discussed, special purpose funds are designed to supplement the heir's lifestyle. These cash resources are not required to support life income but rather are designated to offset unexpected contingencies.

- *Petty cash fund.* How much cash does the heir need in a checkbook to have a sense of financial freedom?

- *Investment opportunity fund.* Liquid assets have become a symbol of financial independence. Many people wish to have adequate liquid assets on hand to take advantage of unexpected investment opportunities. Some define success as that point where opportunity meets

Heir Name	Asset Category	Asset Value
Conrad Miller	Primary Residence	$ 250,000
	Vacation Home	200,000
	Personal Property	100,000
Total for Conrad Miller		$ 550,000
Emma Miller	Primary Residence	$ 250,000
	Vacation Home	200,000
	Personal Property	100,000
Total for Emma Miller		$ 550,000
Total specific assets for heirs		$1,100,000

Exhibit 15.1   Table of Specific Assets for Heirs

preparedness. This fund is intent on making sure each heir is sufficiently prepared to take advantage of unexpected opportunities.

- *Emergency fund.* How much cash is readily available for emergencies? Could the heir withstand unexpected medical expenses or other uninsured loss? What if a grandchild needs immediate financial assistance? How much should be set aside for this?

- *Business opportunity fund.* Should resources be set aside to help the heir get established in business? Many clients accumulate their wealth through growing a personal or family business. Is this an opportunity they might like to provide for their heirs?

- *Vacation fund.* Wisdom is derived from a collection of lifetime experiences. One of the most common and memorable sources of family experience is travel. What amount of financial resources would the client like to provide for each heir in order to increase the quality and quantity of family experiences related to travel?

- *Education fund.* How much should be made available to enhance the heir's education? Is an advanced degree or professional training desirable at some point?

- *Asset acquisition fund.* What assets would the client like to see the heir acquire? Would a larger house or a vacation home be desirable and appropriate?

Once the advisor has developed a special funds definition for each heir, he or she should prepare a report summarizing the total for each heir, as well as the total for all heirs, as illustrated in Exhibit 15.2.

Heir Name	Fund Category	Asset Value
Conrad Miller	Future grandchildren	$ 5,000
	Education	100,000
	Emergency	10,000
	Investment opportunity	10,000
	Petty cash	10,000
Total for Conrad Miller		$ 135,000
Emma Miller	Future grandchildren	$ 5,000
	Education	100,000
	Emergency	10,000
	Investment opportunity	10,000
	Petty cash	10,000
Total for Emma Miller		$ 135,000
Total special funds for heirs		$ 270,000

Exhibit 15.2 Table of Special Funds for Heirs

(ii) Lifetime Income for Heirs. Now that the client has established a minimum resource base for each heir, he or she should consider an income supplement. Use the same procedure as in calculating the financial resources required to maintain the client's desired life income, as shown in Exhibit 15.3.

The advisor should do the following:

- Help the client identify an appropriate supplemental level of income for the heir (e.g., $50,000 after taxes).
- Help the client decide at what rate of inflation the income will likely increase each year (e.g., 3 percent each year).
- Help the client decide when the income should begin and how long the income should continue for each heir (e.g., 25 years). The number

Year	Actual Income	Value in Year-1 Dollars
1	$50,000	$50,000
2	51,500	49,048
3	53,045	48,113
4	54,636	47,197
5	56,275	46,298
6	57,964	45,416
7	59,703	44,551
8	61,494	43,702
9	63,339	42,870
10	65,239	42,053
11	67,196	41,252
12	69,212	40,467
13	71,288	39,696
14	73,427	38,940
15	75,629	38,198
16	77,898	37,470
17	80,235	36,757
18	82,642	36,057
19	85,122	35,370
20	87,675	34,696
21	90,306	34,035
22	93,015	33,387
23	95,805	32,751
24	98,679	32,127
25	101,640	31,515
Total	$1,822,963	$1,001,967

Exhibit 15.3   Projecting Life Income for Heirs

Based on $50,000 annual income, inflated by 3% annually, for a period of 25 years, discounted to year-1 dollars assuming a 5% discount rate.

of years may be based on natural life expectancy or could be limited to a specific term of years.

- Project the income to the end of the term, taking into account inflation (e.g., $1,822,963).

- Discount the projected income stream to reflect the present value, using an assumed after-tax investment (e.g., 5 percent after-tax) rate amount of cash required (e.g., $1,001,967).

(d) Establishing the Inheritance Goal

Once the client has established a financial independence goal for each heir, the individual circumstances of each heir should be considered in establishing an appropriate inheritance. This does not mean the client must treat each heir equally, but rather that it is important to consider each heir's particular financial and social situations. Remember the definition of an appropriate inheritance:

> appropriate inheritance = heir's financial independence goal
> − current financial resources − future contribution from heirs
> − future investment performance

To define an appropriate inheritance, the client must keep all of these factors in mind.

15.2 THE LEGACY GOAL PROFILE: SOCIAL CAPITAL LEGACY GOAL

Once clients identify how much they will need to maintain lifetime financial independence and secure a desired family legacy for heirs, they acquire a sense of freedom to explore their social capital legacy. Social capital legacy represents that portion of the estate not needed to maintain financial independence and not designated for family legacy.

As previously established, there are two forms of social capital: *voluntary and involuntary.* Voluntary social capital is made up of those dollars over which clients make a conscious decision to take responsibility. Consisting of either tax or philanthropic contributions, it represents the lasting impact individuals may have on society by directing their social capital in a manner consistent with their value systems. In other words, these are *self-directed social capital dollars.*

Involuntary social capital consists of those dollars that are involuntarily extracted under the default plan—tax. These *government-directed social capital dollars* represent the mandatory redistribution of social capital that occurs when individuals choose not to take personal responsibility for their wealth distribution.

At this point in the planning process, clients must decide what portion of their social capital will be represented by tax and what portion will be represented by gifts.

In most cases, advisors will be working primarily with assets held in the client's taxable estate. In more complicated cases, advisors may want to consider five possible categories of financial resources:

1. Assets included in the client's taxable estate
2. Assets held in trusts for the benefit of heirs outside the taxable estate
3. Assets previously transferred to heirs
4. Assets held in trust for charity
5. Assets previously transferred to charity

The sum of these five categories represents total available resources. Once total resources have been identified, the following formula should be used to calculate the client's self-directed social capital legacy goal. This definition will be used in drafting the Family Financial Philosophy mission statement.

$$\text{(total available resources} - \text{family legacy goal)}$$
$$\times \text{ self-directed social capital legacy goal \%}$$
$$= \text{self-directed social capital legacy goal,}$$

whereby

- *Total available resources* equals total resources as previously defined.
- *Family legacy goal* equals a client's previously established definition of an appropriate inheritance for heirs.
- *Self-directed social capital legacy goal %* equals the percentage of a client's total social capital identified for voluntary distribution for the benefit of designated charitable and philanthropic purposes.
- *Social capital legacy goal* equals the portion of a client's total financial resources to be divided between gift and tax.

15.3 A BRIEF REVIEW

Family legacy is that portion of a client's total financial resources that is appropriate for transfer to heirs. A separate definition is established for each heir using three components:

1. Clients must identify specific assets they would like each heir to receive. These assets can be real or imaginary, and they represent the tangible portion of each heir's legacy.

2. Clients should identify contingency funds to assist heirs in managing unexpected situations. These imaginary cash funds may never actually be accessed, yet they serve as a cushion for managing the unexpected.

3. Finally, the client must consider an appropriate income supplement. This block of resources is intended to contribute directly to each heir's lifestyle by providing the necessary income for consumption or savings. To place this goal on an equal footing with specific assets and special funds, the income stream is converted into a lump sum of cash in today's dollars.

Once established, the sum total of these dollars represents the client's definition of financial independence for each heir. The advisor now must help the client use this definition to establish a family legacy goal for each heir. This requires the client to take each heir's unique circumstances into account. Advisors should use this goal for the purpose of constructing the client's Family Financial Philosophy.

After the family legacy goal has been established, the client can define the self-directed social capital legacy goal. The first step is to identify what portion, if any, of the client's estate will be allocated to social capital. If the client's family legacy goal is equal to or greater than total available resources, the social capital legacy goal will be zero. If the client's family legacy goal is less than total resources, the difference is available for allocation as social capital.

The final question is whether the client's social capital will be self-directed charitable contributions or paid as tax. Once established, the social capital legacy goal serves as one of the three key financial goals used in drafting the client's Family Financial Philosophy: the financial independence goal, the family legacy goal, and the social capital goal.

CHAPTER SIXTEEN

The Legacy Blueprint

Advisors are aware of the necessity to gather factual information in order to develop an effective estate plan. The legacy blueprint provides a comprehensive methodology for bringing essential information together.

The legacy blueprint information gathering and analysis begins with an inventory and review of financial resources. Once a listing of resources is complete, the blueprint establishes a client's financial status in each level of the pyramid of planning objectives:

1. Financial independence status
2. Family legacy status
3. Social capital legacy status

Chapters 14 and 15 focused on establishing a goal for each of these three areas. This chapter illustrates the results of the client's current plan in each level of the pyramid. Once established, a client's status is compared with the stated goals in each area (see Exhibit 16.1). The difference between each financial status and the goal on that level form the basis for future planning.

16.1 INVENTORY OF FINANCIAL RESOURCES

This step focuses on gathering all available information with respect to the client's current financial position, including all existing planning documents. The greater the detail, the greater the benefit.

The following is an overview of the resource inventory process.

(a) Asset Attributes

At a minimum, the following information should be gathered with respect to each asset owned by the client.

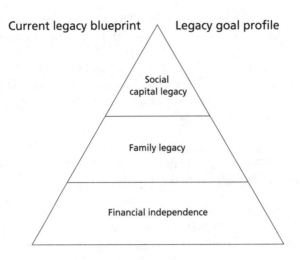

Exhibit 16.1   Pyramid of Planning Objectives

(i) Asset category.   The initial step in creating an inventory of financial resources is to categorize each asset into a specific asset class. This is done by combining assets with common asset attributes into 12 categories.

1. Cash and cash equivalents (checking and savings accounts, money market funds, short-term U.S. Treasury bonds, etc.)
2. Marketable equity securities (stocks, stock mutual funds, etc.)
3. Marketable taxable debt securities (bonds, bond mutual funds, etc.)
4. Marketable tax-free debt securities (municipal and tax-free bonds)
5. Qualified retirement plans (IRAs, Keogh plans, 401(k)s, profit sharing plans, etc.)
6. Residential real estate (primary and secondary residence)
7. Investment real estate
8. Business interests
9. Personal property
10. Life insurance
11. Annuities
12. Other assets (e.g., notes receivable, art collections, etc.)

(ii) Asset ownership.   Once an inventory of financial resources has been established, organize the assets by ownership. For married couples, assets should be divided among husband, wife, joint tenants with right of survivorship, and joint tenants in common and community property.

(iii) Asset beneficiary. Asset categories such as life insurance, annuities, and retirement plans have beneficiary designations. All beneficiaries should be identified for assets in these categories, including primary, secondary, contingent, and so on.

(iv) Asset cost basis. The adjusted tax cost basis should be identified for each asset. This is of particular importance as cost basis is a significant factor in identifying appropriate strategies.

(v) Asset debt. Is the asset subject to direct debt, or has the asset been assigned to collateral? What are the terms of the debt, such as term of years, interest rate, payments, amortization period?

(vi) Asset income, anticipated growth, and realized capital gain. What are the investment return attributes of the asset? What level of income does the asset provide? Will the income increase over time? Is the asset expected to increase in value? What amount of realized capital gains does the asset produce each year?

(vii) Volatility, liquidity, and marketability. Is the asset unusually volatile? What has been the change in its value over the past five years? What has been the largest 12-month change in value? What is the standard divagation of price over the past five years?

Is the asset traded in a public market? Is there an active secondary market for the asset? Will a private sale be required? Are there any restrictions on the sale or exchange of the asset? Is there an emotional attachment to the asset that would prevent a sale?

(b) Liabilities

Does the client have any liabilities or notes payable not identified in association with an asset listed above? What are the terms and conditions of the liability(ies)?

(c) Income Attributes

Once the inventory of assets has been prepared, advisors should identify income sources not associated with specific assets. Items such as salary from employment, deferred compensation, social security, and pension plans should be identified and categorized. Advisors should identify the following attributes for each income source:

- The amount of income to be received
- The term over which the income will be paid
- The frequency of payments (monthly, quarterly, annually)
- Cost of living or other systematic adjustments to the amount of income
- Taxable portion of each income amount
- Reliability of the income source

(d) Net Worth and Cash-Flow Statement

Once assets, liabilities, and income sources have been inventoried, the advisor should prepare comprehensive net worth and cash-flow statements. The net worth statement should clearly establish the gross value, debt, cost basis, net value, and owner of each asset. Advisors should request that the client write his or her initials on the net worth statement to confirm its accuracy.

The cash-flow statement should illustrate income from assets, along with the assumptions used to make the projection for each asset. The cash flow also should list all sources of independent cash flow. Finally, an estimate of potential income tax should be made in arriving at after-tax cash flow. Again, the client should write his or her initials on the cash-flow statement to indicate acceptance of its accuracy.

16.2 REVIEW OF EXISTING PLAN AND DOCUMENTS

Each existing estate planning document (e.g., partnerships, trusts, wills, and so on) should be outlined for specific attributes that affect the client's current plan. If an advisor is an estate planning attorney, he or she should complete this review personally or delegate the review to someone on his or her staff.

Advisors who are not trained as estate planning lawyers may obtain an accurate review of a client's legal documents in one of two ways. First, they can ask the client's current estate planning lawyer for a review of the current documents. This approach will work fine as long as the client's attorney is willing to comply and is operating as a member of the planning team. However, if the client's current lawyer is also the lawyer who prepared the documents, such a review may not be as openly critical of past planning and documentation as an independent review might be.

As an alternative, the advisor might suggest that the client retain new counsel for the sole purpose of reviewing and summarizing the current estate planning documents. Many advisors actually offer this to their clients and then outsource the review to a qualified lawyer for a flat review fee. This is an effective way to produce the required review, as well as to enhance relationships with lawyers.

16.3 ESTABLISHING FINANCIAL INDEPENDENCE STATUS

The client's current financial independence status should be defined and compared with the financial independence goal established in the legacy goal profile segment found in Chapter 14. The legacy blueprint facilitates this process by converting a client's financial resources into a cash equivalent that easily can be compared with the cash requirement identified to achieve a particular client's financial independence goal.

(a) Converting Assets into Cash

The first step in analyzing financial resources is to convert existing assets into a cash equivalent. This puts all assets on an equal footing, where they can be lumped together and compared with requirements for financial independence. Two adjustments are required to convert assets into cash. First, the assets must be appropriately discounted in order to reflect their unique nature. Second, potential future taxes must be taken into account.

(i) Adjustments to reflect potential discounts.   Illiquid assets, or assets in which the client owns less than 51 percent, generally are more difficult to sell than marketable securities. Therefore, these assets should be adjusted to reflect potential discounts from fair market value. Again, ignore assets on the specific asset list. Because the client intends to own these assets into the future and will not rely on them for income, an adjustment is not necessary.

The amount of the discount depends on the particular asset. In some cases, a discount may not be appropriate, while in other situations a discount as high as 50 percent or more may be necessary. A discount of up to 30 percent may be appropriate for illiquid assets such as real estate or partnership interests. In addition, a discount of up to 30 percent may be appropriate for assets in which the client owns less than 51 percent of the controlling ownership. In some cases, multiple discounts will apply. For example, a 25 percent ownership interest in a parcel of raw land would be discounted between 30 and 60 percent, depending on the circumstances.

A discount also may apply to assets that are subject to a restrictive agreement governing the client's rights, or to assets that are inherently volatile or risky. If the client has put a significant portion of financial resources into a single investment, a discount for lack of diversification may be appropriate.

(ii) Adjustments to reflect potential future taxes. The next step is to adjust the value of assets to reflect potential future taxes. First, estimate the potential capital gain tax on appreciated assets. As in the previous calculation, ignore those assets on the specific asset list. Because the client intends to own these assets for the foreseeable future and will not rely on them for income, an adjustment is not necessary.

$$\text{potential tax} = (\text{fair market value} - \text{cost basis} - \text{discounts})$$
$$\times \text{applicable capital gain tax rate}$$

Now estimate the ordinary income tax on retirement plans, IRAs, and other ordinary income assets, such as deferred annuities. With most qualified retirement plans, the cost basis will be zero.

$$\text{potential tax} = (\text{fair market value} - \text{cost basis} - \text{discounts})$$
$$\times \text{applicable ordinary income tax rate}$$

(iii) Estimating the net value of available assets. Net available assets are calculated by subtracting potential tax and discounts from fair market value. To continue the previous example, assume the client's gross assets are $8.75 million with debt of $600,000 and a cost basis of $3,675,000. After adjusting for discounts ($700,000) and tax ($985,000), net available assets are $6,465,000.

(b) Converting Future Income into Cash

Once the client's assets have been converted into a cash equivalent, it is time to determine the value of available income sources. The objective is to convert each future source of income into its equivalent value of cash in today's dollars. Once this is complete, the resource value of a client's assets and income can be combined into a single number representing total available resources.

Consider this example:

An income stream of $75,000 for 30 years without factoring in inflation would equal $2.25 million, or $75,000 times 30. However, if a 4 percent inflation adjustment is used each year for 30 years, the total value increases to $4,206,370. This represents the gross value of the stream of income, after conversion into a lump sum of financial resources.

Next, because not all of this income will be received in the first year, discount the value of payments received in years 2 through 30. This reflects the fact that a dollar received in year 30 is not worth as much as a dollar received today. Completing the example, assuming 4.8 percent after-tax earnings on the client's financial resources, the value of the pension income decreases to $2,017,819. This adjustment puts this stream of income on an equal footing with other financial resources the client has today.

Now, further discount this value to reflect the number of years until the income stream is to begin. For example, if the promised income stream does not begin for 10 years, discount the $2,017,819 from above for 10 years at 4.8 percent. This adjustment ensures that the advisor and client always deal with assets valued in the year of planning. In this example, all income begins immediately and continues for the period specified.

Finally, an adjustment must be made for potential taxes. Continuing with the example, assume total income sources translate into $2,163,753 of available financial resources. To put this on an equal footing with existing cash resources, reduce this amount by the future tax liability. Assuming an ordinary income tax rate of 40 percent, the net after-tax value of this future income is $2,163,753, or $3,606,255 minus $1,442,502 potential income tax.

(c) Estimating Planning Resources

Chapter 14 covered how to estimate lifetime income needs, establish a minimum resource base, and convert assets and income into cash. In Chapter 14, a definition of financial independence was established for a hypothetical client. Exhibit 16.2 details the assumptions used.

Now it is time to calculate the financial independence status.

Excess wealth equals planning resources. Planning resources are determined using the following formula.

planning resources = net asset value + discounted future income
  − taxes − discounts − financial independence
  goal, or

$2,580,926 = $8,150,000 + $3,606,255 − $700,000 − $2,427,502
  − $6,047,826

Assets required to support life income*	$3,539,855
Minimum resource base	
Specific assets value	1,000,000
Special funds value	500,000
Definition of financial independence	$5,039,855
Security fund @ 20% of definition	1,007,971
Financial independence goal	$6,047,826

Exhibit 16.2 Hypothetical Definition of Financial Independence

*Based on $150,000 annual income increasing by 3% each year for 30 years. Reduce to present value assuming a 4.8% discount factor.

Completing the ongoing example, based on the factors established in the hypothetical case, planning resources of $2,679,927 exist. This amount is the "working capital" for achieving planning objectives beyond maintaining financial independence.

The most effective way to monitor how financial independence may change over time is to calculate the percentage of financial independence.

$$\% \text{ independent} = \text{available resources} \div \text{resources required for independence}$$

As this formula indicates, in order to determine the client's financial independence percentage, divide total available resources by total resources required for financial independence. Going forward with the example, this hypothetical couple is 171 percent financially independent, or $8,628,753 \div $5,039,855 = 171\%$.

It is important to note that this calculation is made using the client's definition of financial independence, not the financial independence goal. The goal represents the amount by which the client wants to exceed the definition of financial independence.

Once the current percentage is established, the next step is to compare it with the client's goal for financial independence. In this case, the established goal is 120 percent. Each year, as the goal for financial independence is recalculated, the client's financial independence goal should be used as a measuring stick.

(d) Putting Excess Resources to Work: Conversion to Planning Resources

Recall this definition from an earlier chapter: Values-based wealth transfer planning may be characterized as the irrevocable application of planning resources toward wealth transfer objectives that are consistent with client values. In other words, clients give away what they don't need to people and organizations that will carry on their values.

Similarly, philanthropy may be defined as the irrevocable application of planning resources toward organizations and causes that perpetuate client values. In other words, clients give away what they don't need to nonprofit entities that support their values.

Tax-effective, offensive planning uses planning resources to accomplish planning objectives. In effect, planning resources are excess resources. As previously demonstrated, planning resources are estimated by subtracting the client's financial independence goal from the client's total financial resources. The client's definition of financial independence, therefore, determines how much working capital the advisor has to accomplish planning objectives beyond financial independence.

Carrying the hypothetical case study further, planning resources of $2,679,927 are available to accomplish planning objectives at the second and third levels of the planning pyramid: family legacy and social capital legacy. Effective estate planning will successfully put these excess resources to work.

As Figure 16.3 illustrates, a client's financial independence goal establishes the portion of total resources that must be protected in order to secure the client's desired lifestyle. The financial independence status, on the other hand, represents total available resources. The difference between the two represents resources available for planning at the two higher levels of the pyramid.

If the client has no excess resources, then any concern with complex estate distribution scenarios may yield only marginal benefits. On the other hand, if excess resources have been identified, the advisor has working capital to accomplish meaningful results.

Many of the most powerful planning techniques available for preserving family wealth require an irrevocable transfer. That is, in order to protect clients' financial resources, advisors must help their clients give those resources away, and give them away early. Once they have defined financial independence, it is easy for clients to pour from their proverbial money bag, because they know just how much they can afford to pour without threatening their financial security.

General Observation . . . on excess resources

It is easier to identify excess wealth on someone else's balance sheet than on your own.

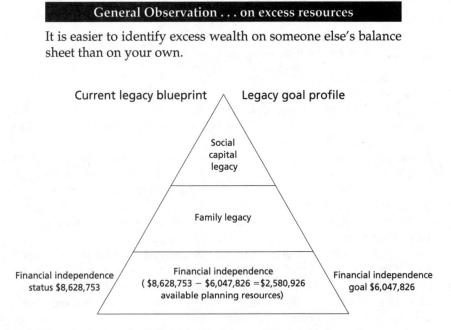

Current legacy blueprint   Legacy goal profile

Social capital legacy

Family legacy

Financial independence status $8,628,753

Financial independence ($8,628,753 − $6,047,826 =$2,580,926 available planning resources)

Financial independence goal $6,047,826

Exhibit 16.3 Pyramid of Planning Objectives—Financial Independence

16.4 ESTABLISHING FAMILY LEGACY STATUS

The client's family legacy status is the dollar amount that would be transferred to each beneficiary of the estate in the event it were settled today, in accordance with the current plan distribution.

(a) Calculating Family Legacy Status

$$\text{family legacy status} = \text{total family financial resources} \\ - \text{transfer taxes paid,}$$

whereby

- *Total family financial resources* equals net value of estate resources *plus* assets held in trust for the benefit of heirs *plus* all assets previously transferred to trusts outside the client's taxable estate *plus* assets previously transferred to heirs.
- *Transfer tax paid* equals all income, gift, estate, generation, excise, and other taxes imposed on the transfer of assets to heirs.

The methodology used in calculating the amount of transfer tax paid is beyond the scope of this book. The author assumes readers have the current capacity to make those calculations or access to resources with such capacity.

(b) Family Legacy Status Percentage

The family legacy status percentage is calculated using the following formula:

$$\text{family legacy status \%} = \text{family legacy status} \div \text{total family} \\ \text{financial resources}$$

(c) Appropriate Family Legacy versus Family Legacy Status

Chapter 15 reviewed a specific methodology for helping clients define an appropriate family legacy. As Figure 16.4 illustrates, the family legacy status indicates how much a client's heirs would receive from the estate if it were settled today without any changes. The difference between the client's family legacy status and definition of appropriate inheritance directs the focus of future planning.

As Figure 16.4 indicates, family legacy status falls short of the family legacy goal. Therefore, planning should move in the direction of strategies that reduce tax and increase family legacy. Alternatively, if the family

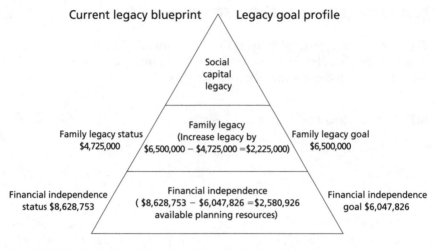

Exhibit 16.4   Pyramid of Planning Objectives—Family Legacy

legacy status is greater than the family legacy goal, there is no need to pursue strategies that increase family legacy. In such a case, planning might focus on strategies that convert government-directed social capital (tax) into self-directed social capital (charitable gifts). In either case, the goal is to close the gap between status and result.

16.5 ESTABLISHING SOCIAL CAPITAL LEGACY STATUS

The client's social capital legacy status is the current allocation of estate assets that would pass to charity or be paid in taxes in the event the estate were settled today in accordance with the current plan. Calculate a client's social capital legacy status using the following formula:

$$\text{social capital legacy status} = \text{self-directed social capital (gifts)}$$
$$+ \text{ government-directed social}$$
$$\text{capital (tax)}$$

For example, if the current plan results in charitable contributions of $1 million and transfer tax payments of $500,000, the client's social capital legacy status would be $1.5 million ($1 million self-directed and $500,000 government directed).

As Exhibit 16.5 illustrates, the social capital legacy sits at the top of the pyramid. The hypothetical numbers indicate that the social capital legacy status is out of alignment with the client's social capital legacy goal. Taken

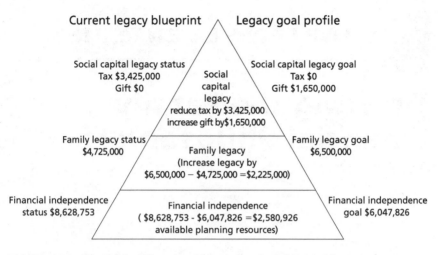

Current legacy blueprint   Legacy goal profile

Social capital legacy status   Social capital legacy goal
Tax $3,425,000   Social   Tax $0
Gift $0   capital   Gift $1,650,000
legacy
reduce tax by $3.425,000
increase gift by$1,650,000

Family legacy status   Family legacy goal
$4,725,000   Family legacy $6,500,000
(Increase legacy by
$6,500,000 − $4,725,000 =$2,225,000)

Financial independence   Financial independence   Financial independence
status $8,628,753   ($8,628,753 - $6,047,826 =$2,580,926   goal $6,047,826
available planning resources)

Exhibit 16.5 Pyramid of Planning Objectives—Social Capital Legacy

in context with the family legacy goal, planning should focus on strategies that have a positive impact on both family legacy and charitable gifts.

16.6 A BRIEF REVIEW

Whereas the legacy goal profile is designed to establish what clients would like to accomplish through planning, the current legacy blueprint illustrates the results of the current plan. The discrepancy between the status and the goal at each level of the planning pyramid determines the appropriate direction for future planning. All decisions should focus on bringing the client status and goal into perfect alignment at any given point in time.

CHAPTER SEVENTEEN

Drafting the Family Financial Philosophy

As previously stated, effective planning requires a solid foundation based on explicit objectives. Advisors who employ values-based planning help clients develop written wealth mission statements that reflect their financial philosophy before recommending specific strategies. This chapter describes how the information gathered through the discovery process is crafted into a written Family Financial Philosophy.

17.1 UNDERSTANDING THE CONCEPT

The Family Financial Philosophy is a compilation of discovery methods reviewed in earlier chapters.

- The legacy interview
- The legacy questionnaire
- The legacy goal profile
- The legacy blueprint

Each method completes a portion of the philosophy puzzle. The interview incorporates the client's unique life experience. The questionnaire enables an advisor to orient a client's values and preferences in a financial context that represents an overall philosophy. The legacy goal profile establishes three key financial goals. The legacy blueprint illustrates the results of the current plan. The following sections describe how these discovery methods are used to define and articulate a client's financial philosophy.

17.2 INCORPORATING THE LEGACY INTERVIEW

The documentation phase of the legacy interview concludes with the development of the legacy biography. This is similar to a traditional biography in that it transcribes the past in a manner that can be understood in the present. However, the legacy biography's primary focus is on the past events and experiences that have helped shape the client's financial philosophy.

By incorporating a client's unique story, the legacy biography plays an integral role in the drafting of the Family Financial Philosophy. Unlike questionnaires that measure information within an anticipated range, the interview process yields a different result each time it is done.

Typically the legacy biography is between two and three pages in length, therefore representing the longest section of a client's financial philosophy. It also is the section likely to portray the greatest number of emotional issues. As a result, some clients may wish to remove or condense the legacy biography section before sharing it with other advisors or even their heirs. In and of itself, this suggests that the advisor who assists a client in the discovery and articulation of a financial philosophy is elevated to a singular status in the client's eyes.

Typical legacy biography paragraphs might read something like this:

> My father worked for his father in the family business. He was always a good provider, but I can remember some really tough times. When business was bad, it had an impact on the entire family. It was as if the future of the whole family ebbed and flowed with the successes and failures of the business.
>
> This is why I decided to take a job with a large company when I graduated from college. I needed to feel a sense of security, and to avoid the constant financial nagging associated with a family business.

Paragraphs such as these effectively lay the foundation for a client's Family Financial Philosophy. They also add the personal touch that reduces the likelihood that another advisor will callously dismiss the written philosophy as unimportant or insignificant.

17.3 INCORPORATING PLANNING AFFIRMATIONS

The legacy questionnaire makes the broadest contribution to the drafting of the Family Financial Philosophy. Because the questionnaire covers such a wide variety of planning issues, it typically serves as the basic platform.

Purpose	Uses of a Family Financial Philosophy
Sources of Wealth	How wealth was accumulated
	Attributions of success
Legacy Biography	The questionnaire does not address the legacy biography
Responsibilities and Obligations	Senses of obligation
Family Philosophy	Personal values
	Special opportunities offered by money
	Opportunities provided by wealth
	Philosophy to impart to heirs (financial stewardship)
	Perspective on talking about money and financial stewardship ("How rich is Dad?")
	Best time to explain potential inheritance or lack thereof
	How to transfer values
Primary Planning Goals	Goals for planning
	Factors that may influence planning
	Estate allocation plans
	Expectations of estate planning
	Views of estate planning
Financial Independence	Definition of financial independence
	What they need today $_____
	What they have as excess $_____
	Thoughts on ownership and/or control
Family Legacy	Current estate allocation reality
	Amount to heirs $_____
	Assessing heirs' stewardship capabilities
	The balance between inheriting and acquiring
	Equal versus fair
	Perspective on transfer during lifetime
	Perspective on transfer to grandchildren
	Effects of transfer on long-term value of inheritance and personal feeling of heirs regarding the process
Social Capital Legacy	Social capital allocation between government or charity by percentage
	Level of personal volunteerism (time, talents, and resources)
	Perspective on charitable gift transfer at death
	Perspective on charitable gift transfer throughout lifetime
	Effectiveness of contributions on positive social change
	Perspective on the amount and level of giving
	Perspective on family foundations
	Perspective on shared philanthropy
	Preferences for philanthropic recognition
	Allocation of $1 million worth of social capital
Acknowledgment	

Exhibit 17.1   Question Value Categories in Relation to Family Financial Philosophy Sections

An advisor should begin the drafting process by categorizing the planning affirmations created in documenting the legacy questionnaire.

As illustrated in Chapter 13, Exhibit 13.1, the questionnaire has been organized around a number of value topics. These value topics are associated with certain elements of the Family Financial Philosophy.

As Exhibit 17.1 illustrates, the planning affirmations literally touch on every aspect of the client philosophy. By organizing the planning affirmations around each section of the financial philosophy, the drafting process begins to take form.

Unlike the interview process, the questionnaire directly relates a client philosophy to specific planning issues. This allows an advisor to draw direct conclusions that characterize a client's financial philosophy.

Although the questions intentionally have been designed in a manner that does not lead a client to a specific conclusion, each question forces a client to choose. Each choice provides the advisor with additional information that is essential to effective planning. Consider this age-old question regarding the division of estate assets among heirs.

What is your opinion about leaving each child the same amount of inheritance? *Check the answer that most closely reflects your view.*

☐ Regardless of his or her individual circumstances or needs, each child should receive an equal share of my estate.

☐ Because of his or her unique circumstances or needs, each child should receive a different share of my estate.

This is one area where clients confront significant emotional barriers to effective decision making. Although issues such as this may be discussed, they rarely are resolved to anyone's satisfaction. The questionnaire facilitates planning by helping clients address and resolve difficult issues. Once resolved, each issue becomes a building block that supports final plan development and implementation. Consider the following sample mission statement paragraph:

> "We have always provided our children with equal access to opportunity, and have confidence in all of our children. We feel fortunate to have progeny with above-average intelligence who are "streetwise" and mature about financial planning. However, we recognize that our children have differing qualifications and interests in creating wealth and that those variations in careers and interests are producing markedly different financial results. Therefore, we would like to develop a plan that provides sufficient flexibility to treat our heirs individually. At the same time, we intend to supplement their future inheritance with lifetime

transfers in accordance with our assessment of their unique situation and needs."

Once incorporated into the written financial philosophy, statements such as this serve as a guide for current and future planning decisions. Of equal importance, they provide the necessary infrastructure for clients to reinforce past, current, and future planning decisions.

17.4 INCORPORATING THE LEGACY GOAL PROFILE

Whereas the legacy questionnaire covers general issues related to financial independence, family legacy, and social capital legacy, the goal profile is a tool for developing specific definitions for each. In practice, few clients can define these three essential planning goals. This provides a significant opportunity for advisors to add value by helping clients wade through the myriad of issues involved. This is the fundamental objective of the legacy goal profile phase of planning.

The legacy goal profile often contributes the most instructive content with which to work when setting the boundaries of the Family Financial Philosophy. Each goal is defined in specific financial terms. Each goal, in turn, establishes a baseline parameter that ultimately governs the direction of future planning. As a client's financial philosophy is prepared, these financial parameters evolve into boundaries that force the planning process to stay within the client's comfort range. Consider the following sample paragraphs.

> "Our present assets and income exceed that which is presently required to maintain financial independence. We intend to have more than sufficient capital to withstand any future unexpected financial or medical disruptions, such as inflation, higher taxes, or long-term sickness and nursing home care. Although we might adjust our lifestyle if assets allow, we do not anticipate a significant change in our spending habits. At this time, we feel comfortable with $150,000 of annual after-tax income and $2 million of liquid assets or marketable securities to address unexpected contingencies.
>
> We would like to see our income grow by 3 percent each year in order to adjust for the impact of inflation. Assuming a 30-year life expectancy and a 5 percent after-tax investment, $3,452,291 of cash resources is required to sustain our income objective. Combined with our $2 million contingency reserve, our definition of financial independence is $5,452,291."

Paragraphs such as these provide an effective guide to advisors as they review and select appropriate strategies for a particular client. They also provide a client with an effective means for evaluating the results of the overall plan. The ultimate objective is to define with absolute clarity the financial boundaries within which a client's advisors must operate.

17.5 INCORPORATING THE LEGACY BLUEPRINT

The legacy blueprint portrays the actual results under a client's current plan. It establishes a base in reality by which a client can guide his or her planning decisions. In preparing the Family Financial Philosophy, the legacy blueprint often is incorporated as a means of contrasting current results with desired outcomes. Consider the following paragraph.

> "Under the present circumstances, we realize that approximately 50 percent of our $14,875,000 in net assets will be lost to estate tax, leaving some $7.5 million of our total estate for our children to share. Although we are not happy to see our estate reduced by tax to this extent, we feel that a family legacy in the range of $7.5 million will be adequate to provide our children with a sufficient financial supplement to achieve their highest goals, dreams, and desires."

In this brief paragraph, the results of the current plan provide a natural opportunity for a client to frame planning decisions in a reality-based context.

17.6 SAMPLE FFP MISSION STATEMENT

The following sections contain excerpts from a sample Family Financial Philosophy. The excerpts are representative of the paragraph sections that would normally be included in a client's FFP. In addition, each sample excerpt is preceded by a general question that describes its primary purpose. These questions help advisors initiate the drafting process for each section of the FFP. The sample paragraphs illustrate what a finished mission statement for a married couple might look like. The section headings represent typical sections of a mission statement.

(a) Purpose

Question: Why have we prepared this mission statement?
This section tells the reader why the mission statement was written. A typical paragraph might read as follows:

> "This document expresses our values and intentions regarding the accumulation, preservation, use, and distribution of our estate. We wish for it to serve as a basis of planning for our professional

advisors. Furthermore, it will articulate clearly to our heirs and others with whom we share it why we have managed and distributed our estate in the manner we have chosen."

(b) Legacy Biography

Question: What past life experiences have helped shape our unique financial philosophy?

This section provides the reader with a unique view of the past, establishing the foundation for the philosophical and financial positions represented in the Family Financial Philosophy.

> "I still remember the first bank account I opened. My father spent countless hours explaining the benefits of savings and how interest would accumulate. When I received the first interest payment, it was like magic. Before long, I had purchased my first share of stock and the rest is history. I have always appreciated the value of saving a dollar."

(c) Sources of Wealth

Question: How did we accumulate our wealth?

This section provides the reader with insight regarding how wealth was accumulated. Typical paragraphs in this section might read something like this:

> "We accumulated our wealth through efforts of personal initiative and hard work, coupled with successful investments. Although we have enjoyed a comfortable lifestyle, we also have been careful to maintain spending at a level well within our means.
>
> We have been diligent in preserving our wealth through sound investment diversification. We have paid our fair share of taxes over the years but also have sought to enhance asset growth and minimize taxes through the ongoing use of legitimate strategies such as qualified retirement plans and tax-exempt bonds."

(d) Responsibilities and Obligations

Question: To whom do we feel a sense of responsibility or obligation regarding the distribution of our wealth?

This section provides the reader with insight regarding the sense of responsibility and/or obligation clients feel with respect to the distribution of wealth. Typical paragraphs in this section might read thus:

"Our first responsibility is to each other—to secure our own financial independence for life and preserve our ability to maintain our desired lifestyle.

Our second responsibility is to our daughters. We have provided them with the best education possible and will continue to nurture their development as financially responsible and mature adults. While we are alive, we will look for opportunities to sustain their knowledge and ability regarding fiscal stewardship.

Our third responsibility is to our community for contributing to our ability to grow and maintain a thriving business. We are also thankful for the rich environment our community provided for raising our children.

Our fourth responsibility is to respect the intrinsic value and memory of our ancestors, our heritage, and our past. Although we inherited little in material assets from our parents, we are indebted to them for the grounding they provided us in the form of positive values, sound ethics, and the worth of personal initiative and hard work, and for their efforts to instill in us a strong sense of self-worth. All of these attributes are more valuable to us than money."

(e) Motivation for Planning

Question: Why are we planning our estate?

This section provides the reader with specific information regarding the primary motivation for planning the estate. What is the number one goal clients are trying to accomplish? A typical paragraph in this section might read as follows:

"Our primary motivation for planning our estate is to reduce tax. It is our objective that any tax savings generated first will be utilized to secure our intended family legacy of $2 million and then will be directed to our designated charitable beneficiaries."

(f) Financial Philosophy

Question: What meaning does money have for us?

This section provides the reader with general information regarding the client's philosophy of wealth. What is important to the clients about money? Typical paragraphs might read like this:

"Up to this point, our wealth has been concentrated in a closely held business. This has greatly simplified the need to venture into other investment areas. However, as we intend to sell the business in the near future, investment management will be a primary concern. We intend to preserve our wealth through sound investment diversification, with an emphasis on long-term growth and professional management.

We have paid our share of taxes over the years, but we have also sought to enhance the growth of our assets through the ongoing use of legitimate tax-saving strategies. With the impending sale of our business, we intend to explore suitable options for limiting the adverse impact of taxes.

We have enjoyed a comfortable lifestyle and plan to continue to enjoy the fruits of our labor. However, we have always been careful not to live beyond our means.

Among those qualities we value most are honesty and integrity, responsibility for actions, respect for others, and spirituality. Among those relationships we value most are family, friendships, and business associates. Among those activities we value most are personal initiative and hard work, personal achievement, education, community involvement, recreation and leisure, and volunteerism."

(g) Financial Independence

Question: What do we need from our money to maintain our financial independence?

Financial independence is at the heart of all financial decisions. This section of the FFP provides the reader with specific information regarding the client's definition of financial independence, and whether or not clients have adequate planning resources. It is important to be specific in this section in order for the mission statement to be meaningful in developing the estate plan. Typical paragraphs might read as follows:

"Our present assets and income exceed that which is required to maintain financial independence. We intend to take full advantage of our wealth, enjoying the finer experiences in life.

At this time, we feel comfortable with $100,000 of annual after-tax income increasing at 3 percent each year. This adjustment will help offset the impact of inflation. In addition, we would like to maintain a cushion of $1 million in case unexpected needs should arise. At the present time, this translates into approximately $2 million of assets. Taking into consideration current available resources of $4 million, we are presently 200 percent financially independent. In other words, available assets are twice that which is required to maintain our lifestyle."

(h) Family Legacy

Question: If we could leave our heirs any amount of wealth, how much would we leave them and why?

A specific family legacy goal is essential to developing an effective estate plan. This section of the mission statement provides the reader with specific information regarding the definition of an appropriate inheritance for each heir. The amounts must be specific in order for the mission statement to play a significant role in the development of the estate plan. Either a percentage of estate assets or a specific dollar amount is appropriate. Typical paragraphs in this section might read thus:

> "We feel a responsibility to conserve assets for heirs in order to ensure that our intended family legacy is achieved. Furthermore, we are willing to commit both cash-flow and assets for the purpose of accomplishing this objective.
>
> We believe each child should receive an equal share of the estate, regardless of individual circumstances or needs. We would like to transfer some assets today but prefer to transfer the majority of our children's inheritance through our estate. Rather than transfer assets to our grandchildren directly, we prefer to transfer assets to our children. They can then determine if it is appropriate to pass a portion along to our grandchildren.
>
> Under the present circumstances, we realize that approximately 40 percent of our $4 million in net assets will be lost to estate tax, leaving some 60 percent of our total estate for our daughters. Although we are not happy to see our estate reduced by tax to this extent, we are confident that a family legacy in the 50 percent range will be adequate to provide our daughters with a sufficient financial supplement to achieve their highest goals, dreams, and desires. At the present time, we feel a family legacy of $1 million for each child would be sufficient for this purpose."

(i) Social Capital Legacy

Question: If we choose to control our social capital, to what organization(s) will we contribute? Why?

This section informs the reader whether clients choose to direct their social capital personally or will allow the government to do it for them. It also specifies what they are willing to do to convert tax into gifts. Finally, it clearly indicates the organizations and causes they would like to benefit through their estate plan. Specific percentages or dollar amounts are essential. Typical paragraphs in this section might be read as follows:

"It is our objective to reduce taxes in favor of charitable gifts where possible, as long as these gifts do not interfere with our ability to maintain our financial independence or provide our desired family legacy (i.e., $2 million total family legacy).

We feel it is important to do our fair share by paying reasonable taxes and have always paid significant personal and corporate income taxes in the past. At this point, we would rather direct money to charity than pay taxes.

We feel good about our philanthropic history. However, thus far in our lives charitable giving and personal involvement with charitable organizations have played limited roles. Now that we have retired and have a satisfactory financial cushion, it is our intent that charity will play a larger role.

To the extent charitable gift strategies can be used to maintain or enhance our financial independence and not interfere with our desired family legacy, we would like to begin the process of philanthropy during our lifetime. In particular, we are interested in charitable strategies that will enhance our annual income and reduce the burden of tax.

Regarding our philanthropy, we prefer to make gifts with a specific purpose in mind and to hold the charitable recipients accountable for fulfilling those objectives. We prefer to contribute to well-established charitable organizations that can demonstrate an ability to effectively use our gifts.

We prefer to be directly involved with the charities we support financially and would like to be directly involved with the work of exploring and/or analyzing problems and shaping promising solutions with our philanthropy. We enjoy being recognized for our philanthropy in order to encourage others to follow our lead.

At this time, we are interested in three areas of philanthropy: health care, education, and our community. At the present time, we have identified three charitable organizations toward which we would like to direct our philanthropy. Although this list presently makes good sense, we wish to reserve the right to adjust our plans, should our feelings change in the future."

The following list is expressed in order of priority:

Our top priority is Anytown Hospital. We intend to direct 50 percent of our self-directed social capital to this organization. This gift is made in recognition of the life-saving treatment Anytown Hospital provided for our daughter Sarah.

The second organization is XYZ University Foundation. We intend to direct 35 percent of our self-directed social capital to this organization.

This gift is made in recognition of the education afforded us by this wonderful institution. The quality of this experience has had a positive impact on our lives and contributed to the lifestyle we have attained. Education is among the pursuits we value most highly.

The third organization is Our Town Fine Arts Museum. We intend to direct 15 percent of our self-directed social capital to this organization. This gift is made in appreciation of the contribution this organization made in teaching our children to appreciate the arts.

(j) Acknowledgment

Question: Can our advisors, heirs, and others with whom we choose to share this document rely on it as a fair representation of our values and opinions regarding wealth?

It is necessary for clients to sign and date the mission statement, as assurance that professional advisors may rely on the document as an accurate reflection of clients' values, opinions, and objectives. The advisor who assists the client in developing the mission statement should also sign the mission statement. A typical paragraph would read as follows:

> "This document accurately reflects our desires and intentions with respect to the management and distribution of our estate. Our advisors shall rely on this document in the preparation and development of a plan that will fulfill our stated mission."

17.7 A BRIEF REVIEW

The Family Financial Philosophy represents a synopsis of the information gathered through the discovery process. The legacy interview, questionnaire, goal profile, and current blueprint each constitute a unique portion of a client's philosophical puzzle. With the puzzle complete, clients can move forward with confidence as they develop a wealth design plan that accomplishes their financial objectives, represents their values, and tells their story.

CHAPTER EIGHTEEN

Completing the Legacy Positive Focus

Now it is time to identify specific consistencies and inconsistencies between the client's current estate plan and the Family Financial Philosophy mission statement. This essential step leads directly to the selection of specific strategies for a client.

18.1 UNDERSTANDING THE CONCEPT

The Legacy Positive Focus provides the foundation for future planning decisions by specifically identifying the gaps between the client's current plan and the goals established in the Family Financial Philosophy. An advisor begins the process by noting the areas where the current plan is consistent with the financial philosophy. This builds client confidence with respect to future decisions by reinforcing the value of past planning efforts.

The Legacy Positive Focus Table has five columns (see Exhibit 18.1). The first lists the goal as iterated in the mission statement. In some cases, an advisor may need to paraphrase the statement; however, it is important that clients can identify the written mission statement as the source of the objective.

The second column, headed Progress Achieved, indicates what progress has been made toward that objective thus far. Here the advisor should focus on any positive steps that have been taken to achieve the objective.

The third column, Further Progress, explains what must be done in order to bring the current plan into alignment with the objective stated in the client's Family Financial Philosophy. This is where the advisor identifies the issues that must be addressed through planning.

Objective	Progress Achieved	Further Progress	Specific Action	Team Member/ Due Date

Exhibit 18.1   The Legacy Positive Focus Table Organization

Under the fourth heading, Specific Action, a client's advisors indicate the specific strategy or strategies that may be utilized to convert inconsistencies into consistencies. This column establishes a task list that the client's planning team will address.

The final column, headed Team Member/Due Date, identifies the team member who is responsible for initiating the strategy and the target date for completion.

It should be noted that the advisor who helped the client develop the Family Financial Philosophy appropriately completes the first three columns. On the other hand, the client's entire virtual planning team typically completes the last two columns. This is essential in order to eliminate bias and to develop a well-balanced plan.

18.2 EMPHASIZE THE POSITIVE

Most advisors make observations with regard to the deficiencies of a particular client's plan. Where do these observations come from? In many cases, they are the result of an advisor's past experiences.

In some cases, the list of observations is referred to as a *sweat track.* Sweat tracks are designed to make a client anxious. Supposedly, anxiety creates fear and fear creates action. Unfortunately, in many cases, fear leads to paralysis rather than action. When advisors emphasize only the negative aspects of planning, the obstacles may seem insurmountable to the client.

Human nature compounds this problem in the mind of the client. By focusing on negatives, the advisor is telling the client that past planning efforts have yielded insufficient results. This may backfire and lead the client to draw the same conclusion with regard to current planning efforts. If nothing positive is going to come from it, then why bother?

The Legacy Planning System is built upon a fundamental tenet of relationship marketing—always emphasize the positive. Advisors should begin by reinforcing the benefit of past planning efforts. There will be plenty of time to illustrate the value of an advisor's service in overcoming plan deficiencies once the client has the stomach to digest any bad news.

18.3 EXTRACT KEY OBJECTIVES FROM THE FAMILY FINANCIAL PHILOSOPHY

In developing the positive focus table, advisors should begin with the client's written Family Financial Philosophy. Reviewing the FFP, the advisor should identify key paragraphs that contain specific action items. At this point, the advisor is looking for information that is specific in nature and can be stated as an objective. Consider the following paragraph:

> "Our present assets and income exceed that which is presently required to maintain financial independence. We intend to have more than sufficient capital to withstand any future unexpected financial or medical disruptions, such as inflation, higher taxes, or long-term sickness and nursing home care. Although we might adjust our lifestyle if assets allow, we do not anticipate a significant change in our spending habits. *At this time, we feel comfortable with $150,000 of annual after-tax income and $2 million of liquid assets or marketable securities to address unexpected contingencies.*"

Although the entire paragraph contains valuable information, the emphasized portion offers specific information upon which advisors can act. Exhibit 18.2 illustrates how this information would be entered in a client's positive focus table.

Objective	Progress Achieved	Further Progress	Specific Action	Team Member/ Due Date
At this time, we feel comfortable with $150,000 of annual after-tax income and $2 million of liquid assets or marketable securities to address unexpected contingencies.	Our present annual after-tax income is $200,000, and we have $4 million of marketable securities.	Our current portfolio of marketable securities is not sufficiently diversified and is trapped by the threat of a substantial capital gain tax if sold. We would like to increase diversification, reduce our market exposure, and minimize the capital gain tax.		

Exhibit 18.2   Sample Entry in The Legacy Positive Focus Table

18.4 TRACING INCONSISTENCIES TO THEIR ROOTS

It is important to trace each inconsistency to its root in the Family Financial Philosophy. This begins with the paragraph in the mission statement and leads to the method or methods of discovery used to uncover the inconsistency. Having a clear understanding of the genesis of the inconsistency will instill confidence in the client, assuring him or her that every step in the planning process has been valuable and has produced results.

The entry made in Exhibit 18.2 easily can be traced to the legacy questionnaire as well as the legacy goal profile. In fact, the statement can be traced directly to the client's response to the following question on the legacy questionnaire.

In order to ensure lifetime financial independence for you (and your spouse, if applicable), please indicate your best estimate of the income and assets you will need, expressed in today's dollars:

Annual after-tax income of $_____, increasing at an annual inflation rate of _____%;

Plus $_____ in additional assets not needed to provide for annual after-tax income.

18.5 REVIEW THE CURRENT LEGACY BLUEPRINT AGAINST KEY OBJECTIVES

Having filled in The Legacy Positive Focus with objectives derived from a client's financial philosophy, advisors should next review the current legacy blueprint for consistencies and inconsistencies. Advisors should remember to start with the positives. For each objective, establish what progress has been achieved thus far. In some cases, this may be none. Yet the mere identification of the objective marks a certain level of progress in and of itself. In such a case, the entry might read, "We have established a specific definition of financial independence."

Now it is time to identify further progress required. This is where inconsistencies begin to develop. Advisors should note, however, that even the inconsistencies should be portrayed in a positive light. The very term *further progress* indicates that some measure of progress already has been achieved.

Reviewing each stated objective, advisors should look for consistencies and inconsistencies with a client's mission statement. Each time an inconsistency is identified, the advisor should make an entry in the corresponding row of the positive focus table that indicates what progress is required to bring the mission statement and plan into alignment. Each time a consistency is identified, the advisor should indicate that no further action is required.

18.6 SUBSTANTIATION

When The Legacy Positive Focus has been completed, it should be carefully reviewed with the client for accuracy. Where appropriate, the advisor should trace the objective to its root in the discovery process. Each line in the table should be substantiated by the client and initialed for accuracy. This is absolutely essential because each entry under *Further Progress* generates the need for strategies that eliminate the inconsistencies between the current plan and financial philosophy. This leads directly to strategy selection, plan design, construction, and execution.

CHAPTER NINETEEN

Plan Design, Construction, and Execution

Chapter 1 advanced the premise that estate planning consists of three steps:

1. Establishing objectives
2. Designing a plan to fulfill the objectives
3. Implementing the plan

Thus far, this book has focused solely on step one, establishing objectives. The creation of The Legacy Positive Focus (see Chapter 18) completes that phase of planning. This chapter touches briefly on steps two and three. A detailed explanation of plan design and implementation is beyond the scope and purpose of this book. Therefore, these pages will summarize one path for maximizing the value of clear objectives, developed in association with David Holaday of The Wealth Design Center, Inc.

19.1 THE LEGACY POSITIVE FOCUS

The first stage of planning focuses on developing clear, concise objectives. In the Legacy Planning System, objectives ultimately are portrayed in The Legacy Positive Focus. The wealth design process begins by emphasizing the attributes of the client's current plan that already are consistent with the Family Financial Philosophy. Then each inconsistency is resolved with an appropriate strategy.

19.2 PLAN DESIGN

(a) Virtual Strategies Design Team

One fundamental objective of values-based planning is to eliminate advisor bias. The virtual planning process accomplishes this objective by applying the concept of unique ability. Review Chapter 9 for a complete explanation of unique ability and the virtual planning process.

The first step in plan design is to create a team of experts who possess the required unique abilities. Because team members generally are selected for their capacity to select and create effective strategies, this is referred to as a *virtual strategies design team*.

A multidisciplinary approach is required for developing a sophisticated wealth design plan. Complex cases will need experts in the fields of law, tax, investments, insurance, financial modeling, and charitable gift planning, to name a few. As a result, the most successful and effective strategy design teams combine several unique abilities for maximum effectiveness.

(b) Strategy Evaluation

The main goal of the strategies design team is to establish an appropriate array of strategies to resolve a client's legacy plan inconsistencies. The team recommends each appropriate strategy based on four criteria:

1. At a minimum, the strategy resolves one inconsistency.
2. The strategy is consistent with the client's strategy risk tolerance.
3. The strategy is consistent with the client's complexity threshold.
4. Sufficient benefit is derived from the strategy to justify the cost of implementation.

(c) Financial Tools

Many strategies require specific financial tools for effective implementation. Therefore, the second responsibility of the strategies design team is to identify and select appropriate financial tools for resolving inconsistencies.

(d) Assets to Fund the Tools

Many wealth design strategies are asset driven. Once strategies and tools have been identified, the next step is to identify appropriate assets for funding. For example, what assets should be transferred to the family partnership? What assets should be transferred to the charitable remainder trust? What assets are most suitable for current gifting to heirs?

(e) Strategy Illustrations

Once strategies have been selected and matched with appropriate funding, the next step is to illustrate the results of the individual strategies. To enhance communication, advisors should use a combination of graphs, text, and numbers.

(f) Cash-Flow and Asset Projections

Following the selection of specific strategies and the clear demonstration of their respective results, the strategies must then be combined into a comprehensive plan. The objective is to identify potential conflicts between strategies and take advantage of unexpected synergies. This is accomplished by developing detailed cash-flow and asset projections.

It is important to emphasize that integrated modeling such as this represents a snapshot of a specific point in time. To ensure that the plan remains effective, the model must be analyzed on a regular and systematic basis. Many clients and advisors agree that an annual evaluation makes sense.

19.3 ADVISOR REVIEW AND FINAL PLAN DESIGN

Once the planning team has developed the preliminary plan, the client's chosen advisors should review design elements in their respective areas of expertise as follows:

- A CPA reviews proposed income statements and balance sheet.
- A foundation board or designated nonprofit professional reviews social capital plans.
- An insurance agent reviews underwriting issues.
- A lawyer reviews the design and drafting checklist.
- A money manager or trust officer reviews the portfolio design.
- A pastor, rabbi, or spiritual mentor reviews family goals and values.

After all advisors have reviewed and signed off on strategies and planning issues in their respective fields of expertise, the final plan should be prepared. This final plan includes individual illustrations of each strategy, as well as integrated cash flows and asset projections.

19.4 PLAN CONSTRUCTION AND EXECUTION

(a) Virtual Implementation Team

With the final plan design complete, the next step is to assemble the virtual implementation team. Given the highly specialized nature of many strategies in circulation today, implementation can be more complex than design. In most cases, some or all of the professionals serving on the strategies design team also will play an appropriate role on the implementation team. On the other hand, additional licensed team members may be needed to implement specific strategies.

(b) Team Responsibilities

Once the implementation team has been selected, team members are assigned their specific responsibilities. In order to facilitate implementation of the wealth optimization plan, each project should have an assigned due date.

(c) Communication

Much like the process of building a house, plan construction and implementation does not always turn out as expected. Therefore constant communication is critical to effective plan implementation. This enables the team to adjust on the fly and adapt the plan design to account for unanticipated obstacles.

(d) Document Drafting and Execution

No less important than communication is to facilitate the drafting and execution of legal documents. Plan implementation requires the timely execution of all legal documents.

(e) Insurance Underwriting

When life insurance is used as a planning tool, a qualified life underwriter must be part of the team. Many advanced strategies rely on the availability of life insurance. Given the complex nature of life insurance underwriting and the variations in underwriting that can be achieved from one company to the next, this can be a tricky process. Therefore, determining the price and availability of insurance as early as possible is essential to effective wealth design and planning.

19.5 EDUCATION AND EVALUATION

An advisor's job is not done when the plan has been designed and implemented. Because the wealth design process is fluid, it requires constant education and evaluation to ensure long-term success. Some of the areas advisors should consider include the following.

(a) Tracking the Plan

In order for any wealth optimization plan to remain optimal, it must be tracked and monitored over time. Inevitably, changes in a client's financial position will alter the optimal relationship among various planning goals. At the same time, general issues such as changes in tax laws and regulations, as well as a client's health, must be monitored.

(b) Monitoring the Goal Status

The legacy goal profile establishes clear goals for financial independence, family legacy, and social capital legacy. In addition, a client's Family Financial Philosophy often establishes a variety of nonfinancial goals. Wealth optimization requires that these goals be monitored over time.

(c) Monitoring Investments and Insurance

Insurance and investment tools are often the engines that drive the strategies. As a result, it is essential that these financial tools be monitored over time to ensure the strategies remain on track.

(d) Managing Assets

Many strategies require the acquisition, sale, or monetization of a client's assets. Selling a closely held business, hedging a client's stock portfolio, or acquiring a new home all are examples of transactions that must be expertly managed.

(e) The Responsibility of Wealth

Along with great wealth comes great responsibility. With no one to focus it, money has an equal probability of producing good or bad results. Because most clients would prefer that family resources have a positive impact on succeeding generations, an effective wealth design plan should constantly reinforce the responsible use of wealth.

(f) Stewardship and Charity

For many families, the development of an effective wealth optimization plan introduces substantial charitable contributions for the first time. This new experience undoubtedly produces new challenges for clients to overcome. Advisors should be prepared to reinforce the importance of philanthropy and assist clients in maximizing the outcome for their family and the organizations they hold most dear.

(g) Youth Advisory Boards

Chapter 8 discussed the benefits of involving children and other heirs in the philanthropic process. The creation of a youth advisory board associated with a client family foundation, support foundation, or donor-advised fund is an excellent way to perpetuate this valuable experience.

19.6 A BRIEF REVIEW

Effective wealth design is built on a solid foundation of objectives. The Legacy Planning System is designed to facilitate that process by developing clear objectives through The Legacy Positive Focus.

In today's complex and changing planning environment, it is essential that advisors have a clearly established model for plan design and implementation. The process described in this chapter outlines an advanced approach to wealth optimization and design. In order to use The Legacy Planning System to its fullest advantage, advisors must have the ability to design, construct, execute, and monitor a plan to accomplish the goals and objectives articulated in the client's Family Financial Philosophy.

CHAPTER TWENTY

Summary and Conclusion

20.1 THE ETERNAL PLANNING PROCESS

Estate planning is more an art than a science. It is inherently unpredictable and filled with emotion. All too often, the dominant emotion is anxiety. Clients venture into a world of complexity outside their comfort zone and are required to make tough decisions, many of them irrevocable. More often than not, anxiety leads to paralysis—and the eternal planning process begins.

As planning paralysis sets in and clients procrastinate, advisors generally follow one of three avenues.

1. They quit and move to the next client.
2. They facilitate the procrastination, while collecting fees.
3. They push toward implementation with increasing vigor.

For obvious reasons, each alternative course of action offers its own unique set of problems. Values-based planning suggests a new approach to managing procrastination: *a planned retreat*. Rather than fight the symptoms, advisors take a step back and search for the source of client procrastination. What are the reasons behind the obstacles?

Although every client has his or her distinct reasons for procrastination, a number of common factors contribute to why so many are trapped in eternal planning.

- Difficulty of the topic: Death and taxes is a subject that many people prefer to avoid.
- Loss of control: For many clients, estate planning signifies a changing of the guard, where privacy is invaded and control shifts from one generation to another.
- Planning dilemmas: The estate planning process requires clients to choose among an array of outcomes, many of which are in direct opposition to one other.

- Complexity: Estate planning requires clients to step outside their area of expertise and rely on the advice and counsel of strangers.

- Too much jargon: Similar to doctors, estate planning professionals often use acronyms and jargon that might as well be a foreign language for clients.

- Separation from resources: Tax-effective wealth transfer requires the irrevocable separation of clients from their wealth, as soon as possible, and forever.

- Emotional barriers: Concepts such as charitable gift planning present clients with an emotional challenge in understanding the benefits.

- Advisor bias: Clients spend considerable time, energy, and money trying to ascertain and eliminate advisor bias.

- Ending the game: For many clients, the end to the process signifies the end of life.

Advisors play a significant role in perpetuating the eternal planning process. A number of common factors contribute to why advisors also find themselves trapped within this process.

- A propensity to make assumptions: In the course of planning, advisors make assumptions based on past experience that often prove incorrect.

- Preoccupation with strategies: Advisors overwhelm clients with technical strategies.

- Mistaking confusion as a need for more information: Thinking they need more detail to understand the strategies, advisors overwhelm clients with too much information.

- Advisor bias: Advisors face considerable bias as they encounter other advisors working with the same clients.

- Codependency: When advisors charge by the hour, they are at risk of becoming codependent on the eternal planning process.

- The economics of success: When compensation is limited to commissions, as it often is, the resulting forward push by advisors tends to produce an equal and opposing force by clients—inertia.

20.2 CONCEPTS AND TOOLS USED IN VALUES-BASED ESTATE PLANNING

Values-based estate planning is a step-by-step process that helps clients define and express their values and objectives regarding money. Well-conceived objectives that are a true reflection of a client's values will en-sure that plan design and implementation can occur with relative ease.

Everyone has values that govern their behavior and relationships in life. It makes sense to rely on clients' values regarding their financial re-sources to guide the decisions made in the planning process. But first clients must be comfortable with what their values are. Most plans begin with numbers and balance sheets. Values-based planning starts by identi-fying what is important to the client.

20.3 THE SEVEN PRINCIPLES OF VALUES-BASED PLANNING

The seven principles of values-based estate planning provide a frame-work for putting clients at the center of and in control of their planning. These seven principles, or planning rules, will lead to a successful and gratifying planning process.

(a) Principle #1: Understand the Hierarchy of Planning Objectives

A pyramid of planning objectives provides a logical and effective progres-sion for the planning process. The value that clients place on (1) financial independence, (2) family legacy, and (3) social capital legacy will lay the foundation for all their planning decisions.

(b) Principle #2: Master the Concept of Social Capital

The concept of social capital redefines wealth and its potential impact on society. Most simply, social capital is that part of an individual's wealth that will be distributed either as taxes or charitable gifts.

(c) Principle #3: Define the Family Financial Philosophy

Wills and trusts describe how estate assets will be distributed. A Family Financial Philosophy explains why. This written wealth mission state-ment expresses clients' values and goals as they relate to wealth and money.

(d) Principle #4: Quantify Financial Independence

The first step in the planning process requires clients to define and quan-tify precisely how much wealth they will need to achieve and maintain fi-nancial independence for the rest of their lives.

(e) Principle #5: Identify an Appropriate Family Legacy

Most people want to leave some part of their estate to family members or others who are important to them. Because passing "value without values" can be detrimental to heirs, it is important to examine issues related to inheritance and specify an appropriate amount for each heir.

(f) Principle #6: Maximize the Social Capital Legacy

Will the clients' social capital legacy be in the form of taxes or charitable gifts? They can choose! Decisions regarding the distribution of excess wealth become easier when they are values-driven.

(g) Principle #7: Build a Virtual Planning Team

The ideal estate planning team is multidisciplinary, with each advisor bringing a unique ability to the mix. Using the values and objectives expressed in the Family Financial Philosophy mission statement as a guide, the planning team works collaboratively to recommend the best possible plan.

20.4 THE LEGACY PLANNING SYSTEM

The Legacy Planning System provides a step-by-step approach to values-based planning. The system eliminates planning paralysis and maximizes the client's control over the process by initially focusing on the first four levels of planning.

1. Gathering data
2. Reviewing the current plan
3. Establishing goals and objectives
4. Developing observations

Within The Legacy Planning System these steps are called the discovery process. The discovery process establishes facts and clarifies ambiguities. To be most effective, this is where the planning process *must* begin—with discovery.

The discovery process is followed by substantiation, where the problems identified in the discovery process are substantiated. Each problem that is substantiated is then addressed with a specific strategy. Next, the strategies are combined into a plan. Finally, the plan is implemented.

The intensity decreases with each new step in the process. Each step builds on the previous step. The Legacy Planning System comprises the following five main components.

(a) Planning Triage

In the triage phase of planning, advisors first establish if the potential for a successful client relationship exists. The next step is to decide between tactical problem solving for immediate needs and an integrated, long-term strategic planning process. The final triage step is the development of a feasibility study that establishes the cost and benefit of planning.

(b) The Discovery Process

The discovery process identifies what is important to the client through the use of four primary discovery methods.

1. The *legacy interview* probes clients' past and present for important events that have helped shape their unique financial philosophy. It then focuses on identifying clients' greatest goals, dreams, and desires. The legacy interview is documented with a legacy biography summarizing key paragraphs and quotes that support the client philosophy.

2. The *legacy questionnaire* provides clients with an opportunity to consider their attitudes, preferences, and philosophy with respect to 39 value areas. The questionnaire process is documented with a list of planning affirmations that represent the individual's or couple's viewpoints in each area.

3. The *legacy goal profile* establishes the three key financial goals found in the pyramid of planning objectives. Through the profile, the financial independence goal, family legacy goal, and social capital legacy goal are established and documented in specific numerical terms.

4. The *legacy blueprint* establishes the results under the client's current estate plan. Following a complete review, the blueprint documents the results of the current plan by clearly establishing financial independence status, family legacy status, and social capital legacy status in specific numerical terms.

(c) The Mission Statement

To help clients maximize the benefits of planning, advisors should begin with the development of a written mission statement that articulates the clients' Family Financial Philosophy. This document expresses clients' core beliefs and values regarding the accumulation, preservation, use, and distribution of wealth. It clearly identifies the appropriate allocation of financial resources among heirs, tax, and charitable gifts, establishes an appropriate level of complexity, and identifies suitable planning strategies.

When planning decisions are based on the objectives set forth in the mission statement, planning strategies will become readily apparent, and clients' estate plans will be fully congruent with their value systems.

(d) Acknowledgment of Existing Consistencies and Inconsistencies

The Legacy Positive Focus is a simple table that identifies and acknowledges each consistency and inconsistency that exists between the written Family Financial Philosophy and the current legacy blueprint. Focusing on the positive, the table quickly establishes progress made thus far and identifies future progress required to bring the client's current plan into alignment with the Family Financial Philosophy mission statement.

(e) Plan Design, Construction, and Execution

Once The Legacy Positive Focus table has been prepared, strategies are selected to address each inconsistency. When appropriate strategies have been determined, they are assembled into a plan that puts everything into focus based on today's goals. Finally, the plan is constructed and executed in accordance with the client's Family Financial Philosophy.

20.5 THE FAMILY FINANCIAL PHILOSOPHY

Clients and advisors who have applied The Legacy Planning System are embracing the Family Financial Philosophy as a unifying tool for the estate planning and wealth management process. Consider these important reasons. The Family Financial Philosophy:

- Provides a context within which clients, their heirs, and professional advisors can better understand clients' deepest values, beliefs, motivations, and goals regarding their wealth
- Stimulates clients to identify and examine the people and entities they hold in the highest esteem, leading to wealth transfer decisions that make sense to them
- Tells heirs why clients have distributed their estate the way they have chosen
- Articulates the client's values to heirs and others
- Prescribes whether the government controls the client's social capital legacy, directing how the wealth will be used, or the client controls it, choosing to direct social capital dollars toward charitable organizations

- Allows clients to remain in full control of the planning process. Through the written mission statement, the client's values, goals, dreams, needs, and desires unmistakably govern the planning process
- Clearly states the client's definition of financial independence, family legacy, and social capital legacy, and expresses objectives within the context of the client's innermost values and beliefs regarding wealth
- Articulates the appropriate allocation of financial resources to each of the three pyramid planning levels—financial independence, family legacy, and social capital legacy
- Streamlines the planning process, leading to effective and timely implementation
- Shapes the balance between self-directed and government-directed social capital
- Eliminates potential biases of professional advisors by explicitly stating the client's values, needs, and objectives, avoiding reliance on commonly assumed objectives
- Provides a context within which to consider the client's social capital potential
- Positions the client and all advisors to use social capital strategically to accomplish planning objectives
- Facilitates a transition from conventional estate planning to client-centered, values-based estate planning
- Establishes an appropriate allocation of wealth among the three beneficiaries of wealth: heirs, government-directed social capital, and self-directed social capital
- Increases congruity between the perception of wealth and the reality of wealth
- Establishes what the client requires to maintain financial independence
- Articulates the appropriate balance between ownership of estate assets and control over estate assets
- Defines an appropriate inheritance for heirs, giving clients peace of mind, and giving their professional advisors the freedom to focus on maintaining financial independence and gaining control over their social capital
- Identifies the congruity, or lack thereof, between clients' values regarding wealth and those of their heirs
- Informs advisors of the client's intentions, saving time and money as they explore appropriate strategies to help the client achieve his or her goals

- Creates the financial freedom to maximize the financial outcome of planning by incorporating both conventional and social capital planning strategies in the fulfillment of the client's clearly articulated goals and objectives

20.6 CONCLUSION

(a) Why Should Advisors Integrate Values-Based Planning into Their Practice?

Three distinct and compelling reasons can be cited:

1. *To build, reinforce, and protect important client relationships.* Values-based planning is a relationship-building process. By helping clients discover what is truly important to them, advisors deepen their relationships to unprecedented levels. The resulting relationship transcends traditional boundaries, and advisors become counselors.

2. *To generate better results for clients.* Values-based planning improves the quality of results. Well-conceived objectives that are a true reflection of a client's values ensure that strategy selection, plan design, and implementation can occur with relative ease and tremendous accuracy. As a result, client confidence increases and maximum results are achieved.

3. *To create a sustainable competitive market advantage.* Today, with the growing use of computer technology and a consumer market that is more savvy than ever before, many estate planning products and services are becoming commodities—easy to access, relatively commonplace, and possessing few distinguishing features. In fact, in many cases, price is the primary distinguishing factor in clients' decisions about who they will retain and what products they will purchase. This creates an increasing problem for advisors. Although it may be possible for advisors to stay ahead of the industry through continuous innovation, there is a more predictable way to combat this trend. Focus on relationship. An advisor's unique capacity to build and maintain lasting relationships is the key to maintaining a competitive advantage. Values-based planning helps advisors refine, package, and deliver their relationship capacity as a valuable service that will protect their market position for decades to come.

(b) Who Should Practice Values-Based Planning?

For the purpose of this book, the term *advisor* has referred to any professional who represents a client's interests above all else. An advisor's chosen profession, whether he or she is an attorney, CPA, trust officer, insurance agent, financial planner, fund-raiser, or investment broker, is irrelevant. What is relevant is the advisor's capacity to provide advice and counsel based entirely on its consistency with clearly articulated client objectives.

For a variety of reasons, advisors sometimes lack the necessary autonomy to meet the definition of *client advisor*. However, those who meet this definition, representing all professional backgrounds, have one thing in common—personal integrity. This is the single most important factor in determining an advisor's capacity to practice values-based planning.

(c) How to Get Started?

The quiz labeled Exhibit 20.1 is a good indicator of whether a client might benefit from values-based estate planning. Advisors who want to test the waters may be surprised at their clients' reaction to it.

Give this quiz to a valued client. If the client answers no to many of these questions and would like to be able to answer yes to them, The Legacy Planning System's values-based tools and methodology will help overcome planning obstacles and move the process forward.

Yes	No	I feel that I understand the estate planning process.
Yes	No	My estate plan accurately reflects my personal values.
Yes	No	My estate plan is based on clear, written objectives.
Yes	No	I have defined how much I (and my spouse, if applicable) will need in order to be assured of financial independence for the rest of my (our) life.
Yes	No	I have identified a specific and appropriate inheritance for my heirs.
Yes	No	I know how much estate tax will be due upon my death, both if my estate were settled today and if it were settled at my normal life expectancy.
Yes	No	I have used the estate planning process as a way to share my values with my heirs.
Yes	No	I understand the concept of social capital.
Yes	No	I have taken the necessary steps to capture and direct my social capital legacy in a way that is consistent with my personal values.
Yes	No	My professional advisors work as a team in developing appropriate strategies for me to consider.
Yes	No	I am confident that my heirs are prepared to manage their inheritance effectively.
Yes	No	I am satisfied with past experiences in making charitable gifts of time and money.

Exhibit 20.1 The Legacy Quiz

Values-based estate planning is fast becoming an industry standard—for good reason. This unique approach to wealth transfer and management puts the client at the center of and in control of the estate planning process. The result is an estate plan that is built around values, ensuring that the legacies clients leave behind are fully consistent with who they are, what they believe, and what is most important to them.

APPENDIX A

The Legacy Questionnaire

Most estate plans begin and end with numbers. The Legacy Planning System employs a unique values-based approach that begins with you and what is most important to you. As you answer the questions in this workbook, you will explore your beliefs, feelings and values about money and its relation to you, your heirs and society at large.

Completing the questionnaire is your first step in crafting a written wealth mission statement—an expression of your Family Financial Philosophy (FFP). Your FFP is the roadmap you and your advisors will rely on to ensure that all estate planning decisions are consistent with your financial values and objectives.

Please note that instructions vary from question to question. Some require you to check the one response that most closely reflects your view. Some ask you to rank the order of importance of your answers. Some ask you to check all the responses that apply. A few require you to fill in the blank. Every question has room for additional comments.

Try to complete the questionnaire at a time when you will not be distracted. Take time to consider your answers carefully, but don't spend too much time on any one question. Be sure to read all choices for each question, as some have very subtle differences. If a question doesn't apply to you, skip it and go on to the next.

Don't become frustrated if you are unable to answer a question or if you are not fully satisfied with your answers. Conflicts and insufficient information are expected outcomes of this process. The idea is to identify issues and concerns so that you can take the necessary steps to address them.

Keep in mind that the more detail and clarification you can provide, the better your FFP will serve as a planning tool. If you are comfortable doing so, use the space for comments to expand on your thoughts or provide additional information that will assist your advisors in developing your plan. The more specific you are, the more effective your ultimate estate plan will be.

When you have answered the questions to the best of your ability, please sign and date the last page. Ideally, couples should each complete a separate questionnaire. You should also sign and date your spouse's completed questionnaire, as an indication that you are aware of how he or she answered the questions.

Return your completed questionnaire to the advisor who gave it to you. He or she will then begin to work with you in the process of crafting your mission statement.

It is important to remember that the amount of time you invest in this process will directly affect its outcome. Trust that your efforts will be well-rewarded!

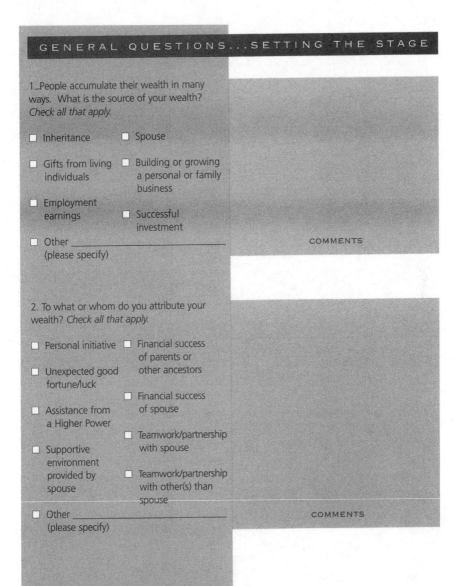

GENERAL QUESTIONS...SETTING THE STAGE

1. People accumulate their wealth in many ways. What is the source of your wealth? *Check all that apply.*

☐ Inheritance ☐ Spouse

☐ Gifts from living individuals ☐ Building or growing a personal or family business

☐ Employment earnings

☐ Successful investment

☐ Other _____ (please specify)

COMMENTS

2. To what or whom do you attribute your wealth? *Check all that apply.*

☐ Personal initiative ☐ Financial success of parents or other ancestors

☐ Unexpected good fortune/luck

☐ Financial success of spouse

☐ Assistance from a Higher Power

☐ Teamwork/partnership with spouse

☐ Supportive environment provided by spouse

☐ Teamwork/partnership with other(s) than spouse

☐ Other _____ (please specify)

COMMENTS

3. What personal values are of the greatest importance to you at this time in your life? *Check the 5 most important.*

☐ Ethical values, such as honesty, justice, fairness

☐ Personal values, such as modesty, loyalty, faithfulness

☐ Emotional values, such as compassion, kindness, generosity

☐ Public values, such as good citizenship, community involvement, government service

☐ Economic values, such as financial responsibility, frugality, stewardship

☐ Financial values, such as material possessions, independence, social standing

☐ Spiritual values, such as inner spirituality and meditation, faith, religious commitments

☐ Work values, such as effort, punctuality, competence, professional achievement

☐ Physical values, such as health, relaxation, quiet time alone, exercise

☐ Cultural values, such as music, visual arts, travel

☐ Relational values, such as family, friends, work associates

☐ Philanthropic values, such as contributions of time and money to care for others

☐ Recreational values, such as sports, leisure activity, hobbies, family vacations

☐ Educational values, such as study, self-improvement, academic achievement

☐ Other (please specify) _____
_____

COMMENTS

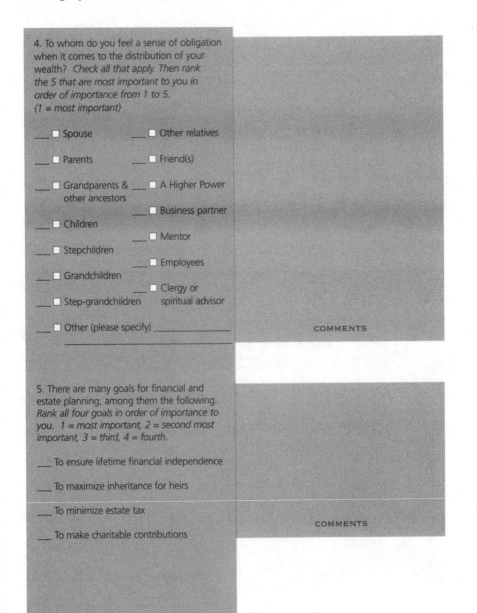

4. To whom do you feel a sense of obligation when it comes to the distribution of your wealth? *Check all that apply. Then rank the 5 that are most important to you in order of importance from 1 to 5. (1 = most important)*

____ ☐ Spouse   ____ ☐ Other relatives

____ ☐ Parents   ____ ☐ Friend(s)

____ ☐ Grandparents & ____ ☐ A Higher Power
       other ancestors
                       ____ ☐ Business partner
____ ☐ Children
                       ____ ☐ Mentor
____ ☐ Stepchildren
                       ____ ☐ Employees
____ ☐ Grandchildren
                       ____ ☐ Clergy or
____ ☐ Step-grandchildren   spiritual advisor

____ ☐ Other (please specify) _____

COMMENTS

5. There are many goals for financial and estate planning, among them the following. *Rank all four goals in order of importance to you. 1 = most important, 2 = second most important, 3 = third, 4 = fourth.*

____ To ensure lifetime financial independence

____ To maximize inheritance for heirs

____ To minimize estate tax

____ To make charitable contributions

COMMENTS

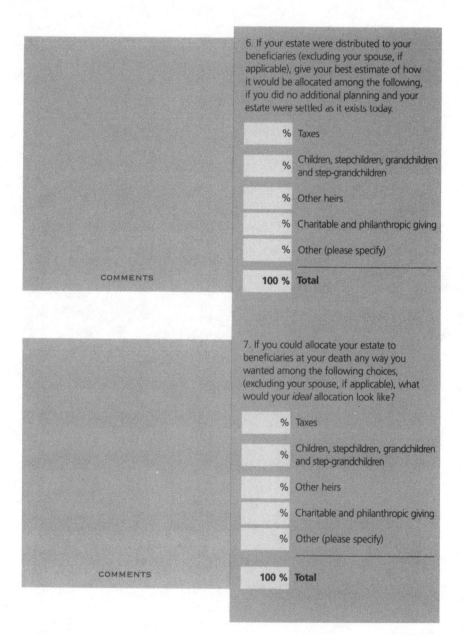

6. If your estate were distributed to your beneficiaries (excluding your spouse, if applicable), give your best estimate of how it would be allocated among the following, if you did no additional planning and your estate were settled as it exists today.

%	Taxes
%	Children, stepchildren, grandchildren and step-grandchildren
%	Other heirs
%	Charitable and philanthropic giving
%	Other (please specify)
100 %	Total

COMMENTS

7. If you could allocate your estate to beneficiaries at your death any way you wanted among the following choices, (excluding your spouse, if applicable), what would your *ideal* allocation look like?

%	Taxes
%	Children, stepchildren, grandchildren and step-grandchildren
%	Other heirs
%	Charitable and philanthropic giving
%	Other (please specify)
100 %	Total

COMMENTS

8. How likely are the following to influence you in the creation or revision of your current plan? *Rank all five choices in order of importance to you. (1 = most important; 5 = least important)*

Having better understanding about:

____ my current financial status.

____ the future needs of my family.

____ the tax benefits of giving to charitable or philanthropic organizations.

____ tax-effective estate planning options.

____ what I would like to accomplish with my financial resources.

COMMENTS

FINANCIAL INDEPENDENCE...HOW MUCH DO I NEED?

9. Which statement most closely reflects your definition of financial independence? *Check one box only.*

☐ I have no clear picture of whether I am financially independent.

☐ I am not yet financially independent.

☐ I am financially independent but have no excess wealth.

☐ My present assets and income exceed what I need for financial independence.

COMMENTS

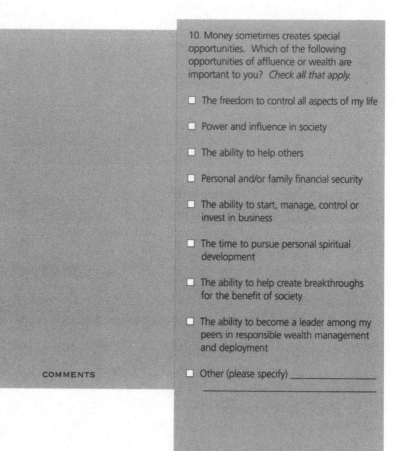

10. Money sometimes creates special opportunities. Which of the following opportunities of affluence or wealth are important to you? *Check all that apply.*

☐ The freedom to control all aspects of my life

☐ Power and influence in society

☐ The ability to help others

☐ Personal and/or family financial security

☐ The ability to start, manage, control or invest in business

☐ The time to pursue personal spiritual development

☐ The ability to help create breakthroughs for the benefit of society

☐ The ability to become a leader among my peers in responsible wealth management and deployment

☐ Other (please specify) _____

COMMENTS

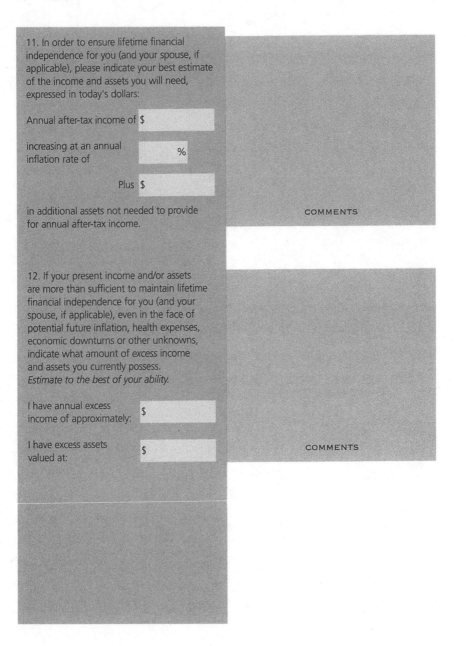

11. In order to ensure lifetime financial independence for you (and your spouse, if applicable), please indicate your best estimate of the income and assets you will need, expressed in today's dollars:

Annual after-tax income of $ _____

increasing at an annual inflation rate of _____ %

Plus $ _____

in additional assets not needed to provide for annual after-tax income.

COMMENTS

12. If your present income and/or assets are more than sufficient to maintain lifetime financial independence for you (and your spouse, if applicable), even in the face of potential future inflation, health expenses, economic downturns or other unknowns, indicate what amount of *excess* income and assets you currently possess. *Estimate to the best of your ability.*

I have annual excess income of approximately: $ _____

I have excess assets valued at: $ _____

COMMENTS

COMMENTS

13. Which statement most closely reflects your thoughts regarding your willingness to give up ownership or control of assets? *Check one main answer only, along with any applicable subcategory.*

☐ I am uncomfortable with any strategy that interferes with my direct ownership or interferes with my ability to spend income and principal.

☐ I am comfortable relinquishing ownership as long as I maintain control,

   ☐ *and* retain access to *all* income.

   ☐ *and* retain access to *sufficient* income to maintain my financial independence.

   ☐ *regardless* of access to income (i.e., I can continue to manage the assets).

☐ I have no concern about relinquishing ownership or control of assets.

FAMILY LEGACY...WHAT DO I WANT TO LEAVE MY HEIRS?

Your "family" may be traditional or non-traditional. Whatever your personal situation, please skip any questions that are not relevant to your particular family situation.

14. Which statement most closely reflects your view regarding your responsibility to conserve assets for heirs? *Check one main answer only, along with the applicable subcategory.*

☐ I feel no particular responsibility to conserve assets for heirs,

    ☐ *and* would prefer to spend my assets during my lifetime.

    ☐ *however*, I am satisfied to have whatever is left of my estate pass to heirs upon my death.

    ☐ *however*, there are certain amounts I would like to leave specific heirs.

    ☐ *nevertheless*, I intend to plan my estate in a manner that will maximize my heirs' inheritance.

☐ I *do* feel a responsibility to conserve assets for heirs and to plan my estate in a manner that will maximize their inheritance,

    ☐ *however*, I am not willing to commit current cash flow or assets for that purpose.

    ☐ *and*, I am willing to commit current cash flow or assets for that purpose.

COMMENTS

15. If there were no limit to the amount of wealth you could leave your heirs other than spouse, what is the sum total dollar amount you would leave to them?

COMMENTS

$

16. You may have developed a philosophy regarding financial stewardship that you may wish to impart to children and other heirs. *Check all of the following that are important to you.*

☐ Focus on long-term growth

☐ Ensuring proper investment diversification

☐ Adherence to asset allocation

☐ Minimizing the impact of taxes

☐ Limiting investment to things that I understand

☐ Avoiding deals that appear too good to be true

☐ Assessing and taking appropriate risk

☐ Living within one's means

☐ Being frugal

☐ Strategic debt management

☐ Freedom from debt

☐ Focus on investments in a closely held business

COMMENTS   ☐ Other (please specify) _____

_____

17. There are various perspectives regarding whether to discuss family financial resources with children or other heirs. *Check the statement that most closely reflects your view.*

☐ It is not appropriate to disclose family financial resources to children or other heirs.

☐ It is appropriate to disclose family financial resources to children or other heirs only after they have demonstrated a level of financial maturity and have reached the age of _____ . (please specify)

☐ It is appropriate to disclose family financial resources to children or other heirs only after they have demonstrated a level of financial maturity.

☐ It is appropriate to disclose family financial resources to children or other heirs, regardless of financial maturity and age.

COMMENTS

18. Regarding their specific potential inheritance, when is the best time to reveal your estate plan to children or other heirs? *Check the statement that most closely reflects your view.*

☐ Heirs should be informed of their potential inheritance only after they reach age _____ . (please specify)

☐ Heirs should be informed of their potential inheritance only after they reach age _____ (please specify) and have demonstrated a level of financial maturity.

☐ Heirs should be informed of their potential inheritance when they receive it and not before then.

COMMENTS

19. You may be concerned that your children lack the necessary skills to manage wealth. Which statement most closely reflects your view? *Check one main answer and any applicable subcategory.*

☐ I believe my children *do not* possess the necessary skills to manage wealth and,

    ☐ I *do not* feel a responsibility to prepare them to do so.

    ☐ I *do* feel a responsibility to prepare them to do so.

    ☐ I prefer to pass assets in trust, or by another means that assures professional management.

☐ I believe my children *do* possess the necessary skills to manage wealth,

    ☐ *but* I prefer to pass assets in trust, or by another means that assures professional management.

    ☐ *and* I feel comfortable they will manage their wealth effectively.

☐ I am unsure of the interest level, skills and ability my children have to manage wealth.

COMMENTS

20. How much inheritance should you leave your children? *Check the statement that most closely reflects your view.*

☐ Regardless of their children's individual needs, parents should leave children the maximum possible inheritance.

☐ Parents should leave a large enough inheritance so that their children could do anything they want, but would still have to be productive.

☐ Parents should leave children the minimum inheritance required to meet their children's individual lifestyle needs.

☐ Parents should not leave children an inheritance under any circumstances.

COMMENTS

21. What is your opinion about leaving each child the same amount of inheritance? *Check the answer that most closely reflects your view.*

☐ Regardless of his or her individual circumstances or needs, each child should receive an equal share of my estate.

☐ Based on his or her differing circumstances or needs, each child should receive a different share of my estate.

COMMENTS

22. What do you think about transferring assets to children and/or other heirs during your lifetime? *Check the answer that most closely reflects your view.*

☐ I prefer to transfer assets to my heirs as soon as possible.

☐ I prefer to transfer some assets today, but will wait to transfer the largest portion of my estate at my death.

☐ I prefer to transfer all assets at my death.

☐ I prefer to transfer all assets only at the death of both my spouse and me.

☐ Other (specify) _____
_____

COMMENTS

23. If applicable, how do you feel about transferring assets to your grandchildren? *Check the answer that most closely reflects your view.*

☐ I prefer to leave my estate to my children; they can then determine if it is appropriate to pass a portion of the assets along to my grandchildren.

☐ I am primarily concerned with providing for my children; however, if sufficient assets were available, I would consider leaving a portion of my estate directly to grandchildren.

☐ I would like to make assets available for both children and grandchildren, with the flexibility to respond to their varying needs.

☐ I would prefer to distribute the remainder of my estate to my grandchildren.

☐ I do not choose to transfer assets to grandchildren.

COMMENTS

24. There are numerous ways to transfer your family financial values to children and other heirs. *Check the three that are most important to you.*

I prefer to:

☐ Actively discuss the importance of specific financial values.

☐ Demonstrate values by how I lead my daily life.

☐ Establish a family mission statement.

☐ Involve children in charitable giving and volunteering.

☐ Establish or use an existing family foundation or other family charity.

☐ Become involved as a family in a spiritual community.

☐ Encourage children to work, in order to learn the meaning of money.

☐ Involve children in the family business.

☐ Hold regular family meetings.

☐ Use rites of passage and family celebrations.

COMMENTS

25. How does the transfer of family assets
to children also affect the wealth you seek
to preserve? *Check all of the statements
with which you agree.*

☐ If I give my children too large an inheritance,
   they are likely to lead less productive lives
   and may even suffer a loss of self-worth,
   as well as a lack of respect from others.

☐ I am concerned that if I leave a large
   inheritance to my children, they may spend
   it unwisely, or otherwise lose it through
   divorce, lawsuits or poor financial advice.

☐ I believe I should leave all my wealth
   to my children under their control.

☐ I believe my children must earn their
   own wealth, and that as a parent and
   the wealth holder, I should direct its use
   toward organizations that will perpetuate
   my values now and after my death.

☐ I am concerned that my children will be
   resentful of me for the rest of their lives
   if I do not leave them a large inheritance.

☐ Although I am aware that my children
   presently feel "entitled" to my wealth,
   I believe they will get over any
   disappointment if their inheritance
   fails to meet their expectation.

☐ I believe my children will develop more
   positive values if I do not leave them
   significant wealth.

☐ Unlike my own parents, who were unable
   or unwilling to leave me a significant
   inheritance, I want to give my children
   the advantage money provides.

COMMENTS

☐ Other (specify) _____

_____

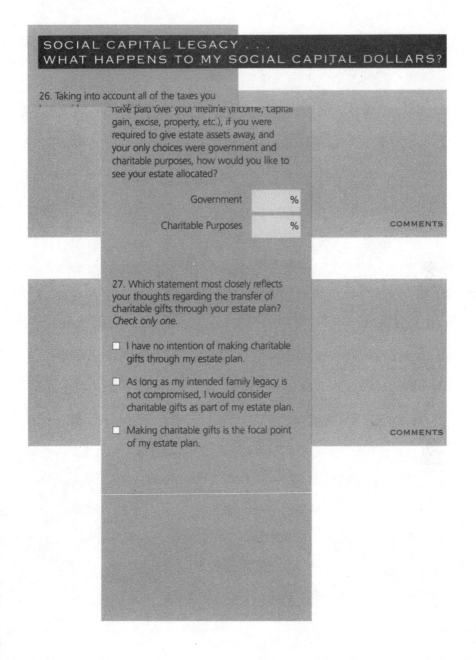

SOCIAL CAPITAL LEGACY . . .
WHAT HAPPENS TO MY SOCIAL CAPITAL DOLLARS?

26. Taking into account all of the taxes you have paid over your lifetime (income, capital gain, excise, property, etc.), if you were required to give estate assets away, and your only choices were government and charitable purposes, how would you like to see your estate allocated?

Government	%
Charitable Purposes	%

COMMENTS

27. Which statement most closely reflects your thoughts regarding the transfer of charitable gifts through your estate plan? *Check only one.*

☐ I have no intention of making charitable gifts through my estate plan.

☐ As long as my intended family legacy is not compromised, I would consider charitable gifts as part of my estate plan.

☐ Making charitable gifts is the focal point of my estate plan.

COMMENTS

28. Which one main statement and its subcategory most closely reflect your level of involvement with charitable organizations, including volunteer time and money?

☐ I have had little or no involvement with charitable organizations, and

    ☐ involvement is a low priority for me at this time.

    ☐ I would like to be involved, but simply don't have the time.

    ☐ I would consider becoming involved, if the "right" organization asked me.

    ☐ I would like to be more involved, but need help determining the best way and place to do so.

    ☐ I have definite plans to become involved or more involved.

☐ I have had moderate involvement with charitable organizations, and plan to

    ☐ maintain my current level of involvement.

    ☐ decrease my current level of involvement.

    ☐ increase my current level of involvement in the future.

☐ I have been active with charitable organizations, and

    ☐ plan to continue at my current level of involvement.

    ☐ plan to increase my level of involvement.

    ☐ feel I've done my part and plan to decrease or discontinue involvement.

COMMENTS

29. What do you think about transferring assets for charitable purposes during your lifetime? *Check the answer that most closely reflects your view.*

☐ I prefer to make charitable gifts during my lifetime, so that I can enjoy watching the impact of my philanthropy firsthand.

☐ As long as my financial independence and intended family legacy are not compromised, I would consider making charitable gifts during my lifetime.

☐ I prefer to make charitable gifts during my lifetime, as long as they enhance my financial and estate plans.

☐ I prefer to make charitable contributions through my estate plan, so that I do not give up control of my assets during my lifetime.

☐ I have no intention of making charitable contributions.

COMMENTS

30. On a scale of 0 to 10, how satisfied are you with the current effectiveness of your charitable gifts of money and time in improving the well-being of others?

Not at all   Extremely
satisfied   satisfied

0   1   2   3   4   5   6   7   8   9   10

Why or why not?

COMMENTS

COMMENTS

31. Which statement most closely reflects your view regarding the level of charitable contributions you make? *Check one main answer and any applicable subcategories.*

☐ I am comfortable with my current level of charitable contributions.

☐ I plan to decrease my current level of charitable contributions.

☐ I plan to increase my current level of charitable contributions.

☐ I am likely to increase the overall level of my charitable contributions if the following occurs: *Check all that apply.*

  ☐ My net worth increases.

  ☐ Tax incentives increase.

  ☐ I find more time to study and think strategically about my charitable giving.

  ☐ I find a new and worthy cause about which I feel especially passionate.

  ☐ I have a better understanding of the positive impact my current donations are making.

  ☐ I find out that I have more financial resources than I, or my family, will ever need.

32. Some families establish personal or family foundations through which they channel their charitable contributions. *Check the statement and any applicable subcategory that most closely reflects your view.*

☐ I am attracted to the idea of a personal or family foundation.

☐ I am interested in a personal or family foundation, but would prefer a less complicated alternative.

☐ I have already established a personal or family foundation and,

    ☐ so far, have been disappointed.

    ☐ have been satisfied, but feel there is room for improvement.

    ☐ have found the process compelling and rewarding.

COMMENTS

33. Which of the following statements reflect your view regarding the process of family or "shared" philanthropy? *Check all that apply.*

☐ Family or shared philanthropy does not fit with my charitable planning objectives.

☐ I want my family to be involved with me in my charitable activity.

☐ I want my children to work together in a single family foundation.

☐ I would like for my children to establish their own foundations.

☐ I would like my children to make decisions on their own regarding philanthropy.

☐ I believe philanthropy is better carried out individually or, at most, as a couple.

COMMENTS

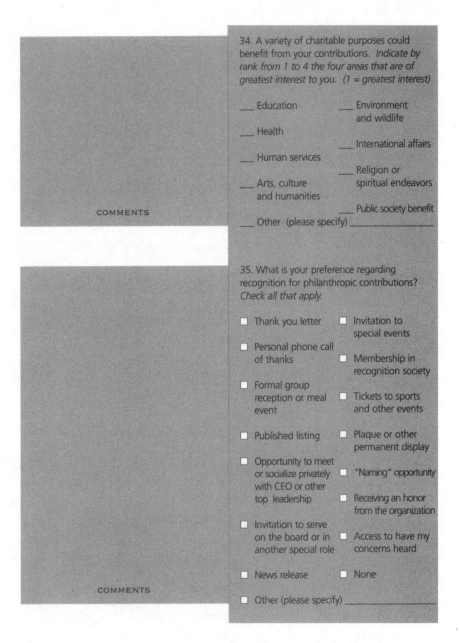

COMMENTS

34. A variety of charitable purposes could benefit from your contributions. *Indicate by rank from 1 to 4 the four areas that are of greatest interest to you. (1 = greatest interest)*

___ Education   ___ Environment and wildlife

___ Health

___ Human services   ___ International affairs

___ Arts, culture and humanities   ___ Religion or spiritual endeavors

___ Other (please specify) _____   ___ Public society benefit

35. What is your preference regarding recognition for philanthropic contributions? *Check all that apply.*

☐ Thank you letter   ☐ Invitation to special events

☐ Personal phone call of thanks   ☐ Membership in recognition society

☐ Formal group reception or meal event   ☐ Tickets to sports and other events

☐ Published listing   ☐ Plaque or other permanent display

☐ Opportunity to meet or socialize privately with CEO or other top leadership   ☐ "Naming" opportunity

☐ Receiving an honor from the organization

☐ Invitation to serve on the board or in another special role   ☐ Access to have my concerns heard

☐ News release   ☐ None

☐ Other (please specify) _____

COMMENTS

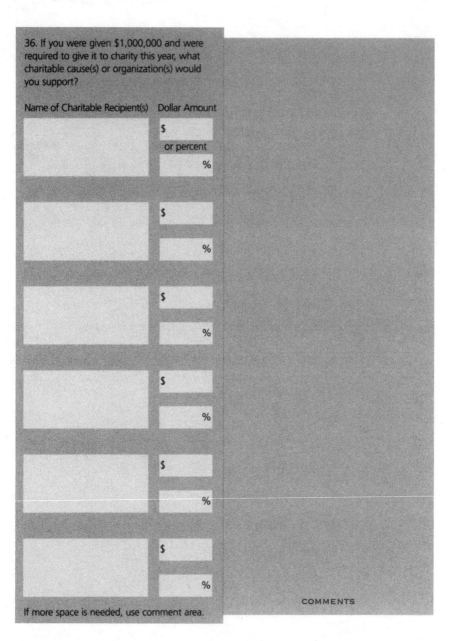

36. If you were given $1,000,000 and were required to give it to charity this year, what charitable cause(s) or organization(s) would you support?

Name of Charitable Recipient(s)	Dollar Amount
	$
	or percent
	%
	$
	%
	$
	%
	$
	%
	$
	%
	$
	%

If more space is needed, use comment area.

COMMENTS

IN CONCLUSION . . .

37. The Legacy Planning System results in
the creation of a written Family Financial
Philosophy (FFP). Once complete, how
would you envision using this document?
Check all that apply.

☐ I would want to use the FFP as a personal
guide for my/our estate planning decisions.

☐ I would want to share the FFP with
my children.

☐ I would want to share the FFP with heirs
other than my children.

☐ I would want to share the FFP with those
charitable causes and organizations that
I support.

☐ I would want to share the FFP with my
professional advisors.

COMMENTS

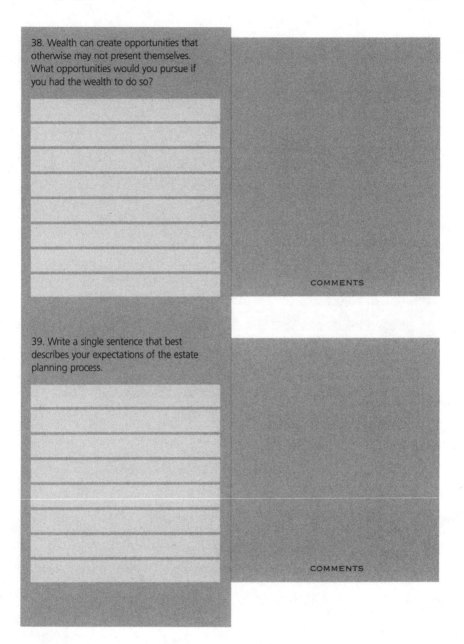

38. Wealth can create opportunities that otherwise may not present themselves. What opportunities would you pursue if you had the wealth to do so?

COMMENTS

39. Write a single sentence that best describes your expectations of the estate planning process.

COMMENTS

ADDITIONAL THOUGHTS AND COMMENTS

Your signature indicates that you are comfortable with the answers you have provided in this questionnaire and that (if applicable) you are aware of the manner in which your spouse answered the questions on a separate form. Your answers will provide the foundation for creating your personal Family Financial Philosophy.

Please print and sign your name(s).

#1

Print Your Name

Signature

Date

#2

Print Your Name

Signature

Date

APPENDIX B

The Legacy Interview Guide

The most effective interview process combines the use of questionnaires and face-to-face interviews. From these two information sources, the planning advisor elicits patterns and themes with respect to individual or family history, values and beliefs. This guide is designed to help the advisor plan and conduct the personal interview.

THE PERSONAL INTERVIEW

The personal interview is an integral part of The Legacy Planning System™. It follows the compilation of answers to The Legacy Questionnaire™ and expands further on the client's biography in preparation for writing the initial draft of the client's Family Financial Philosophy mission statement.

By asking thought-provoking questions, you will help your clients clarify values, as well as resolve any conflicts or differences that may exist between spouses. It is recommended that you audio tape the interview. Such a tape not only will guarantee the preservation of your clients' exact words, but also will ensure that all relevant information is captured, along with the emotion associated with the responses.

The following lists of question topics will guide you in helping your clients identify and express their personal life experiences and value systems, and then further relate these to their convictions and objectives regarding their wealth.

Check L M or H to indicate whether your client shows a Low, Medium or High level of interest or emotion with respect to the topic.

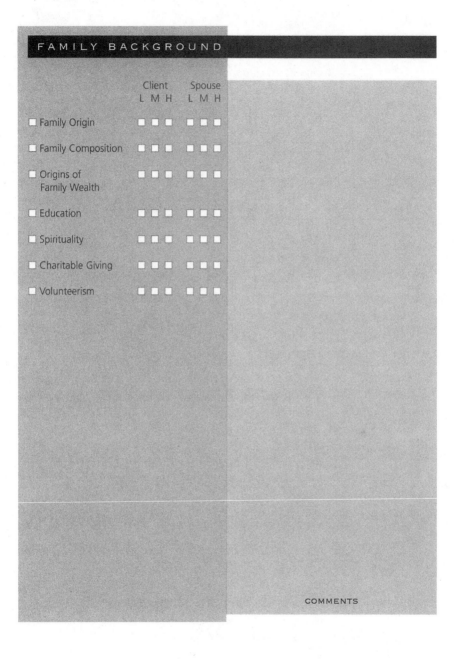

FAMILY BACKGROUND

	Client L M H	Spouse L M H
☐ Family Origin	■ ☐ ■	■ ☐ ■
☐ Family Composition	■ ☐ ■	■ ☐ ■
☐ Origins of Family Wealth	■ ☐ ■	■ ☐ ■
☐ Education	■ ☐ ■	■ ☐ ■
☐ Spirituality	■ ☐ ■	■ ☐ ■
☐ Charitable Giving	■ ☐ ■	■ ☐ ■
☐ Volunteerism	■ ☐ ■	■ ☐ ■

COMMENTS

GROWING UP

	Client			Spouse		
	L	M	H	L	M	H
☐ Financial Security	☐	☐	☐	☐	☐	☐
☐ Growing Up Wealthy	☐	☐	☐	☐	☐	☐
☐ Growing Up Poor	☐	☐	☐	☐	☐	☐
☐ Taboo on Talking About Money	☐	☐	☐	☐	☐	☐
☐ Learning About Money	☐	☐	☐	☐	☐	☐
☐ Education Experiences	☐	☐	☐	☐	☐	☐
☐ Early Work Experiences	☐	☐	☐	☐	☐	☐
☐ Family Values	☐	☐	☐	☐	☐	☐
☐ Major Influences	☐	☐	☐	☐	☐	☐
☐ Spirituality	☐	☐	☐	☐	☐	☐
☐ Charitable Giving	☐	☐	☐	☐	☐	☐
☐ Volunteerism	☐	☐	☐	☐	☐	☐
☐ Family Partners in Decision-Making	☐	☐	☐	☐	☐	☐
☐ Professional Partners in Decision-Making	☐	☐	☐	☐	☐	☐
☐ Benchmarks or Turning Points	☐	☐	☐	☐	☐	☐
☐ Financial Goals as a Child	☐	☐	☐	☐	☐	☐
☐ Business/Professional Goals	☐	☐	☐	☐	☐	☐

COMMENTS

THE PRESENT

	Client L M H	Spouse L M H
☐ Family Structure	☐ ☐ ☐	☐ ☐ ☐
☐ Business/Professional Resume	☐ ☐ ☐	☐ ☐ ☐
☐ Origins of Personal Wealth	☐ ☐ ☐	☐ ☐ ☐
☐ Meaning of Money	☐ ☐ ☐	☐ ☐ ☐
☐ Perceptions About the Wealthy	☐ ☐ ☐	☐ ☐ ☐
☐ Taboo on Talking About Money	☐ ☐ ☐	☐ ☐ ☐
☐ Teaching About Money	☐ ☐ ☐	☐ ☐ ☐
☐ Family Partners in Decision-Making	☐ ☐ ☐	☐ ☐ ☐
☐ Professional Partners in Decision-Making	☐ ☐ ☐	☐ ☐ ☐
☐ Distribution of Resources	☐ ☐ ☐	☐ ☐ ☐
☐ Social Responsibilities of the Wealthy	☐ ☐ ☐	☐ ☐ ☐
☐ Family Values	☐ ☐ ☐	☐ ☐ ☐
☐ Spirituality	☐ ☐ ☐	☐ ☐ ☐
☐ Charitable Giving Resources	☐ ☐ ☐	☐ ☐ ☐
☐ Volunteerism	☐ ☐ ☐	☐ ☐ ☐
☐ Benchmarks or Turning Points	☐ ☐ ☐	☐ ☐ ☐

COMMENTS

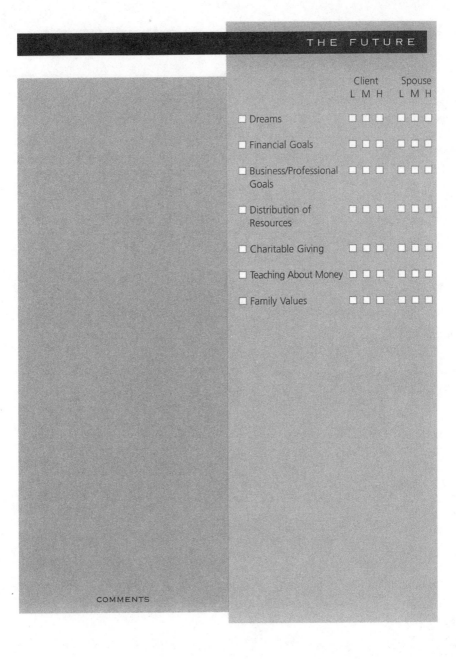

THE FUTURE

	Client L M H	Spouse L M H
☐ Dreams	☐ ☐ ☐	☐ ☐ ☐
☐ Financial Goals	☐ ☐ ☐	☐ ☐ ☐
☐ Business/Professional Goals	☐ ☐ ☐	☐ ☐ ☐
☐ Distribution of Resources	☐ ☐ ☐	☐ ☐ ☐
☐ Charitable Giving	☐ ☐ ☐	☐ ☐ ☐
☐ Teaching About Money	☐ ☐ ☐	☐ ☐ ☐
☐ Family Values	☐ ☐ ☐	☐ ☐ ☐

COMMENTS

ADDITIONAL THOUGHTS AND COMMENTS

Interviewing the Affluent: A Guide to Asking the Right Questions*

Interviewing the affluent requires the combined use of questionnaires and personal interviews, from which the advisor elicits patterns and themes with respect to an individual's or family's history, values, and beliefs. This guide will help the advisor plan and conduct the personal interview.

(a) The Personal Interview

The personal interview is an integral part of The Legacy Planning System. It either precedes or follows the compilation of answers to The Legacy Questionnaire and expands further on the biography of the client in preparation for writing the initial draft of the client's Family Financial Philosophy mission statement. The interview may be thought of as a semiorganized conversation in which advisors learn what they need to know in order to help clients accomplish their legacy.

Asking thought-provoking questions helps clarify the client's values and deepen mutual understanding between spouses. Audiotaping the interview not only guarantees that the client's exact words are preserved but also helps to capture the emotion associated with the responses. Some clients appreciate a copy of the tape and transcript as an autobiographical memoir they can share with their children and grandchildren.

---

*The questions in this guide were developed by Paul G. Schervish, Social Welfare Research Institute, Boston College.

CONDUCTING THE INTERVIEW

The interview is essential to capturing information in preparation for writing the mission statement. The key is to ask questions that give clients a chance to tell you where they have come from, where they are now, and where they hope to go. Simply inviting them to "tell me a bit more" gives them that rare opportunity to tell someone who appears truly interested those significant details they hardly ever get a chance to recount. Dwell a while longer on any topic that has an emotional undertone or is an important benchmark or turning point.

OVERVIEW OF INTERVIEW QUESTIONS

The questions that follow will provide the basis for sensitively drawing out a client's story. Don't be apprehensive by the number and detail of the questions. These questions will help advisors get a feel for the type of information they need in order to prepare the Family Financial Philosophy mission statement.

It may be helpful to keep in mind a simple schematic understanding of the interview questions.

- **Interview goal**—To get as many details as are relevant for understanding the clients' past, present, and future
- **Family backround**—Key people, ideas, emotions, and events that surrounded and shaped the construction of the financial pyramid for the family in which the clients grew up and that left a mark on the clients' life
- **Adult past**—Key people, ideas, emotions, and events that surrounded and shaped the construction of the financial pyramid for clients and their own families and that left a mark on the clients' life
- **Present**—Key people, ideas, emotions, and events that surround and shape the configuration of the financial pyramid for clients and their own families and that are leaving a mark on the clients' life
- **Future**—Key people, ideas, emotions, and events that surround and shape the reconfiguration of the financial pyramid for clients and their own families and that clients want to mark their life and legacy
- **Throughout**—Watch for and ask about the *dilemmas* they face (the mixed and sometimes conflicting emotions, ideas, and activities that clients try to pursue simultaneously and the *strategies* clients pursue to deal with the dilemmas)

The Interview Questions

The following questions will provide the basis for sensitively drawing out clients' stories. Don't be put off by the number and detail of the questions. The list of questions is merely to help you get a feel for the types of information needed to prepare the Family Financial Philosophy mission statement. Several opportunities to obtain the needed information will become evident in working through drafts of the mission statement with clients.

Growing Up

I. Family origins: your parents growing up
   A. Family
      1. Tell me about your family? Who are they and where do they come from?
         a) Grandparents?
         b) Parents?
         c) Their brother(s) and sister(s)?
         d) Other key relatives or friends?
      2. How is your family distributed throughout the United States? The world?
      3. Did you live near your extended family?
      4. Is there anything unusual or unique about your family origins?
      5. What is the single most important factor that defines your family origins?
   B. Economic background of your parents
      1. What did your grandparents do for work?
      2. Were your parents particularly poor or wealthy when they were growing up?
      3. Did your grandparents have any significant wealth?
      4. What allowed them to accumulate that wealth?
   C. Education: parents
      1. Through what level of school were your grandparents and parents educated?
      2. Did they attend private or public?
      3. Was education an important value in their family?
      4. How was education paid for?

II. Family background: you growing up
   A. Tell me about your family?
      1. Your brother(s) and sister(s)?
      2. Other key relatives or friends not already mentioned?
      3. When growing up did you live near your extended family?
      4. Was there anything unusual or unique about your family when you were growing up?
      5. What is the single most important factor that shaped your growing up?
   B. Financial security/insecurity
      1. What did your parents do for work?
      2. Were you particularly poor or wealthy growing up?
      3. Did you feel financially secure growing up?
      4. What made you feel secure? Insecure?
      5. Was there ever a time when you were scared?
   C. Growing up wealthy
      1. What was it like growing up wealthy?
      2. Did your parents themselves have significant wealth?
      3. What allowed them to accumulate that wealth?
      4. Did you openly discuss your financial situation with friends?
      5. How did this affect your relationship with friends?
      6. Did you ever feel guilty as a result of your family wealth?
      7. What specific advantages did wealth provide?
   D. Growing up poor
      1. What was it like growing up poor?
      2. Did you openly discuss your financial situation with friends?
      3. How did this affect your relationship with friends?
      4. Did you ever feel embarrassed as a result of being poor?
      5. What specific disadvantages did being poor cause?
   E. Taboos on talking about money
      1. A lot of people say that money is or was never discussed directly in their family. Was that true in your experience?
      2. Do you think there is a taboo in your family against talking about how much money you or your family has, or how you use it?
      3. If so, why do you think that is? What is this phenomenon about?

F. Learning about money

 1. How did you first learn to manage your money?

 2. Who taught you about money or how you should spend it?

 3. Did this change as you became more experienced and, if so, how?

 4. What was this process?

 5. How are you dealing with your children about being wealthy or handling money?

G. Educational experiences

 1. Through what level of school were you educated?

 2. Through what level of school were your siblings educated?

 3. Did you attend private or public school?

 4. Where did you go to school?

 5. Did you receive a good education?

 6. Was education important in your family?

 7. How was education paid for?

H. Family values

 1. Did your family ever openly discuss family values?

 2. What are the most important values you learned while growing up?

 3. Who taught them to you?

 4. Did they teach by example or instruction?

I. Major influences

 1. What were the major influences on you while you were growing up?

 2. Did you have any mentors?

 3. What significant event do you recall from your childhood?

 4. What is the single most important event you recall from your childhood?

J. Spirituality

 1. Was spirituality or religion an important part of your upbringing?

 2. What impact has this had on you?

K. Charitable giving

 1. Was charitable giving an important part of your upbringing?

 2. What impact has this had on you?

    L. Volunteerism and community involvement

        1. Was volunteerism or community involvement an important part of your upbringing?

        2. What impact has this had on you?

    M. What were your financial, career, or business goals as a child?

Adult Past

  I. Marriage and family

    A. When were you married and to whom?

        1. Describe your spouse's background: family, education, career.

        2. Describe any key personal or financial aspects of your spouse's life.

    B. How many children do you have and when were they born?

  II. Business and professional life

    A. Goals and aspirations

        1. When you were starting out, did you have any business, professional, or financial goals that you wanted to achieve, and, if so, what were they?

        2. Describe your business or career history. Sketch your business activity from its beginnings to the present.

        3. Have your goals changed over the years, and, if so, how are they different now? Do you think you will have different goals in the future?

        4. What do you *like least* and what do you *like best* about the business or professional activities that you have just described?

    B. Business/professional resume

        1. Could you begin by telling me a little about your personal and professional background?

           a) Education/occupation

           b) Other pertinent information

        2. When you think about your personal and professional biography, are there particular events or developments that had a significant impact on your life in a positive or negative way?

        3. Let's talk a bit more about your current business activity.

           a) When was the business founded?

b) Who founded the business?

c) How many family members are actively involved in the business?

d) What type of working relationships do they have?

e) How many family members are not actively involved in the business?

f) What type of relationship do you have with those family members who are actively involved?

g) Do you have a business succession plan in place?

h) What is your future plan for the business?

III. Origins of personal wealth

A. Could you briefly describe the process by which you have made or are now accumulating your wealth?

B. If inherited, what is the origin of money in your family?

C. If self-made, what is the nature of your money-making activities?

D. Other comments

E. Are there any particularly positive or negative experiences specifically related to being wealthy that have had a significant impact on who you are?

IV. Investment background

A. How have you invested your money?

B. What types of investments have provided you with the best return?

C. Did you invest the money yourself?

D. How did you make the decision to invest?

V. Benchmarks or turning points (If not answered already.)

A. What would you say are the major influences or benchmarks that made you who you are?

The Present

I. Family

A. Tell me about your children.

B. What do they do for a living?

C. Where do they live?

D. Do they have families of their own?

E. What things do they like to do?

    F. Where do they go on vacation?

II. Perspectives on life and wealth

    A. Financial security

        1. Do you consider yourself financially secure?

        2. What does this mean for you?

        3. When did you decide that you were financially secure?

        4. Has being financially secure produced any negative or positive changes in your life?

    B. Spirituality

        1. Is spirituality or religion an important part of your life?

        2. Please describe the important aspects of your spirituality or religion.

        3. What impact has this had on you?

    C. The effectiveness and significance of wealth

        1. What do you think is the most important thing money can give you?

        2. What *can't* it give you?

        3. Given your current level of wealth (and business success), what motivates you to continue the process of investing and accumulating more?

        4. Why?

        5. Do you consider yourself a wealthy person?

        6. What does this mean to you?

        7. Do you experience any regrets or guilt about your status as a wealthy individual?

        8. Do you experience any regrets or guilt about how you obtained or have used your money?

        9. Have you had to compromise your principles or beliefs in order to use your wealth productively?

III. Distribution of resources

    A. Budget categories

        1. Can you tell me, in general terms, what you spend your money on? General categories?

        2. Why do you divide it up that way?

        3. Is this on an annual basis?

        4. How do you decide how to manage your money and to use it for different purposes?

5. Do you have a budget?

6. Is there any other kind of decision-making framework you use? (i.e., how do you decide how much money to spend on yourself versus investments, gifts to heirs, charitable contributions, or other general categories mentioned in previous question?)

B. Potential changes

1. How do you think you will be spending your money in five years?

2. Do you foresee any changes from how you spend it today?

3. Are you likely to change your priorities?

4. Do you think you will spend more or less on certain things?

5. Do you anticipate spending money on anything in the future that you don't currently spend your money on?

6. Can you think of anything you do not have today that you would purchase if money were no object?

C. Potential hazards

1. In order to keep pace with inflation, at what rate would you like to see your income increase each year?

2. What happens if you live longer than you expect?

3. What happens if your investment performance fails to meet your expectations?

4. What happens if inflation exceeds your expectations?

D. Future

1. Looking ahead to the future, do you have any plans or agenda for how you will accumulate, use, or dispose of your money, say five to ten years from now?

2. How about when you retire?

3. Have you thought about or made provisions for the use of your money when you die?

IV. Philanthropy

A. Charitable giving

1. Is charitable giving an important part of your life?

2. What was your first large gift?

3. How did you decide to make this gift? What motivated you to start giving at that point? What impact has this had on you?

4. Since then, what has been your pattern of charitable giving?

    a) To whom do you make your major contributions and why?

    b) About how much do you give each year to charity?

5. Thinking about the past 12 months, in general, what kinds of gifts did you make to different groups, individuals, or issues? Can you give me some examples?

    a) To whom did you give?

    b) How much?

    c) In what form? (e.g., trust, bequest intention, outright charitable donation, gift of stock, gift of real estate, corporate gift, and so on)

    d) What is a typical gift size?

    e) Do you tend toward large gifts? Small gifts?

    f) How did you decide on the amounts?

    g) Why did you make past gifts?

        (1) Simply because you were asked?

        (2) Was it part of a plan?

        (3) Was there "pressure" by a friend or associate?

6. Satisfaction with gifts

    a) Did past gifts make you happy?

    b) Were they satisfying?

7. Effectiveness of gifts

    a) What has been the outcome of past gifts?

    b) Have the charitable recipients followed through on their promises?

    c) How do you hold the charity accountable?

    d) Do you require written feedback?

    e) Do you withhold future support if accountability becomes an issue?

8. Most important gift

    a) Of all the things you gave money or time to last year, which do you consider your *most important* gift? Which was the most significant or meaningful to you personally?

    b) Why?

    c) Was this also your largest gift?

    d) If not, why not?

9. Are there any particular areas, projects, or causes to which you are deeply committed?

    a) Do you give to them regularly and, if so, why? If not, why not?

    b) How are these gifts different from your one-time gifts?

10. What groups or causes *don't* you give to? To whom do you say no, and why?

11. What criteria do you use in making decisions about whether or not to give? (e.g., types of issues, effectiveness, or certain characteristics of the group)

12. How do you determine the maximum amount you will give away?

13. Has it ever occurred to you to give all your money and assets away?

14. Have you ever thought about setting up a foundation to meet your philanthropic or social goals?

    a) If yes, what are your thoughts about doing so?

    b) If not, why not?

15. Do you think your pattern and motivation for giving is similar to your friends, other family members, or others in your economic and social class?

16. Do you see your pattern of giving as being distinctive or unique in any way, and, if so, how?

17. Has giving in a distinctive way been important to you, and, if so, why?

18. Do you generally retain any control or discretion over the gifts that you give?

19. Do you prefer to stipulate how your gifts should be used, and, if so, what are those stipulations?

20. If you prefer to retain control over how your gifts are used, what is your concern in doing so? Or, if control is not a concern of yours, why is this?

21. Have you had past negative experiences with charities?

22. If so, what caused these negative experiences?

23. How can they be avoided in the future?

24. Do you typically initiate the gift or respond to a request?

25. Do you prefer to make gifts unrestricted?

26. Do you prefer to make contributions for capital projects, current programs, or endowment?

    B. Volunteerism and community involvement

        1. Besides making charitable contributions, is volunteerism and community involvement an important part of life?

        2. Do you also donate time or advice or lend your name or endorsement to various groups or efforts? If so, please describe your involvement.

            a) What kinds of things do you do?

            b) How much time do you give?

        3. What is your feeling about giving time rather than, or in addition to, money?

        4. What impact has your volunteering and community involvement had on you?

V. Communicating financial values

    A. Are there taboos or inhibitions regarding talking about money or wealth in your family?

    B. What did/do you try to teach your children about the use and abuse of money in their lives?

        1. What values are important to you?

        2. To whom do you attribute these values?

        3. Are these values reflected in your current estate plan?

        4. Do you believe your heirs share your values?

        5. If you could transfer one value to your heirs, what would it be? Why?

VI. Financial decision making

    A. Family partners in decision making

        1. Do you discuss financial matters or decisions with any family members, friends, or other relatives, and, if so, whom?

            a) Spouse?

            b) Children?

            c) Other family members or relatives?

            d) Friends?

            e) Business associates?

        2. What do you discuss with others?

        3. How involved are they?

        4. What degree of influence do they have in the final decision?

        5. What types of advice do you seek?

    B. Professional partners in decision making

    1. Do you discuss financial matters or decisions with any professional advisors, and, if so, whom?

        a) Attorney?

        b) Investment manager?

        c) Financial planner?

        d) Planned giving officer?

        e) Trust officer?

        f) Insurance agent?

    2. What types of advice do you seek?

    3. How involved are the advisors?

    4. What degree of influence do advisors have in your final decisions?

VII. Views and perspectives

  A. Perceptions about wealth and the wealthy

      1. Do you think that there are different kinds or groups of "wealthy" (e.g., do you distinguish between inherited wealth and self-made wealth)?

      2. If so, what are these distinctions?

      3. Do you think money means different things to these different groups?

      4. Where do you see yourself as fitting in?

      5. Are there special personal or social activities (e.g., related to lifestyle) associated with being wealthy in our society?

      6. What do you think the majority of people in the country think about people who are wealthy?

      7. Is there any particular stereotype of the wealthy that you think most people hold?

      8. In what ways have you personally experienced this stereotyping?

      9. Does it bother you?

      10. How would you go about changing people's impressions of the wealthy?

  B. Social responsibility of the wealthy

      1. Do you think wealth carries with it certain social obligations or places pressure on the wealthy in general?

      2. Do the wealthy owe anything to those who do not have much at all?

3. Do you personally feel any particular responsibilities being a wealthy person, and, if so, how do you deal with or meet those responsibilities?

4. Do you think of yourself as being in any particular social class, and, if so, which one?

5. Why do you say that particular class? (Advisor: Probe for criteria of class membership such as income, occupation, education, lifestyle, etc.)

6. What other social classes are there, and how would you describe the people in them?

7. If everyone had the same income and amount of wealth, would we still have class difference?

8. Do you think the wealthy (rich, upper class) are different from other social classes besides the fact that people in that class have more money? If so, what makes them different? (Advisor: Probe for responses relative to influence, power, responsibility, lifestyle, culture.)

9. If it were possible to change the class structure in any way we wanted, what changes would you like to see occur? Do you foresee any changes in the class structure occurring?

C. The roles of government and the market in economic matters

1. Do you think that our society could provide wealth for everyone, and, if so, why hasn't it?

2. Do you think it is possible to eliminate poverty?

3. Is the elimination of poverty desirable?

4. Do you think those who are not poor benefit from the fact that there are poor people?

5. Are there any particular social needs in our country that you think should be addressed?

6. In terms of addressing those social needs, do you think that there are those that should be the responsibility of government and those that should be the responsibility of the private sector?

7. If so, who should be responsible for what?

8. Are there areas in which the government is presently involved that you think it should stay out of, and, if so, why?

9. Some people say the decisions made and policies implemented by the federal government reflect the broad interests of the citizenry as a whole. Others argue that they

essentially reflect the influence of special interest groups. Which view do you agree with the most?

10. If the latter, which groups do you think have the most influence over the federal government?

11. If you could design a utopian society, one in which everything would be arranged according to your ideals, what would it look like?

The Future

I. Dreams and goals

A. Financial goals

1. If money were no object, what is the one thing you would most like to do?

2. What are your financial goals for the future?

3. How do you see your financial situation changing in the future?

4. What is your first financial priority for the future?

B. Business or professional goals

1. What professional milestones have you yet to accomplish?

2. Do you envision changing the amount of time allocated to work?

3. Are there any additional resources (staff, technology, etc.) that are essential to your future success?

4. What additions will your résumé show three years from today?

C. Distribution of resources

1. Do you intend to allocate your resources differently in the future?

2. What will be the most dramatic change?

3. Why are you making these changes?

D. Charitable giving

1. How do you foresee your giving being different in the future from what it is today?

2. Are there any projects that you would fund today if you had adequate financial resources?

E. Teaching values about life and money

1. Do you have any new things you want to teach your children or grandchildren about life and money?
   a) What is your objective?
   b) Have you begun yet?
2. Would you like family values to be reflected in your planning in the future?

DON'T FORGET

The development of the typical estate plan does not reflect an in-depth understanding of clients' innermost thoughts, dreams, goals, and desires. Certainly each advisor achieves this desired level of performance and relationship at one time or another. The goal is to make this approach the norm, rather than the exception.

DON'T WORRY

Competent advisors already possess the basic skills of a good listener, advisor, and counselor. If they didn't, they would not be in this line of work. Helping clients sort through the myriad of issues relating to their wealth is not unlike helping a good friend overcome a problem. Remember to treat clients with the same respect and concern as you would a friend or family member. The results will speak for themselves.

The Legacy Goal Profile

he planning process is driven by three intrinsic objectives: (1) the need for *financial independence*; (2) the desire to leave a *family legacy*; and (3) the desire to make a difference or, put another way, the desire to have a positive impact on society through a *social capital legacy*.

FINANCIAL INDEPENDENCE

Your client's first and most basic planning objective is to identify and maintain *financial independence*. Simply stated, your clients achieve financial independence when they have accumulated and preserved all they would ever need to maintain their desired lifestyle. Generally expressed as a unique combination of annual income and minimum resource base, financial independence answers the question, "What do I want from my wealth for the rest of my life?"

FAMILY LEGACY

Once they *define and achieve* financial independence, your clients likely will want to shift their attention to wealth distribution, or what we generally call estate planning. This level of planning determines the "family legacy" – what they will leave for heirs. In the most effective, comprehensive plan, a family legacy is *predetermined* as that portion of the estate identified as *appropriate* for transfer to heirs. During this phase of the planning process, you help your clients deliberately and carefully specify an inheritance amount for each estate beneficiary.

SOCIAL CAPITAL LEGACY

Once you have helped your clients identify how much they will need to maintain lifetime financial independence and secure a desired family legacy for heirs, they will have acquired a sense of freedom to consider their "social capital legacy." Social capital legacy represents that portion of the estate not needed to maintain financial independence and not designated for family legacy.

There are two forms of social capital - *voluntary and involuntary*. Voluntary social capital is made up of those dollars over which we make a conscious decision to take responsibility. Consisting of either tax or philanthropic contributions, it represents the lasting impact your clients may have on society by directing their social capital in a manner consistent with their value systems. In other words, these are *self-directed social capital dollars*.

Involuntary social capital consists of those dollars that are involuntarily extracted from us under the default plan - tax. This represents the mandatory redistribution of social capital when your clients do not take personal responsibility for their wealth distribution. These are government-directed social capital dollars.

In the most effective estate plan, each of the three objectives – *financial independence*, *family legacy* and *social capital legacy* – is carefully examined and specified.

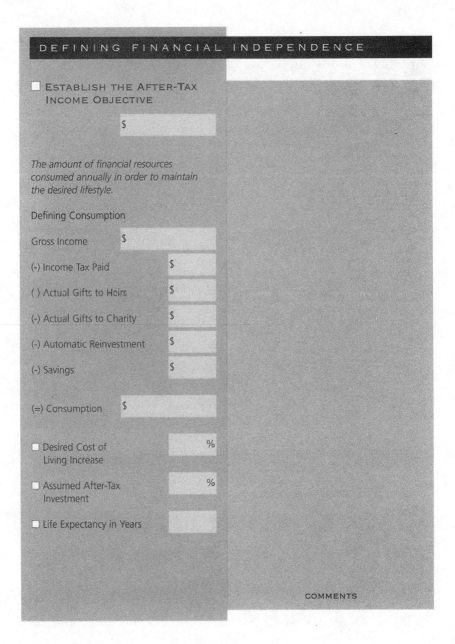

DEFINING FINANCIAL INDEPENDENCE

☐ ESTABLISH THE AFTER-TAX
   INCOME OBJECTIVE

   $ _____

*The amount of financial resources
consumed annually in order to maintain
the desired lifestyle.*

Defining Consumption

Gross Income $ _____

(-) Income Tax Paid $ _____

( ) Actual Gifts to Heirs $ _____

(-) Actual Gifts to Charity $ _____

(-) Automatic Reinvestment $ _____

(-) Savings $ _____

(=) Consumption $ _____

☐ Desired Cost of   _____ %
   Living Increase

☐ Assumed After-Tax   _____ %
   Investment

☐ Life Expectancy in Years _____

COMMENTS

☐ SPECIFIC ASSETS

$ _____

*Assets that are presently owned, and will
be owned in the foreseeable future, such
as a primary residence or second home,
personal property, antiques and collectibles.
For the purpose of determining financial
independence, do not rely on these assets
for providing either liquidity or income.*

Asset Category	Value
1	$
2	$
3	$
4	$
5	$
6	$
7	$
8	$
9	$
10	$

COMMENTS

☐ SPECIAL PURPOSE FUNDS

*Funds designed to supplement the
desired lifestyle. These cash resources are
not required to support the life income
objective, but rather are designated to
offset unexpected contingencies.*

Asset Categories

Petty Cash Fund	$
Investment Opportunity Fund	$
Emergency Fund	$
Business Opportunity Fund	$
Asset Acquisition Fund	$
Vacation Fund	$
Education Fund	$
	$
	$
	$

COMMENTS

DEFINING AN APPROPRIATE FAMILY LEGACY

☐ ESTABLISH AN AFTER-TAX
INCOME OBJECTIVE FOR
EACH DESIGNATED HEIR

*To identify an appropriate income
supplement for each heir, use the same
procedure used in calculating the financial
resources required to support the client's
desired life income.*

☐ Assumed After-Tax Investment   %

☐ Desired Cost of Living Increase   %

Heir	Income Goal	Term
	$	yrs
	$	yrs
	$	yrs
	$	yrs
	$	yrs
	$	yrs
	$	yrs
	$	yrs
	$	yrs
	$	yrs
	$	yrs
	$	yrs
	$	yrs

COMMENTS

□ SPECIFIC ASSETS

Total .$

Heir 1	Heir 2	Heir 3

Asset Categories

1		
$	$	$

2		
$	$	$

3		
$	$	$

4		
$	$	$

5		
$	$	$

6		
$	$	$

7		
$	$	$

8		
$	$	$

COMMENTS

☐ SPECIFIC ASSETS

Total $ _____

Heir 4	Heir 5	Heir 6

Assets Categories

1

| $ | $ | $ |

2

| $ | $ | $ |

3

| $ | $ | $ |

4

| $ | $ | $ |

5

| $ | $ | $ |

6

| $ | $ | $ |

7

| $ | $ | $ |

8

COMMENTS

| $ | $ | $ |

☐ SPECIAL FUNDS

Total $ _____

Fund Categories

Heir 1	Heir 2	Heir 3

Petty Cash

$	$	$

Investment Opportunity

$	$	$

Emergency

$	$	$

Business Opportunity

$	$	$

Asset Acquisition

$	$	$

Vacation

$	$	$

Education

$	$	$

$	$	$

$	$	$

$	$	$

COMMENTS

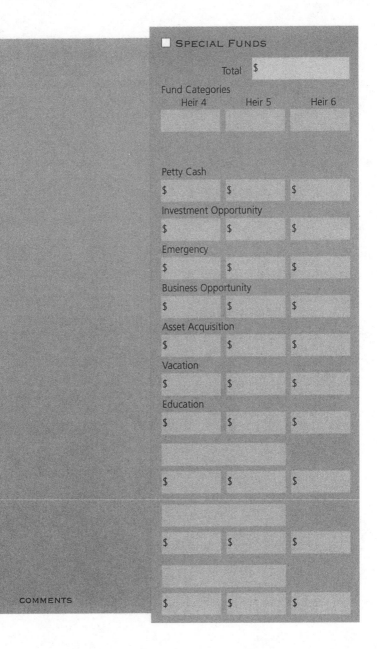

☐ SPECIAL FUNDS

Total $

Fund Categories

Heir 4	Heir 5	Heir 6

Petty Cash

$	$	$

Investment Opportunity

$	$	$

Emergency

$	$	$

Business Opportunity

$	$	$

Asset Acquisition

$	$	$

Vacation

$	$	$

Education

$	$	$

$	$	$

$	$	$

COMMENTS

$	$	$

☐ GOVERNMENT-DIRECTED

Involuntary social capital dollars are transferred from the client's estate under the default plan, tax. This results in a mandatory redistribution of social capital that occurs when clients do not choose to take direct responsibility for its distribution. These social capital dollars are government-directed.

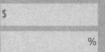

$

%

COMMENTS

☐ SELF-DIRECTED

Consisting of either tax or philanthropic contributions, these dollars can create a lasting impact on society when clients choose to direct their social capital in a manner consisitent with their value system. These social capital dollars are self-directed.

$

%

Organization	Percentage
	%
	%
	%
	%
	%
	%
	%
	%
	%
	%
	%
	%
	%
	%

COMMENTS

Index

Visit us on the World Wide Web

NONPROFIT
Resource Center

www.wiley.com/nonprofit

Our nonprofit Web site features

• **A nonprofit catalogue** where you can order and search for titles online. View book and author information about our management, law/tax, fund-raising, accounting, and finance titles.

• **A threaded discussion forum** that provides you and your colleagues with the chance to ask questions, share knowledge, and debate issues important to your organization and the sector.

• **Over 500 free forms and worksheets** to help run any nonprofit organization more efficiently and effectively. Forms are updated monthly to cover a new key area of nonprofit management.

• **Useful links** to many nonprofit resources online.

The Wiley Nonprofit Series brings together an extraordinary team of experts in the fields of nonprofit management, fund-raising, law, accounting, and finance. This Web site highlights our new books, which present the best, most innovative practices being used in the nonprofit sector today. It also highlights our established works, which through their use in the day-to-day operations of thousands of nonprofits have proven themselves to be invaluable to any nonprofit looking to raise more money or improve their operations, while still remaining in compliance with all rules and regulations.

For nearly 200 years, Wiley has prided itself on being a publisher of books known for thoroughness, rigor, and readability. Please browse the Web site. You are sure to find valued titles that you need to navigate the new world of nonprofit action.

Wiley Nonprofit Series